The technique of television news

Ivor Yorke

Focal Press
London and Boston

Focal Press

is an imprint of the Butterworth Group

which has principal offices in

London, Boston, Durban, Singapore, Sydney, Toronto and Wellington

First published 1978
Second edition 1987

British Library Cataloguing in Publication Data
Yorke, Ivor
    The technique of television news.—2nd ed.
    1. Television broadcasting of news
    2. Television—Production and direction
    I. Title
    791.45'5   PN4784.T4
    ISBN 0-240-51253-7

Library of Congress Cataloging in Publication Data

Yorke, Ivor
    The technique of television news.
    (The library of communication techniques)
    Bibliography: P.
    Includes index.
    1. Television Broadcasting of news.   I. Title.
II. Series.
PN4784-T4Y6   1987   070.1'9   87-321
ISBN 0-240-51253-7

PN
4784
.T4
Y6
1987
c.2

Cover photograph courtesy BBC Central Stills
Photoset by MC Typeset Limited, Chatham
Printed and bound by Robert Hartnoll Ltd, Bodmin, Cornwall

Foreword

If that keen young man who managed, despite the odds, to safely deliver some bad news to his monarch — and was promptly executed because nobody liked the message he brought — was a contemporary figure, it would be a safe bet that he was a broadcasting journalist.

Certainly, after more than thirty years in broadcast journalism, I am keenly aware that we do not rank high in the Establishment Popularity Stakes.

The reason is no more complicated than the recognition that it is our job to present fact and truth, with clarity, dispassion and neutrality, however inconvenient or dismaying much of that information may be.

Journalism is about discovery and disclosure. But good journalism is *responsible* journalism. Anyone can make up a story and present it attractively, with a bold headline that screams for attention — most of the London daily newspapers are expert at it. As in modern politics, so it is with Fleet Street journalism: respect for fact and truth is no longer a prime qualification for employment.

That I believe so strongly in the need for responsible journalism is only one of the many reasons why I welcome this revised edition by Ivor Yorke of his *Technique of Television News*. It is an excellent piece of work, produced by a master of his craft, who has spent many years writing, editing and producing television news programmes. Now, as the BBC's Head of Journalist Training, he passes on that breadth and depth of experience to a new generation of young lions who have yet to learn their skills.

I can speak with personal knowledge of Ivor Yorke's abilities, for he was a senior member of my staff when I was Editor of BBC Television News: we work together again, since the training of journalists is part of my overall responsibility for the standards of journalism throughout the Corporation.

This book reflects the concern for the maintenance of the highest standards of journalism that must be the hallmark of the good practitioner. Words must mean what they say, and say what they mean. Research into a story, an item or a programme can no longer be merely copper-bottomed: in a world seemingly populated by those who prefer less than full disclosure of fact and truth, people ever ready to discredit the journalist and journalism, facts have to be platinum-plated.

And that, of course, is as it should be, for the journalist who cannot stand over his story to the last comma discredits not only himself, but a proud and worthwhile profession that demonstrates over and over again how great a force for good it can be.

Every day, huge numbers of citizens turn to television for their news. The credibility of television news remains outstandingly high. The trust of the public in what we produce for them is in itself the greatest accolade any group of professionals could ever receive.

The techniques of television news, the practicalities and the methodology of translating raw information into comprehensible, cogent, and fluent presentation, can nowhere be better discerned and discovered than in this splendid book.

Alan Protheroe
Assistant Director General, BBC

Preface to second edition

The first edition of this book, in 1978, happened to coincide with the beginning of a revolution in television news. Nearly a decade later, that revolution is not only still going on, it shows no obvious signs of slowing down.

The signs are there for anyone who cares to see. Electronic news gathering, whose sensational impact ended more than 20 years' domination by the 16 mm film camera, has already found its three-quarter inch standard tape size challenged by half-inch, with quarter-inch also a reality. Ever more magical properties are being built into each succeeding generation of the computerized 'paint box' systems which have transformed news graphics into works of electronic art. Manufacturers of the television newsroom computers which started to spring up in the early eighties are looking ahead to the days when, as a matter of routine, a production instruction buried within a journalist's script will automatically roll a videocassette recorder or select a still from the memory of a digital frame store.

Continuing change in television news has not been confined merely to the area of technology. The loosening of the grip of programme schedulers, the move towards all-news or specialist news channels (particularly as a result of cable and satellite) and the growing influence of news programme presenters behind as well as in front of the camera, combined with the subtle shift of emphasis from brief, 'hard' news items to longer explanation and interpretation, have served only to emphasize how deeply the revolution has taken hold.

The aim of this second edition is to bring up to date as many of those changes as may be relevant to the journalists whose working lives are affected by them, and to predict — as far as that is ever possible — what may be in store over the next few years.

In this dual mission I have been helped by many busy people who gladly gave up their precious spare time to write copious notes, read the manuscript in part or in full, and offer their constructive advice.

In particular I should like to record my special thanks to three colleagues: Duncan Herbert, for his painstaking explanation of electronic picture editing at home and abroad; Bill Nicol, one of that hardy breed of globe-trotting news cameramen, for leading me gently through the practical differences between the film and ENG eras; and Sandy McCourt, for his invaluable guidance on aspects of computerized graphics. Many of the detailed suggestions they made influenced my approach to certain matters, although the responsibility for any mistake in interpretation is, of course, my own.

I would also like to express my gratitude to all those who generously allowed me to quote direct from work in which they hold the copyright; to the numerous equipment-makers who provided useful technical information or illustrations; to Adrian Scott of BASYS and Professor Phillip O. Keirstead for sharing their expertise in newsroom computing; Derrik Mercer, late of Channel 4 News, for help during the run-up to the publication of his own work on media matters; Graham Milloy, manager of BBC Central Stills; Denis Donovan; Alex Swan of Turner Broadcasting; the Cable Authority in London; the Federal Communications Commission in Washington; Communications & Information Technology (CIT) Research; John Heuston; Geoff Sarbutt; Greg Philo; Zdenek Stepanek of Intervision News, OIRT; Ron Onions of Visnews; Kim Baumgartner of COMSAT; Charles Barrand, Head of News, Europa Television; David Wilson of BBC Teletext; ORACLE Teletext; Alan Protheroe, a past editor of BBC Television News, now Assistant Director General, for agreeing to write the foreword; Gerald Dorey of Focal Press, for his encouragement and interest; and my wife, Cynthia, and children Sarah and Judith, for stoically accepting my abdication from normal family life and responsibility for the second time while this latest project took shape.

Finally, I have to acknowledge the important contribution made by modern technology towards the production of this book: the fact that a tiny cupboard in a bedroom had to serve as an office for several months only increases my enthusiasm for the microcomputer, word processor and printer as ideal tools for the writer. If only they could make the coffee.

Ivor Yorke
London

Contents

Contents

The library of communication techniques

Film

The technique of documentary film production
By W. Hugh Baddeley

The technique of editing 16 mm film
By John Burder

The technique of the film cutting room
By Ernest Walter

The technique of film editing
Compiled by Karel Reisz and Gavin Millar

The technique of film music
By Roger Manvell and John Huntley
(revised by Richard Arnell and Peter Day)

The technique of professional make-up for film,
television and stage
By Vincent J.R. Kehoe

The technique of the motion picture camera
By H. Mario Raimondo Souto

The technique of special effects cinematography
By Raymond Fielding

Television

The technique of lighting for television and motion pictures
By Gerald Millerson

The technique of special effects in television
By Bernard Wilkie

The technique of television news
By Ivor Yorke

The technique of television production
By Gerald Millerson

Sound

The technique of the sound studio
By Alec Nisbett

The technique of radio production
By Robert McLeish

Introduction

Television is commonly a target for attack by the politicians, press and people of many countries. Some educationists see its cumulative effect as a major factor in the breakdown of respect that children are previously supposed to have had for their parents and teachers. Some moralists believe it has contributed to sexual permissiveness, alcoholism, violence, vandalism and drug-taking. Television has been said to reduce the great issues of the time to trivia, to blunt the senses against man's inhumanity to man, to disrupt family life, to act as a soporific for the 'working classes', and to set back the standards of reading and writing in schools. Sneered at by its detractors as the 'goggle-box', the 'idiot tube', 'chewing gum for the eyes' and 'a vast wasteland of useless rubbish', it joins package holidays and fast food in the pillory for being too popular by half.

Countless books have been written in an attempt to understand the phenomenon. Many have examined the political and social impact of the medium through the internationally renowned broadcasting organizations: some have dealt with its history, growth and potential. Others have devoted their pages to the exploits of those who make their living from it, or have dissected television technology in general or specific terms.

In this welter of words, the documentary and current affairs broadcasts in Britain have been examined under the microscope often enough. But it is only in the past few years that writers, politicians and sociologists have begun to concentrate seriously on television news, the daily programmes which attract vast audiences for their coverage of events of international, national and local importance.

The ability of these programmes to influence public opinion was probably not recognized until the mid sixties, after the broadcasters had demonstrated that new communications technology, combined with a willingness among some services to co-operate regularly in the exchange of news material, could make pictures of almost any significant event available beyond national boundaries within hours. Once world audiences had shared the Kennedy assassination, student riots, Watergate, terrorism and various wars including Vietnam and the Middle East, nothing could ever be the same again.

By the eighties, anyone who still remained sceptical about the power of television news must have had all doubts swept aside by the astonishing, spontaneous public response to the appearance in October 1984 of harrowing pictures of famine in Ethiopia. The impetus for the creation of the Band Aid relief fund and all that has followed in an attempt to alleviate the suffering of millions can be attributed directly to the reports seen on the news bulletins of an estimated 400-plus broadcasting organizations. That television journalism could be a power for good was in this case unarguable.

For most of its recent existence, though, television news has been under attack for what are considered to be its less positive virtues. Much of the criticism echoes the tone of a speech by Spiro T. Agnew, at Des Moines, Iowa in November 1969, during his term as Vice-President of the United States. In the course of it he created a flutter by drawing attention to American television news people as 'a tiny, enclosed fraternity of privileged men elected by no one', who created national issues overnight, had a free hand in 'selecting, presenting and interpreting the great issues of our nation', and elevated some men from obscurity to national prominence within a week, while ignoring others.

His comments were seen at the time as important to the international debate about television, for they also helped bring into focus criticism being voiced in other countries by those who believed similarly that journalistic interpretation of events did not always reflect the world as they knew it (or as they might prefer to know it). It has since become fashionable to suggest that a like-minded fraternity in Britain selects the news from within a narrow spectrum restricted by its members' own upbringing, education and social attitudes. Depending on the critic's own political standpoint, television news is either unnaturally obsessed with gloom and doom, having been infiltrated by extreme left-wing sympathizers as part of a wider conspiracy to destroy moral values and the established order of things (a strike by broadcast journalists in the summer of 1985 over a BBC decision to put off transmission of a documentary it had made about Irish extremists would have done nothing except confirm that view), or is so dominated by white, middle-class males that opponents of the established system are rarely shown in anything but a bad light if they are shown at all.

The Glasgow University Media Group has published a series of books critical of television news[1], particularly in its coverage of industrial and defence matters, and has also produced a video examining the reporting of the year-long miners' strike which brought scenes of violence between pickets and police into people's living rooms night after night during 1984–5. The group's conclusion is that television journalists accepted too readily the employers' view of the dispute, including press statements giving the number of miners said to have reported for work each day. The union regularly disagreed with the figures, but the group suggests that another reason television stays with official sources and the normal channels is that 'it is safer'.

[1] *Bad News* (Routledge & Kegan Paul, 1976); *More Bad News* (Routledge & Kegan Paul, 1980); *Really Bad News* (Writers' and Readers' Publishing Co-operative, 1982); *War and Peace News* (Open University Press, 1985).

'Powerful interests such as the government, Whitehall or the police expect to be routinely consulted by the media. They take it for granted that their briefings and press releases will be used, and that they can feed information into the system. In practice they can define what issues are given important treatment. People who wield power don't show much liking for alternative news and don't much like to be criticised or embarrassed by journalists.'[2]

Some of the group's work has in turn come under academic fire[3] for alleged exaggeration and the drawing of sweeping conclusions from miniscule evidence. But the miners' strike is typical of the 'big' or sensitive story which from time to time intensifies interest in, and criticism of, the way television news goes about its business.

Very occasionally, the criticism is fundamental enough to warrant being met head on. In the autumn of 1986, BBC Television News executives took the unprecedented step of issuing a line-by-line rebuttal of charges made public by the ruling Conservative Party. The complaints, detailed to the point of challenging certain words used in the headlines, were about the way the *Nine O'Clock News* had covered a controversial American bombing raid on Libya six months earlier. Overall public assessment of this bout of linen-washing was that if the politicians lost the argument they succeeded in making the journalists justify their actions to the audience to an extent previously unknown.

In June 1985, an American TWA airliner carrying more than one hundred people was hijacked in the Middle East. Some of the passengers were released, one American aboard was murdered, and others were spirited from the aircraft as it sat on the ground at Beirut airport. For the next two weeks, as the American government negotiated for the hostages' release, the country's three television networks were locked in private combat to bring their viewers the most detailed coverage. The biggest journalistic scoop of the crisis was scored by ABC, which got agreement to interview the pilot and two of his crew under the eyes of a gunman in the cockpit.

Later, pictures and interviews with other hostages at bizarre news conferences hosted by Lebanese Shi'ite militiamen appeared on prime time news programmes in a way which suggested to many that the journalists had allowed themselves to be cleverly manipulated by people who had a clear understanding of how they operated and how their appetite for the story could be satisfied at the same time as motivating American voters to exert pressure on their President. So a new word passed into the language: terrorvision. And people started to ask if there would have been any hostages if there had been no cameras in Beirut. Some journalists began to wonder the same thing, and waited to see if the lessons would be learnt by those conducting future acts of terrorism. In the meantime, a few weeks after the event, one answer seemed to be provided by the British Prime Minister, Margaret Thatcher, herself the target of an assassination attempt the previous year. In a London speech she suggested that the media should starve the terrorist and the hijacker of 'the oxygen of publicity' on which they depended and went on to ask for the establishment of a voluntary code of conduct under which broadcasting and the press would agree

[2]*Coal Board News, Television and the Coal Dispute* 1984–5.
[3]*TV News — Whose Bias?*, Professor Martin Harrison (Policy Journals, 1985).

(eventually releasing a limited version for transmission) leaving to kick their heels 400 journalists — nearly 250 from the American networks alone — who had assembled within a day or two.

Again, as with the Falklands, an accident of the geography made the restriction easy to enforce, although it did not prevent some journalists from making unofficial, ultimately unsuccessful attempts to get to the action by themselves. It was not until several days later that the news caravan was allowed into Grenada, and then under some supervision. What made the episode all the more disturbing to the critics of this policy was that the United States had long been held up as the shining example of an enlightened, information-free society, and they believed that Americans had a right to know what the government they had elected was doing in their name.

One side effect of the Grenada incident was that it became relevant to and part of the British study, which also drew on the experience of journalists covering some of the other main international conflicts since Korea — Suez, Vietnam and Lebanon. The authors pointed out that the media has grown, from 550 accredited correspondents at the time of the D-Day landings in 1944 to 3500 at the London economic summit of 1984.

Derrik Mercer, author of the sections of the report dealing wth the Falklands, NATO and the future, says this, plus the scale and nature of modern communications, means that governments and the military must 'recognize reality'. A practical relationship must be developed in peace time, because 'a crisis or war is no time to try to develop understandings between what are essentially different interests'. He argues for 'a modicum of trust' between the two sides, with the authorities aware of the limitation that, because of the competition which exists between various parts of the media, no agreement could be watertight. The international nature of the media has to be understood, he says, because normal methods of accreditation would not be possible at the time of a crisis in Europe.

'Television would be there, like it or not. And not all would be on 'our' side. Many would be neutral, some hostile. As for controlling what they did in a period short of all-out war — some European countries have press freedom built into their constitutions.'

Even so, as the furore over the coverage of the Falklands recedes with the passage of time, there is little evidence to suggest a radical change in the military belief that television *would* be unable to avoid the limitations imposed on it in time of war. If journalists and their camera crews wished to reach inaccessible battle zones, the only way to get there would be by courtesy of the military; and help would be granted only on the understanding that those seeking it would be prepared to abide by whatever rules were laid down.

The response of many television journalists to offers of help with coverage has often been one of considerable suspicion, especially when applied to some of the international spectaculars involving world politicians and statesmen. Questions have begun to be asked about the value of these events and the attitudes of those in authority who are happy to welcome the cameras when it suits them, but who seek to keep them out when matters of real importance occur. The mirror image of that attitude can be seen in the large number of countries where reporting is not 'free' in any sense. Given that television in many parts of the world is controlled or funded by governments, it is not difficult to appreciate that many news services are able to produce nothing except what is officially sanctioned. In addition, 'foreign' camera crews and reporters cannot fly in with their equipment to anywhere they please and expect to start work. Some countries simply refuse to allow them entry; visas to get into others may take months, and when permission is finally granted the presence of 'minders' may be so inhibiting that the reports which are made may be no more informative than those old-fashioned cinema travelogues.

One effect is that some events about which there is no independent confirmation might just as well not have happened, for while pictures of, say, a serious accident on a foggy West German autobahn would be available to the rest of the world within an hour or so as a matter of routine, some disaster which wiped out an entire African village might go unreported because no cameras were there until months afterwards. In this way it is still possible for whole areas of the world to remain ignorant of what is taking place in others, either by reason of geographical accident or through the deliberate actions of governments anxious not to let any event of an unfavourable nature be seen by outsiders.

As an insurance, among the first things some governments or their agents will do when contemplating something nasty will be to threaten, imprison or expel any journalists considered likely to be an embarrassment to them. Sometimes it is done quite blatantly, as when the South Africans banned all except officially approved reporting of its internal strife in an attempt to curb what it saw as the 'vicious and venomous' coverage by foreign television news crews, whose presence, according to the minister responsible for law and order, was 'a catalyst for further violence'.

The ban, applying to riots, strikes, boycotts, attacks on people and property as well as action by the security forces, prohibited the televising, photographing, recording or drawing of scenes of conflict in districts covered by emergency regulations, except with the permission of the Commissioner of Police. Penalties for contravention included the confiscation of equipment, a fine or prison. Significantly, the moves came at a time when the satellited pictures of growing unrest and police counters to it were beginning to turn international opinion against South African apartheid even more strongly, proving that the tendency to blame the messenger for the message was still alive and well.

The newspaper world, meanwhile, has maintained its morbid interest in the fortunes of television and television news, developing a love-hate relationship which allows the gossip columnists to dig deeply for the dirt while, simultaneously, other pages within the same issue may devote columns to programme previews, reviews and personality interviews. For although some journalists writing about television news display a distressing lack of understanding of the subject, they are at least cute enough to realize that television news *is* news. There is no disguising their glee when, as happens often enough, it has some internal strife, falls foul of authority, makes mistakes, shows outward signs of foolish over-spending, or offends in some other way. This attitude should come as no surprise, even to ex-newspapermen like myself, who once fondly believed that all journalists were brothers. Newspapers in general have a vested interest in seeing public confidence weaken in those to whom they lost the fight long ago. William Small of CBS News once summed it up this way:

> 'The tube is an easy target. There is a waiting audience, swelled by intellectual snobbery and professional envy, that warmly greets new attack on television. The envy reflects television's kidnapping of [the] exciting and powerful roles once exclusively the province of the printed press. Television in the world of reality is too important and too powerful to be left to its practitioners or its critics. It is also too complicated to be reduced to simple generalisations, critical or not.'[7]

There is, as it happens, a fierce and continuing internal debate about the role, purpose and methods of presentation of television news, but the journalists engaged in it are invariably unable to recognize themselves or their motives from the pictures painted in sociological analyses, believing that the professional judgements they apply as they seek honestly to interpret the happenings of an immensely complicated modern world defy convenient labels or categorization. And they are equally surprised by the contention that they are pursuing a *religious* task, in the strict sense of the word, as they try to put matters into context for their viewers.[8]

The fact remains that very few attempts have been made to study in detail the problems, processes and techniques involved in bringing news to the screen several times a day, 365 days a year. Admittedly it is not an easy subject to explain. Television news cannot be easily dismissed as 'radio news with pictures' (as some broadcasting organizations trying to set it up for themselves have discovered to their cost) or as identical to any other branch of the television business. It has been described as a kind of electronic jigsaw puzzle which, like other puzzles, makes no sense until it has been completed. Taking a few separate pieces at random is rather like examining the big toe and thumb and expecting them to give an accurate picture of what the entire human body looks like. In television news, the most important pieces of the jigsaw are people, operating within their own limited spheres of influence along parallel lines which converge only at times of programme transmission.

How those pieces fit together may not greatly interest the professional critics or many who make up the daily viewing audience, but it *does* concern those journalists for whom television companies all over the world are continuing to provide worthwhile and stimulating careers.

It also concerns their employers who, fully aware of the ever-mounting pressure upon them from all sides to produce fair, accurate programmes of a professionally high standard, need the journalists they engage to be expert and reliable. For in television news, the craft of writing clearly and succinctly has become only part of the battle. Much of the rest of it has to do with the bewildering battery of electronic equipment and strange jargon which needs to be mastered properly before a single word is written. This means the journalist must understand the nature of television, what he is doing, why, and how his own role fits in with that of the rest of the team.

[7]*To Kill A Messenger, Television News and the Real World*, William Small (Hastings House, 1970).
[8]*No Good News is News — Through the Camera Darkly*, Colin Morris (The Hibbert Lecture, 1986).

More than ever before, all that has to be achieved in the full glare of the public spotlight, and the clear implication is that any journalist who intends to take his responsibilities half seriously should ensure that his motives are seen to be above reproach. Sadly, the fun days of television news have gone; too much is at stake. So while it may be considered a denial of personal freedom, I genuinely believe it is not too much to ask any television news journalist voluntarily to stay free from formal allegiance to any political party or sensitive cause. As for 'committed' journalism of any hue, that has always seemed to me to be counter-productive, because one part of the audience is inevitably going to be alienated.

For all these reasons and more, every journalist planning to make a career in television must be attuned to the demands of an exacting occupation. That means a certain amount of formal training, which has become more important than ever as television techniques advance and which, significantly, seems to escape more or less unscathed when economies are demanded in other areas.

Regrettably, even in these enlightened days of adult education, the word 'training', so far as it applies to journalism, is one for which too many old newspapermen still have only contempt. To them, the idea that any kind of journalist can be made rather than born is anathema, suggesting a succession of unthinking stereotypes pouring from the same mould. They are wrong. Training does not seek to restrict the free thinker from thinking freely about his work or anything else; training in television news technique sets out to equip the recipient of it with the knowhow and confidence to employ the marvellous technical resources which are about to become the tools of his or her trade.

The experienced newcomer to television news might have been employed on a weekly or daily newspaper, a news agency or radio station. The novice might have been recruited straight from university or elsewhere outside, and needs initiation into journalistic fundamentals as well as the special skills needed for television. All types of recruit have the same thing in common; they need to learn, preferably as swiftly as possible, *how*.

What follows in this book is not intended as a substitute for a properly run training scheme led by expert professional tutors fresh from operational duties. It makes no claim to be comprehensive, especially as the terminology, systems and equipment in use are bound to vary considerably according to the importance and financial resources of the station concerned. Neither can it attempt to standardize procedures for news selection and judgement because no standard is universally accepted.

Every news team jealously guards its own, based on its status within its parent broadcasting organization and on the principles guiding that organization's role within the social and political system of the country it serves.

What this book *is* intended to be is a first reader in television news style and production technique by one working journalist for others venturing into the most exciting field of mass communication. The emphasis throughout is on what it is important for journalists or aspiring journalists to know about how television news works at a practical level, together with enough background to put it into the modern context. It is an attempt to help newcomers fit the pieces of the electronic jigsaw puzzle together in as painless and non-technical a way as possible.

1

The electronic jigsaw puzzle

Among the inevitable first questions asked of all journalists by outsiders is 'How do you get your news?' For those working in television the answer is by no means a simple one, as so much depends on the financial and technical resources each news service is able to put into its news-gathering effort. The smaller and poorer, with little of their own to call on, may well find themselves almost totally dependent on 'second-hand' material passed on by the sister radio services often run in parallel under the same roof, or on the international television news agencies. The large, prestigious 'independents' with fat budgets are able to buy a great deal of exclusivity.

How television gets its news

Between the two extremes there lies a vast amount of common territory open to world news organizations in general, whether they are engaged in putting the word out over the air waves or on the printed page. In Britain, for example, there are the regular postal deliveries, each of which produces its share of publicity hand-out material prepared by government departments, political parties, public relations firms, private companies, industrial and social organizations. To this rich harvest can be added 'house', trade and business magazines, official statistics, advance copies of speeches, invitations to exhibitions, trade fairs, inaugurations, openings, closings, the laying of foundation stones and other ceremonies of varying importance. Well-established fixtures — parliamentary sessions, court sittings, state visits, sports events and anniversaries of all types — join the queue with scores of other public and semi-public events which are carefully weighed for their potential interest.

Those surviving the first hurdle are noted in diaries of future events for more serious consideration nearer the day. These so-called 'diary' stories or their immediate consequences (follow-ups) probably account for the majority of news stories which appear on television and in newspapers. The rivals to television news, whether they come in the shape of other newscasts, radio, magazines, daily or weekly papers, are scoured for titbits on which to build something bigger.

Staff, freelances and stringers
Journalists working either for themselves or for other publications offer suggestions (for which they expect to be paid) on a fairly regular basis. Freelances or 'stringers' they are called, and there are whole networks of them, wooed by news editors against the day that a really big story breaks in their area. It is the stringers who provide much of the basic news. With good contacts among local police, politicians and businessmen, they are usually first on the scene of any important event in their community, and are swift to pass on the information to their larger brethren. Local or specialist news agencies, concentrating on crime reporting, sport, finance and so on, also add their contributions, but it is the larger concerns in this particular field which provide most of the bread-and-butter written information and still photographs (some transmitted by wire) on a regular basis to the broadcasting organizations and the press.

Subscribers obtain their domestic news from the British national agency, the *Press Association* (*PA*, founded 1868) which is owned by the chief provincial newspapers of Britain and the Irish Republic, and which supplies a complete service of general, legal, parliamentary, financial, commercial and sporting news. *Exchange Telegraph* (*Extel*, 1872), which for many years ran a parallel general service, now concentrates on financial and sporting topics. *Reuters* (London-based since 1851) is the main source of foreign news, with full-time staff based in more than 70 countries. It is a publicly owned company whose shareholders mainly represent press interests. *The Associated Press* (*AP*) and *United Press International* (*UPI*) are British subsidiaries of American news agencies, and also serve the broadcasting organizations and the press. All are now making increasing use of the sophisticated computer display systems which are available to the world's newsrooms.

The agencies themselves rely for their material on either full-time staff journalists or on the hundreds of stringers who owe first loyalty to the publications employing them. The end product of all their work can be seen every day in the hundreds of thousands of words which pour out from the tape machines clicking away next to the newsroom.

This material is analogous with the raw meat fresh from the butcher. Some of the fat has been trimmed off but otherwise it is left for the customer to cook as he pleases. Television throws it to its news-writers (sub-editors) to be chewed, swallowed and then regurgitated into another meal more easily digested by the viewer sitting cosily at home. Newspapers treat agency copy as merely one of the ingredients from which their staff general reporters eventually produce their own masterpieces to satisfy their readers' proven tastes. These general reporters, traditionally under the wing of the news editor, are also deployed to cover the various diary items day by day, or may be detached for longer periods to work on projects or campaigns of special interest to their publications.

The television news equivalents, fewer in number than their counterparts on individual Fleet Street newspapers (from which many of them have graduated) are used mainly on the diary or follow-up assignments offering the most picture-worthy possibilities. They are also engaged in spot news stories broken first by the agencies, but in either case the television news reporter has to work as part of a team.

There is a cameraman to take the pictures, a recordist to capture the sound and, where interior locations are involved, possibly a lighting assistant to supply enough artificial illumination by which the film or tape can be shot. Without these or other forms of technical help, the reporter is powerless to produce much that is worthwhile for television. Conversely, camera crews are often briefed to cover stories without reporters, relying on their own judgements for the detailed choice of coverage. There are also single-operator units. These have obvious limitations, but the development of the 'cam-corder', a very lightweight electronic system which combines camera and integral audio/video cassette recorder, has made what's called in the trade the 'one-man band' a much more practical proposition for some news services.

Other staff newspeople are specialists in particular areas of news. Regarded as experts after years of devoting themselves to a single subject and building up highly placed personal contacts, they themselves become reliable sources for much that is important. The political editor, fresh from an off-the-record chat over lunch with a government minister; the industrial correspondent, back from talks with acquaintances influential within business, industry or the trade union movement — each is ideally placed to begin piecing together information which might well develop into a big news story, perhaps not today or tomorrow but next week.

This handful of specialist correspondents, as members of recognized groups or associations of journalists working in the same field for different news outlets, enjoy confidential 'lobby' briefings from governments, and are on the regular mailing lists of professional bodies sending out material of a technical or restricted nature.

The television news organizations are also able to rely fairly heavily on their own out-stations, which in turn may employ specialist correspondents, staff and freelance reporters and camera crews. Material originated locally can be pumped into the network news programmes live, or recorded on to videotape for replaying at some convenient point later on. The BBC central television newsroom is served by national production centres in Scotland, Wales and Northern Ireland, plus eight main television newsrooms in provincial England. All are partly in business for the purpose of providing the national news with items deserving wider than purely local coverage, although forays by teams from headquarters are by no means discouraged. It is also a two-way process. BBC TV News contributes from London to the 25 minute regional daily news magazine programmes, sometimes supplying its own facilities and staff including the specialist correspondents, sometimes allowing network facilities to be used by regional people travelling down specially for the occasion. In all these cases, the contributions may be 'live' or be recorded at the receiving end for local transmission later.

The BBC controls four national radio networks centred on Broadcasting House in London, more than 30 local radio stations, and Bush House, headquarters of external service broadcasting, from any of which ideas and some sound-only coverage can be picked up for use when required.

It also operates its own internal news agency, the General News Service, which evaluates all incoming news material from its own and other sources, relaying the most important through a computer called the MSS (Message

Switching System) and about 200 news teleprinters from the radio newsroom at Broadcasting House.

A particularly valuable part of the GNS service, known as 'Rip 'n' Read', makes complete summaries of national and international news available for immediate re-broadcast by local and regional BBC stations which lack the resources or time to compile their own. GNS is also responsible for another internal system by which some offices are alerted to service messages or news flashes over a loudspeaker network. Yet another source is the corporation's monitoring service, which passes to BBC television and radio newsrooms information collected from a round-the-clock listening service to the radio broadcasts of foreign stations — often the quickest and most reliable way of obtaining international 'official' news.

Independent Television News has natural links with the 15 commercial television programme companies and the 40-plus local radio stations operating under the umbrella of the Independent Broadcasting Authority. It also has teams based in the north and midlands of England, but it is otherwise a chiefly centralized organization, priding itself on an ability to act swiftly in the movement of people and equipment from London around Britain and beyond.

Foreign news sources

On the foreign side, some staff journalists are employed permanently away from base in any one of a small number of important centres. These, by the nature of international affairs, are those considered to be the most likely to produce a steady stream of news stories of interest to viewers at home and, equally important, are themselves at the crossroads of the world's international communications systems: New York, Washington, Hong Kong, Jerusalem.

Maintaining a permanent overseas base anywhere is an extraordinarily expensive business. Every correspondent needs transport, an office, some ancillary help and somewhere for him and his family to live. His children may need to be educated. And all that is before he files a single story. So the value of each foreign news bureau is kept under continuing close scrutiny by those who have to foot the bill for it, and changes are made to keep pace with the emergence of new areas of special interest. As a result, adjustments in the mid-eighties have tended to produce more offices in eastern Europe and southern Africa.

Like his counterpart at home, the foreign specialist sees that he understands the language, meets the right people, reads the local papers, watches television, listens to radio and gets himself accredited as the official representative of his television station at home. This, as a rule, will ensure a constant flow of information to be sifted for use as background material to items transmitted later on.

Though based for convenience in one place, the foreign correspondent might well have a huge territory, perhaps a whole continent, to cover. This means having to travel thousands of miles to reach stories breaking in remote areas. Time differentials frequently weigh heavily. The correspondent may have to work through the night to produce the goods for bosses for whom it is still daytime. He will probably wear two watches, one keeping local time, the other 'home' time to remind him constantly of deadlines. With skill, experience and good fortune, the foreign correspondent will become an accepted part of the local scenery, sometimes as an honoured guest. Elsewhere, there may be hostility thinly disguised as toleration. The correspondent's home is bugged, the telephone tapped. He and his wife are followed. Eventually, he commits what the government of the country regards as a professional indiscretion, and is expelled.

If that does not happen, after a few years in the same place, he is likely to be summoned home and re-assigned by employers who fear he may become too comfortable to remain an objective observer.

Where full-time television newspeople are not based, the foreign equivalent of the home stringer is frequently used. Sometimes this is a local national serving any number of overseas outlets. Often he is a foreigner himself. He may be a freelance accepting occasional commissions outside his normal field, or a staff correspondent of one publication which, in an effort to keep down the costs involved in maintaining a presence abroad, allows him to supply material to others. In addition to all these permutations, in the case of the BBC there are also staff working abroad for radio, and these can be borrowed by the television side where occasion demands.

In some foreign centres, the television news representative has easy access to locally based camera teams who are hired for a daily fee. In one or two particularly busy areas for news, crews are employed on a permanent or semi-permanent basis, and some of these provide highly sophisticated equipment and facilities which almost amount to studios in their own right. The material they shoot is usually shipped home by air for editing and transmission, although there are increasingly occasions when the nature or immediacy of the story dictates that it is handled locally, using hired staff, and then transmitted through the global communications system. This saves many hours, and is being used more and more widely by those television organizations that see news as a highly perishable commodity and consider the outlay for the hire of satellite time to be money well spent.

International news agencies
The other main users of the global system are the international television news agencies which supply the foreign material for hundreds of news programmes throughout the world.

Their links with the main networks give them immediate access to a staggering choice of first-class news material, and they also employ their own staff and freelance camera crews in important centres.

For the poorer news services, unable or unwilling to meet the expense of assigning their own staff to foreign stories, agency coverage is relatively cheap and usually perfectly adequate in terms of coverage quality, whether broadcast in its entirety and supplemented by sub-titles, or reduced in length and transmitted alongside a locally written commentary from the paperwork accompanying every film or tape.

The biggest agency is probably *Visnews*, which began life in 1957 as the British Commonwealth International Newsfilm Agency, and is owned by

Reuters, the BBC and several Commonwealth broadcasting organizations. Part of its operation is to supply by satellite or videocassette a daily service of news and sport to more than 400 broadcasting stations. It is also involved in *BrightStar*, a permanent satellite link between Britain and the United States. In addition Visnews operates its own network of camera crews, many of whom have made an important contribution to the coverage of world events. It was the head of Visnews' African Bureau, Mohamed Amin, whose pictures in 1984 alerted the outside world to the scale of the Ethiopian famine.

Visnews' main rivals are *Worldwide Television News* (*WTN*), formerly UPITN, which was established in 1967 as a partnership between the television department of United Press International and Independent Television News of London. It is now owned by ITN, ABC of the United States and the Nines Network of Australia. WTN has more than a dozen bureaux around the world, its full-time staff and 400-strong freelance network supplying news and features by satellite and videocassette to broadcasters in over 100 countries. Both agencies have ambitious expansion plans. Visnews have experimented with *World News Network*, a centrally run news channel which would be available to subscribers in their own language.

WTN, too, is interested in producing its own programmes for cable and satellite. International competition already exists. Material from the *Cable News Network*, established in Atlanta, Georgia, in 1980, is screened in more than 20 countries outside the United States, in addition to the European service it began in 1985.

Much of this agency material has the merit of being the first pictorial record of an important news story to which the wealthier services may decide to despatch their own staff units later on. Even when they do, the agencies are relied upon to continue their coverage for the rest of their clientele. The agencies are also important sources for historical or background items for news programmes. Potted biographies, moving pictures and still photographs of events and places previously, or likely to be, in the news are rapidly made available when occasion demands, even though the material may consist of no more than a single, portrait-type photograph of an obscure politician, or a few precious seconds of film or tape.

Archives

Most television news departments maintain their own archives, largely built up from material they have already transmitted. In some cases the 'library' is run by a picture editor alongside his normal duties, and consists of a few cans of film kept on the cutting room shelf, half a dozen videocassettes and a drawer of 35 mm colour slides. At best, others have become sophisticated storehouses of stills, film and videotape. These represent hundreds of thousands of separate news items, each carefully catalogued and indexed by trained full-time staff to ensure that the user has accurate and immediate access. The storage of this mass of bulky material in conditions where it will not deteriorate itself provides an enormous headache, especially as so much film is now transferred to videotape for transmission, and the regular pruning necessary demands thoroughness without carelessness. This is no mean task when there is constant pressure to make room for new additions.

Vast libraries of press cuttings and previously broadcast news scripts are also collected under the supervision of qualified staff. With literally millions of pieces of paper involved, the problem here again is the obvious one of storage space. One solution has been to transfer older cuttings to microfilm, another to rely more on computer databases, including commercial 'on line' systems offering information on specialist topics.

To this wide and fascinating mix of home grown and expensively gathered news material can be added the occasional unexpected bonus — the 'tip-off' from a member of the public, or the amateur with a holiday snap or home video which turns out to be a genuine exclusive for the organization lucky enough to get it. Video material is now so widely used that some news programmes serving huge or remote areas have encouraged the creation of extensive networks of enthusiastic amateurs on constant look-out for news items they can pass on for broadcast use.

Who does what in television news

If television news is a jigsaw puzzle, then most of the pieces represent highly skilled technicians with special contributions to make towards building up the final picture. For in modern industrial jargon television is 'labour intensive', which means that a large percentage of what it costs to run such an organization is spent on the wages bill. Value for money is therefore essential.

Purely local broadcasting, frequently run on a shoestring budget, demands nothing if not versatility from its people. In its mildest form, this is likely to give an executive senior managerial and administrative duties as well as editorial ones. It may mean an engineer operating a television camera in the studio one day and a videotape recording machine the next, or all journalists reading as well as writing their own material.

In extremes this versatility requires the reporters physically to edit pictures as part of a normal day's work, and cameramen to write commentaries for some of their own material.

National news programmes, too, are not necessarily free of the need to be economical in their use of staff resources. One senior news editor in the Caribbean spends the first two-thirds of the day as a news-gatherer and writer for the main evening news and the remaining third as studio director. In the late seventies, a West European television news service was still operating without any permanent journalistic staff at all, apart from the chief editor. The writing for the main bulletins was undertaken by journalists who had already completed a full day's work elsewhere. Even among the more fortunate, it is not uncommon for television news to have to share such basic services as camera crews, picture editors, equipment and transport with sister departments within the same organization, even though obvious problems arise from the need to serve more than one master.

At the other end of the scale, the television news department has the exclusive use of its own separate staff, studios and technical equipment. In the BBC, for example, it has a specially built wing of the Television Centre in West London, but remains part of a public corporation responsible for a vast range of television and radio output. Independent Television News, with headquarters in Wells Street, Central London, is a separate non-profit making company owned and financed by 15 of the British independent programme companies, and is charged under the Television Act with the responsibility of producing national news programmes for the country's commercial network. The exception is the breakfast operation run by *TV-am*, which set up its own news service from scratch and found it extremely costly.

Chiefly because of the demands made on them to produce programmes at least three or four times a day each week, these and other 'big league' news organizations each need full-time staffs totalling several hundred. These are divided into smaller groups of specialists — cameramen, reporters, picture editors, studio directors, graphics designers, newsroom journalists, newsreaders, etc., who rarely if ever stray from their own clearly defined duties.

These sections may then be arranged into two broad categories, one responsible for gathering the news (*intake* or *input*), the other for its selection and final shape on the screen (*output*). See Fig. 1.1.

The entire editorial machine is notionally under the control of the most senior output people on duty — usually the editors of the daily programmes. At one time it was fashionable to give the responsibility for each day's news coverage, treatment and output to a single person under what was known as the 'editor for the day' system. The main benefit was seen as the continuity it provided, for each editor's spell on duty was 12 hours or more, covering the transmission of several (shortish) news bulletins.

The current view generally acknowledges that it is virtually impossible for anyone to take charge of more than one main news a day, because programmes are longer, more technically difficult, and differ in style and content from others within the same stable. In any case there would scarcely be enough time to give proper consideration to one newscast

THE ORGANIZATION OF TELEVISION NEWS

INTAKE/INPUT (News-gathering)	OUTPUT (News processing)
Home and foreign assignments organizers	Programme editors
Reporters and correspondents	Newsroom editorial and clerical staff
Operations organizers (technical)	Newsreaders/presenters
Camera crews	Picture editors
Facilities engineers	Graphic designers
Despatch riders	Video and stills archivists
Diary planners	Studio production and technical staff

Fig. 1.1. Typical division of responsibilities in a large news organization, with one group of people concentrating on news-*gathering*, the other on news-*processing* and production. Many roles are combined in smaller news operations.

before the next one became due. So even though they may be sharing some of the staff and facilities, the editors of programmes within the same organization are working towards separate goals.

In the mid eighties, ITN, one of the world's big five television news organizations (the others being their British rivals the BBC, and the three American networks ABC, CBS and NBC) were running four weekday news programmes, each of different duration and each with a clear and different identity from the rest.

Each programme editor is supervised from a distance by the senior executives who head ITN, and who are ultimately responsible for its overall activities. But at an operational level the daily chain of command extends from the programme editors to the other departments which provide their individual skills to order.

The news-gathering machine

Aside from his operational duties on the day, the editor of a programme also has to shoulder a degree of responsibility for anticipating what will appear on the screen. Lengthy planning meetings are held daily, weekly and monthly, at which the meticulously compiled diaries are considered event by event under the guidance of the domestic and foreign news executives whose job it is to deal with the logistics of news coverage for the whole of the output.

At this stage each editor is really gazing into the crystal ball, trying to foretell what the programme on his next duty day will in part contain, even though it is clearly understood by all concerned that the most expensive, carefully laid plans will be scrapped at the last moment should a really important story break unexpectedly. It is a hazard readily accepted by everyone, not least by those who may have spent many hours 'setting up' interviews or obtaining permission to cover news items which may never be seen.

Such flexibility is a routine but essential part of the news-gathering process, which is relatively slow under even the most favourable conditions, although the speed of communication has improved considerably.

It has long been recognized that coverage for factual television programmes has to be organized well in advance to ensure that people and equipment are properly positioned as an event takes place. To that extent it is far simpler to call off coverage than it is to lay it on at the last moment.

Home assignments
The main responsibility for either eventuality rests with the duty *News Editor* or *News Organizer** manning the home assignments desk as the mainstay of that part of the operation dealing with domestic subjects (which invariably account for a greater proportion of air time than foreign news items). With these journalists, through the programme editors and the department heads, rest the moment-to-moment decisions of when to

---

* These are operational titles. Broadcasting organizations have different names for the same post.

send staff reporters and camera crews on assignments or when to rely on regional or freelance effort to produce the goods. The news organizers often see themselves, somewhat cynically, as the 'can-carriers' of news departments. They are meant to have the mental agility of chess grand masters in moving pieces (in this case reporters and camera crews) into position before events occur, at the same time making sure that enough human resources remain available in reserve to deal with any important new events which may arise.

The work also demands a certain intuition about the workings of senior colleagues' minds. In briefing reporters, for example, they are expected to know instinctively how any one editor would wish an assignment to be carried out, down to the detail of questions to be asked in interviews.

The role of the news organizer/editor is generally restricted to arranging on-the-day coverage, much of which is based on plans previously laid by other members of the department.

The duties of the *Planners* include the submission of ideas for, and treatment of, the various items. But the routine calls chiefly for a well-developed news sense. This must be keen enough to isolate, from an embarrassing wealth of incoming information about subjects for potential coverage, that tiny proportion which has some small chance of reaching the screen.

Much of the planners' time is spent making telephone calls to arrange interviews, to verify whether what seems interesting on paper will actually stand up to the closer scrutiny of a camera, and to evaluate whether the various ingredients, as discussed, are likely to result in a clear and balanced report eventually being transmitted. Once the broad details have been agreed, each item, now formalized under a one- or two-word code name it will keep until it reaches the screen, is added to the internally circulated list of subjects for prospective coverage. At a still later stage, arrangements may have to be made to collect any useful documents or special passes needed on the day, so that the process of collecting the news may be carried out as smoothly as possible.

Planning for longer-term or particularly complicated assignments may well be conducted by special units created within the news-gathering department on an ad hoc or permanent basis. Big set-piece events such as important overseas tours, summit meetings, elections, party political conferences or conventions lasting several days, call for highly detailed organization in advance if the eventual coverage is to be comprehensive. It may be necessary to establish temporary headquarters away from base, committing substantial numbers of staff and technical resources to ensure that the main story and any side-issues are properly reported.

The spin-off from all this effort may well be extended reports within the regular news programmes or 'specials' in their own right.

The same units may also be responsible for preparing background items and for keeping the profiles/obituaries of prominent personalities up to date — in fact for almost anything that helps programme editors avoid an unsatisfactory scramble to get something on the air.

Working in close harmony with the rest of the intake department are the staff concerned with the technical side. An executive variously named the *Field Operations Organizer, Assignments Editor/Manager* or *Camera Unit*

Manager allots the camera crews and lighting assistants to their duties, with or without reporters, probably keeping in touch by means of two-way radio telephone systems installed at base and in the camera vehicles. His empire also includes the *FACs* (*Facilities*) staff, the new breed of engineer whose role is to supply the communications links between base and the camera crews on the road.

The big, sophisticated intakes also employ clerical staff whose duties include booking studio time and facilities for material originating from regional and other outside sources, plus a small posse of motor-cyclists who play an indispensable part in the urgent collection of videotapes and still photographs.

Covering the world
Foreign news is also usually considered to be part of intake, its small presence at head office the tip of a formidable iceberg made up of staff correspondents resident abroad, a world-wide network of stringers, and close ties with friendly broadcasting organizations able to conjure words and pictures from virtually anywhere in the globe at very short notice. The department is probably headed by the *Foreign News Editor*, a senior journalist whose professional interests are expected to extend beyond the boundaries of his own organization into the multi-national 'clubs' established to provide regular, free-flowing exchanges of news material between member countries.

On a formal basis the foreign editors or their very senior colleagues of BBC TV News and ITN take their turns to act as co-ordinators for the European club — the European Broadcasting Union's Eurovision News Exchange. It is a ten-day task twice a year, and involves taking charge of the daily conference hook-up at which offers of coverage are made or requested, the decisions being reached between international colleagues without the need for anyone to leave his office.

The routine administrative load is shared by *Deputy* or *Assistant Foreign Editors*, while operationally the better-off can afford to staff the foreign assignments desk with two or three *Foreign Duty Editors*, working in rotation. These are the equivalent of the news organizers on the domestic side, providing a link between the news-gatherers in the field and the programme editors at home. The despatch of normally home-based staff on 'fire-brigade' assignments is a matter for negotiation between the more senior members of the department.

The last link in the foreign chain is the *Foreign Traffic Manager* or *Satellite Operations Organizer*, who makes the detailed arrangements for the collection of material from abroad, and who needs to be in frequent direct contact with other broadcasting organizations, especially during the regular conferences between 'club' members. The residents of the foreign traffic desk are also renowned for their encyclopaedic knowledge of the procedures for organizing satellite communications at very short notice — a talent in demand when important news suddenly breaks at awkward times in the world's most unexpected places.

The three faces of output

Despite the growth of news-gathering operations over recent years, television news output remains bigger and more complicated, relying as it does on the resources provided by three separate services functioning under the loose headings of editorial, production and technical.

Among the craftspeople who work in these three groups lies the same sort of generally friendly rivalry which exists between a newspaper's journalists and its printers. But all are acutely aware of the fact that, however expert in their own field, no one group alone is capable of taking the material produced by intake and putting it on the screen.

Decision-making begins and ends with the *Programme Editor/Producer* who, as the senior member of the editorial team, is usually based in the newsroom, where communications with the rest of output and intake are most easily maintained. According to personal style, each editor exerts a different amount of influence to ensure that the programme follows its intended course. But with so many calls upon his time and so many loose ends to be tied during an often frantically busy few hours, responsibility for the detailed organization tends to be led by a senior lieutenant, the *Chief Sub-editor* (*Senior Duty Editor* in BBC TV News and radio) whose function is very similar to that of his newspaper counterpart.

The chief's responsibilities are defined most simply as those of quality controller and time-keeper. Quality control begins with the briefing of the newsroom writing staff, perhaps six or eight people of different seniority, who are preparing the individual elements within the programme framework. It continues with the checking of every written item as completed so that all the strands knit together in a way which maintains continuity while avoiding repetition, and language and programme style are kept on an even keel throughout the programme. This may mean striking out or altering phrases, perhaps even re-writing whole items composed in haste by people working under intense pressure.

Also, as a journalist of great experience, the chief sub-editor has further value as an editorial long-stop, preventing factual errors creeping through in a way which would ultimately damage the credibility of the entire programme.

Since few scheduled television news programmes are regularly open-ended, the chief sub-editor's talents are meant to include a facility for speedy and accurate mental arithmetic, essential for his other role as time-keeper. Steering a whole programme towards its strict time allocation is no mean feat, especially as so much depends on intuition or sheer guesswork about the duration of segments which may not be completed until the programme is already on the air.

For this reason the chief continually has to exhort those entrusted with the individual items to restrict themselves to the 'space' they have been allotted. A typical half-hour news programme might contain 12 or more separate stories varying in importance and length. An unexpected 10–15 seconds on each would play havoc with all previous calculations, resulting in wholesale cuts and alterations. These, in turn, would probably ruin any attempts to produce a rounded, well-balanced programme.

A further stage in the chief sub's time-keeping duties comes during transmission itself, when the appearance of late news may call for what newspaper people know as 'cutting on the stone'. In the case of television this is the deletion of material to ensure that, whatever changes have to be made, a programme does not over-run its allocation of air-time, even by as little as a few seconds.

Many editors find it more sensible to entrust the responsibility for timing the programme to a member of the production staff, especially if organizational demands are such that they have to combine the duties of both producer and chief sub-editor.

But since the decision is always about what as well as how much to omit, journalists elsewhere keep the chore to themselves, perhaps somewhat reluctantly in some cases, as many are notoriously ham-fisted when it comes to dealing with figures. Technology is coming to their rescue. Business-type calculating machines which work in minutes and seconds already exist, and the recent development of electronic newsroom systems has opened up a vast new range of facilities, one of which allows the computer to adjust programme timings automatically on a video screen as items are added or cut.

Before too long television chief sub-editors or their counterparts the world over are likely to have foresaken their pencils for good as they sit at computer terminals calling up scripts created by their colleagues working from similar keyboards around the newsroom.

Newspaper terminology has also been borrowed to title another role in the newsroom's output operation. The *Copytaster*, a senior post on any journal, is less so in broadcasting. The duties are largely confined to keeping individual writers fuelled with news agency tape about stories already chosen for inclusion by the editor/producer, although the wise old hands are much valued for their ability to spot the odd item worth following up for special treatment.

The copytaster spends much of his time sifting through the paper output of half a dozen or more news agencies — a thankless, never-ending task which is becoming gradually less arduous as the teleprinter gives way to the video screen. This is helping the many news services which operate without a central copytasting system, as wire copy can be fed direct to the writers by computer.

The journalist newcomer to television news is more than likely to join the newsroom's pool of writing staff, usually the largest single group within the editorial side of output.

In local television, their work is almost sure to include intake responsibilities, including the assigning of reporters and camera crews. Some may also appear on screen. On national programmes they are known as *News Producers, Sub-editors, News editors, Scriptwriters, News-writers* or simply *Writers*, depending on the organization for which they work, yet the tasks they are called upon to perform are bound to be broadly similar.

Within the limits of responsibility as defined by their senior colleagues, they assemble the components which make up every programme item, selecting still photographs, artwork and videotape, writing commentaries and liaising closely with contributing reporters and correspondents. The most senior are often put in charge of small teams of other writers to create larger programme segments from particularly complex news items comprising different elements. The most junior, supervised carefully by the chief sub-editor or another parent-figure, may contribute only a few seconds of air-time from a pile of news agency copy. Some writers go on to develop expertise in other areas of television technique and, as a result, are occasionally called upon to display their talents as field-producers, directors or reporters on the screen.

The news-writer's role is one which has evolved over the years to keep pace with the changing styles of the news programmes themselves, and the development of equipment which demands the acquisition of new skills. As the journalistic backbone of output, linking production and technical staff with the news-gathering effort supplied by intake, the news-writers exert considerable influence over what the viewer eventually sees on the air.

Production output

Until the late seventies it scarcely seemed possible to imagine the world's television news programmes exchanging their trusty 16 mm sound cameras and fast-process colour film for lightweight electronic hardware and three-quarter or half-inch magnetic videotape. But they embraced the technological revolution with enthusiasm when it came and swept film aside in an astonishingly short time. Some of the traditional crafts went out with the celluloid, though fortunately most of the practitioners were retrained to cope with the all-electronic medium.

The film editors, for example, became *Picture Editors*, adapting their skills to continue working closely with the writers from the newsroom, viewing and assembling the raw video material into coherent story lines within lengths dictated by their programme editors. Edited picture stories may run for a few seconds or several minutes according to importance, and as with the editorial side of output, the senior, more experienced are given the most complicated items to assemble. The junior staff handle those involving the simple editing of minor stories (which may never get on the air) and material copied from the archives.

Dubbing Mixers, drawing on libraries of sound effects recorded on to disc or magnetic tape, add extra sound tracks to synchronize with the edited pictures. Other production staff are closely concerned with the operation of the studio control room, the central point through which all programmes are routed.

The main occupants of the studio itself are the *Newsreaders*, *Newscasters*, *Anchors* or *Presenters*, the public faces of the programme on whom the success or failure of any news service may be said to depend.

Although reading other people's written work aloud for limited periods each day might not seem either particularly onerous or intellectually demanding, consistently high standards of news reading are not easily reached, and there are other pressures to offset the undoubted glamour image of the job. Many of those with strong journalistic backgrounds are also becoming more involved with their programmes, to the extent that they now have a role in the decision-making as well as writing a large part of their own material.

Unseen by the viewer, other studio staff have their own duties: the *Prompter Operator*, tucked away in a corner at the controls of a machine which enables the presenter to speak the script apparently from memory;

Studio Cameramen, operating the four or five electronic cameras providing the link with the viewing audience; and the *Floor Manager*, supervising the whole studio operation and using a headphone-microphone set to stay in touch with colleagues sitting facing a bank of preview monitors in the control room on the other side of the studio's glass wall.

Although the technical responsibility for every programme rests with a *Senior Engineer*, the creative head of the control room on transmission is the *Studio Director*, who co-ordinates all the resources offered by the three areas of output. Helping to fuse these together at the critical moment is a *Production Assistant* to control the exact timing of different elements, a *Vision Mixer* to press buttons on a console introducing the visual selections as made by the director, and a *Sound Engineer* to bring in the accompanying audio feeds from microphones, tapes, records, additional sound tracks, etc. Slight errors or delays in reaction by any member of this team are instantly translated into noticeable flaws on the screen.

Two other creative groups come within the category of production: *Graphics Designers/Artists* are engaged full-time on the provision, in accepted 'house' style, of all artwork used in television news. This is increasingly computer-based and includes maps, charts, diagrams and lettering for identifying people on the screen. *Stills Assistants* research and maintain a permanent, expanding library of photographic prints and slides, some of which are taken by staff *Photographers*, who are assigned to supplement material provided by freelances and the international agencies.

Technical output

Distinction between the production and technical faces of output are frequently thin, since both demand common skills. This is perhaps most noticeable in the case of *Videotape Editors*, who have both output and intake responsibilities, and are expected to combine technical mastery over highly sensitive electronic recording machines with an awareness of the editorial values of picture and sound which matches that of the picture editors, with whom they are increasingly considered to be interchangeable.

The ability to reach this standard has lifted much videotape editing for news to heights at which the assembly of very complex items, particularly from foreign sources, is achieved with remarkable accuracy and speed.

On a daily basis, the technical staff are directly responsible to a senior colleague from the engineering department for the maintenance and operation of equipment. Their first aim is to ensure the highest possible technical standards, but at the same time to remain flexible in outlook, for compromise is necessary where picture and sound material may be poor in quality but regarded as high in news value.

Engineering tasks, though rarely sharing the limelight, are nevertheless central to the existence of any programme. Without them the carefully constructed jigsaw puzzle of television news would fall apart.

News OB units and electronic news gathering

Engineering staff also provide the main manpower for one or any number of news OB (*Outside Broadcast*) units, scaled-down versions of the teams which supply multi-camera picture and sound coverage, often live, of major set-piece events. Standard OB units consist of several vehicles

HOW TV NEWS GETS ON THE AIR

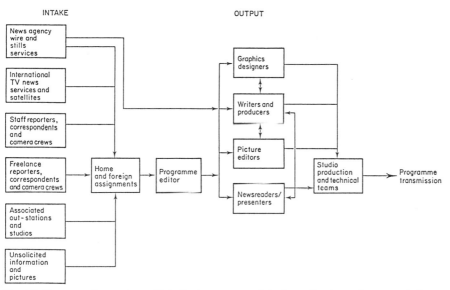

Fig. 1.2. Progress of news items. Note the importance of the home/foreign assignments desks as the chief link between incoming sources and the output editorial and production teams.

containing both conventionally mounted and portable electronic cameras, several hundred feet of cable, videotape recorders and generators. A news OB, responding through intake to matters of immediate concern, might have to manage with up to six technicians, a single member of the production staff (a director), two or three cameras, a videocassette recorder and two medium sized vans, one acting as a mobile control centre. Once in position, news OBs are ideal for coping with events where more than a single camera is needed.

That brings us finally to the so-called 'Lightweight Revolution', brought about by the introduction of ENG (Electronic News Gathering), a self-contained video system consisting of a highly portable battery-operated camera and accompanying videocassette recorder. *ENG Crews*, usually made up of two people, are technically under the management of their intake desks, yet the raw material they produce is fundamental to the existence of news programmes and therefore to the output editors. The ENG system is versatile enough to be used in any one of several ways: the picture can be recorded onto the videocassette and then physically sent back to base for editing, linked electronically from fixed or mobile microwave points or bounced off strategically placed receiving aerials in urban areas, and/or — most exciting of all — transmitted 'live' into news programmes while they are taking place (see Fig. 1.2).

2

Writing for television news

The first thing to be said to the apprehensive newcomer about writing for television news is that there are any number of broad guidelines but very few hard and fast rules. This makes sound commonsense in a medium where so much depends on instant reaction in the field or in the newsroom, up to the time of programme transmission.

Television style

The television news department of the British Broadcasting Corporation, the pioneers of illustrated news on television, still has no formal style book. Shortly after his appointment, as part of a new-broom exercise, one executive head did launch a brief blitz on what he considered to be the sloppy use of language which had crept into the daily programmes. In 1979, during its 25th anniversary year, a senior writer laid low by an accident was asked to spend his convalescence producing a guide aimed at encouraging reporters and newsroom journalists to think more clearly about what they were writing. On a more regular basis, a growing newsroom log tries to signpost any editorial pitfalls as they present themselves, and there exist certain established programme styles in the area of type-faces, colours and formats of news artwork. But the writers are otherwise free of the straitjacket into which much newspaper material is forced by the tyranny of the style book.

On my very first morning as a trainee reporter with a London suburban weekly, I was given a 50 or 60 page hard-cover volume to treat with the same reverence as I would the bible. It told me that, among other things, I was always to spell the word *organize* rather than *organise*, that the title *Councillor* had to be abbreviated to *Cllr.*, *Alderman* to *Ald.*, that it was not the *High Road* or even the *High Rd.*, but the *High-road*, and so on.

In later years I worked in a newspaper office where the length of each paragraph had to be *one* sentence . . . in another office, *two*. These sentences, it was made clear, must not begin with the definite or indefinite article, or with the word *But*, and that it was a journalistic crime, punishable by ridicule, to refer to the *18-year-old* defendant in a court case when, all along, we really meant the *18 years old* one.

All that may seem very trivial, and in many ways indeed it is. But the fact remains that so far as the printed page is concerned uniformity and consistency within the columns are considered more likely to please the reader than to repel. Haphazard changes of type face or different spellings of the same word in the same or succeeding issues are guaranteed to irritate and annoy, and experts in design are much sought after to bring discipline and good order to newspaper pages so that the reader's eye may be led smoothly from one item to another.

By its nature, television news cannot expect to do precisely the same. While it is certainly both desirable and possible to lead the viewer from event to event by the proper use of visual signposts, combined with careful phraseology, what occurs within the brief time-scale of many a broadcast news item is open to each viewer's personal interpretation of what is being seen and heard.

It is this extra dimension which helps to place television in its unique position among methods of communication. A newspaper's verbatim report of an important political speech will give a clear record of what is said . . . a newspaper reporter's word picture will give, at one remove, an interpretation of what is meant. A direct radio broadcast will enable what is said to be heard complete with repetitions, hesitations and 'bad' grammar.

But only the television viewer, sitting in the comfort of his own home, is given the full information from which to make a personal assessment of the *way* things are said, together with the sidelong glance and nervous twitch which accompanies the confident-sounding delivery.

Unfortunately, it is extremely probable that the viewer will be shown a relatively small sample on which to base that judgement, as it is freely accepted by television newspeople that the 'whole' story, however important, can rarely, if ever, be told within the context of a routine 25 or 30 minute news programme sandwiched between the domestic comedy show and the detective serial. Even if there were no pictures and the presenter read continuously for an entire half hour, it would not be possible to pack in more than about 5500 words — fewer than the front page of the London *Times*.

However long they might like to linger over recounting events of the day, television news journalists are acutely conscious that, through no fault of their own, they have to be ultra-selective, both in the number of items put on the screen and the amount of time devoted to each. Critics outside and inside television news are convinced that these factors in themselves result in restrictions on the type of material which can be included, and that a direct comparison shows up a remarkable similarity between the content and treatment of news transmitted on the main programmes of the two national broadcasting organizations in Britain.

Whether or not this is entirely true, there is little doubt that the time element does impose an important form of constraint on the newsroom-based journalist in particular. Yet whether it has only negative influence is arguable.

The need to condense forces continuing re-assessment of the merits of individual items as they develop, ensures economy in the use of words, and discourages length for its own sake. Above all, it sharpens the newsman's traditional ability to recognize those facts which cry out for inclusion from those which do not, and if standards are not to slip, the movement towards longer news programmes will occur without allowing flabbiness to creep in. Application of a developed news-sense is, however, only one half of the newsroom journalist's task. The other half, probably more important, is to put across the chosen facts in a way that every television viewer can readily understand. It does not mean pandering to the lowest common denominator of intelligence, but it does pose a problem that does not apply to the printed word.

The newspaper reader fed with a regular diet of the *Daily Mirror* or the *New York Post*, for example, soon learns to expect every issue to be treated in the same bright and breezy style with which he has become familiar. The regular subscriber to the *Times* or the *Washington Post* will come to expect the treatment to be sober and more discursive. Television news has to satisfy both readerships at the same time.

Helping the writer to do that is a powerful double-edged weapon — the capacity to let the viewer see and hear events for himself. That advantage must not be squandered, either by the use of technical wizardry for its own sake (so complicating otherwise uncomplicated issues) or by the presentation of written material in a way which appeals to only one half of the intellectual spectrum. Ed Murrow, one of the most outstanding of all broadcast journalists, recognized that fact long ago when he told CBS radio reporters to use language which would be understood by the truck driver yet not insult the professor's intelligence.

Today's sophisticated audience has become accustomed to hearing everyday words and phrases used in films, the theatre and on television. The news is no exception. It must be told in an authoritative, yet friendly and informal way which attracts and maintains interest without going as far as page three of Rupert Murdoch's *Sun*. Even though the total audience may add up to millions, the writer should be encouraged to think small, perhaps imagining people in groups of no more than two or three. Conversational language (not slang), preferably used in short, direct sentences, should be the aim. The point which even experienced television journalists keep in the front of their minds is that their efforts will be totally wasted if the viewer does not immediately grasp what is being said, particularly when moving or other illustration is competing with the spoken word. The admission may be painful to journalists, but the old cliché that one picture is worth a thousand words has more than a ring of truth.

The newspaper reader can always return to the printed sentence. If necessary he can pore over a dictionary. But words once uttered on television (or radio, of course) are beyond recall. A viewer left wondering about the meaning of what has been said at the beginning of a sentence will probably be too distracted to comprehend what is being said at the end of it. That applies to every television news item, without exception, and almost the greatest crime that any journalist in the medium can commit is to leave any part of the audience in confusion about what is meant. The onus is on the writer, always, to put across the spoken word in as clear, simple and direct a way as can be managed.

Some very old hands maintain that one of the best ways of achieving this is not to 'write' scripts at all, but to dictate them to typists to ensure the use of natural-sounding language. (When computer systems take over there may not be any newsroom typists, but there will be nothing to stop writers trying out their scripts on each other.)

Of course it is far simpler to set down the principles for direct writing than it is to carry them through, especially where some government publications, wordy official announcements or complicated economic or industrial subjects are concerned. Indeed official gobbledygook is so prevalent, groups of language lovers exist to try to combat it. Until they succeed in stamping it out altogether the television news-writer is left with a single, over-riding test to apply. Does *he* understand what he is writing? If he doesn't, neither will the viewer.

The successful news script probably also has as much to do with proper mental preparation as it has with an ability to put words together in a clear way. The journalist working in television must be already tuned in to the task ahead before anything is written. Watching yesterday's programmes, this morning's before setting off to work, listening to the radio on the way in and reading the newspapers every day may at times be regarded as chores to be avoided, but the journalist who is not well-informed and up to date on a wide range of current subjects is unlikely to be genuinely authoritative when it comes to informing others. The sacrifice of 'pleasure' reading for 'duty' reading is an unavoidable necessity of professional life.

That each journalist should be keenly aware of what is going on in the world will appear to be stating the obvious. It is a matter for regret that an astonishing number are ill-informed about subjects they consider to be beneath them, and are proud of it.

There is also a proper routine to be observed once the writer is given the day's assignments in the newsroom. Where applicable, there are the relevant newspaper cuttings, reference books and pamphlets to be consulted, coverage details to be discussed with correspondents contributing from abroad or with reporters conducting interviews or constructing 'packages', changes of emphasis to be watched on running stories. Where pictures are concerned, a close check needs to be kept on progress from location to editing suite. In other words, unlike the newspaper sub-editor whose role is similar but not the same, the television news-writer does not simply sit still and wait for things to occur. By the time the moment comes to put words on paper or screen, the journalist should be in complete control of the shape and content of that part of the programme for which he is responsible.

Equally important is every writer's recognition that his own contributions, however important, represent only one fraction of the broadcast. There must be conscious awareness of the preceding and following items in the order of transmission so that, where appropriate, the right phrases may be used to smooth the transition from one subject to the next.

Knowledge of what is in the rest of the programme ought to be automatic, but it is not. Editorial staff often admit that they are so engrossed in their own particular duties that they are completely unaware of what their colleagues around them are doing.

It is a standing sick joke that the day will come when a writer handing down bulletin pictures of a VIP opening some prestige project will be happily working away in an editing suite, blissfully unaware that, on his way back to the office, that same VIP has been run over by a passing steamroller or blown up by a terrorist bomb.

Finally, although both the television and newspaper journalist trade in words, what ultimately distinguishes one from the other may be seen as a matter of arithmetic. The newspaper sub-editor calculates in *space* — ems, ens, points and columns. The television writer works in *time* — minutes and seconds, and the formula that three words of English take one second for a professional to read aloud on the air provides the fundamental basis of all news writing for television. This takes into account not only the slight variations in pace between readers, but also the different lengths of words used in normal, spoken language. It has, despite the scepticism of successive generations of newcomers to television news-writing, proved itself remarkably accurate, and it is equally adaptable to other languages when calculated in syllables instead of whole words.

Reader on camera

The most simple method of telling the news on television is for the presenter to read the writer's words direct to the viewer through the television camera and the microphone in the studio. In the terminology of television, the reader becomes *on camera* (*on cam.*). In BBC TV news terminology the reader is said to be *in vision*, which makes the written item itself a *vision story*.

All television news programmes contain varying numbers of vision stories, most of which are the products of heavily edited news agency tape or information from other sources. Sometimes they are complete in themselves; more often they are used as a base from which the newsreader launches some visual material, hence the frequent use of the term *vision/on camera intro.* Theoretically, although a vision story may be of any duration, and it is in any case impossible to generalize about 'ideal' lengths, editors of news programmes have a tendency to keep them to within reasonable limits for fear that the programme presentation as a whole may seem to lack pace and variety. It is also felt that long vision stories, those going much beyond a minute (180 words), do not make the fullest use of television's possibilities. Conversely, there is believed to be little point in producing a vision story shorter than two sentences, as anything less seems unlikely to register with the viewer.

Superficially, there may appear to be very little difference between the vision story, the newspaper article, or even the piece of agency tape torn from the teleprinter. In fact there are essential variations. The opening paragraph of any newspaper item will make a point of establishing four main facts — who, what, where and when, as in the typical example:

Luton, Bedfordshire, Thursday.
Three men armed with shot guns forced their way into the High-street branch of Pitkin's Bank here this afternoon and held staff and customers hostage for nearly an hour while two other members of the gang stripped the vault of an estimated quarter of a million pounds in cash and jewellery from safe-deposit boxes . . .

An attempt to follow precisely the same pattern on television, with so many facts packed into a very short space of time would almost inevitably lead to confusion in the viewer's mind. Shuffling the identical details into a different order, the television newswriter should attempt to explain the incident in much the same kind of simple, easy manner he would use to a group of friends:

> There's been a big bank raid in Luton, about 30 miles from London. An armed gang held customers and staff hostage for nearly an hour before making off with cash and jewellery worth about a quarter of a million pounds. The bank, a branch of Pitkin's . . .

Using the same technique, even such complicated subjects as the monthly Trade Figures or Retail Price Index need hold no terrors for the writer, even if both sets of statistics were to arrive for publication at the same time:

> The economy's continuing to show signs of improvement, according to two new sets of official figures. For the sixth month running Britain sold more abroad than ever before, and prices in the shops have dropped again.

Once that basic message has been put across, the i's can be dotted and the t's crossed with diagrams prepared by the graphics department. But it is accepted that opening sentences do represent one of the most difficult areas for writers seeking a compromise between impact and full comprehension. There is, for example, nothing much wrong with this sentence:

> Railway fares are going up by ten per cent on most routes in the autumn.

Yet if heard with anything less than full attention at least one of the four facts may be missed. The alternative leaves little margin for error. First, the viewer is hooked:

> Railway fares are going up again.

Then firmly landed:

> The increases, averaging ten pence in the pound on most routes, take effect in the autumn.

Of course there are occasions when this approach would be considered far too soft and tentative. The television newswriter must then talk in bold headlines:

> Five hundred and twenty people have been killed in the world's worst air crash.
> Ronald Reagan has been re-elected.
> The Government has been defeated in the Commons.

The transition from these to less momentous events is sometimes best achieved by the use of a form of words most easily described as a *side heading*, to signify change of pace and subject:

> Next, the economy . . .
> At home . . .

In the Middle East . . .
Now sport.

The phrases in themselves are perhaps just beginning to be considered clichés, but they remain good examples of the kind of language that can be used as signposts to smooth the way between items.

There also comes a moment in an event that has been reported for several successive days when it is desirable to resort to easily understood shorthand by way of an opening phrase. In that way, the progress of world-wide efforts to alleviate the suffering of starving Africans became:

The Ethiopian famine

and the break-in at the Democratic Party's Washington headquarters, which eventually led to the overthrow of a President, was identified as:

The Watergate scandal

long before the revelations ceased. In each case three little words were sufficient to make any viewer sharpen the senses ready for the latest news about items which had already aroused considerable interest.

In the context of short news programmes, this shorthand technique is most effective. But there are clear dangers: first in the assumption it makes of the audience's knowledge of what has already happened; secondly, in the case of complicated issues, the background may be easily forgotten. After a while, for example, the dispute about bonus payments and overtime rates for 150 of the 2000 production line workers at the Rusting Cars Company is handily telescoped into

The Rusting Cars strike.

A week later, with the dispute escalating into component shortages and lay-offs at other motor factories, the viewer may be forgiven for having lost sight of the original problem. So in these cases it is necessary to go back over the entire ground, however much some editors might consider it a waste of precious air time.

But, whether it concerns an old event or a new one, the writer's aim must always be that an opening sentence of any vision story hits the target first time. The viewer must be properly alerted to matters of interest and importance by the skilled use of words which, in their effect, have the reader bawling from the screen: 'Hey, you! Watch *this!*'.

Adding illustration

The first stage in making the simple vision story more interesting for the writer to construct — and the point at which television starts to exploit its inherent advantage — comes with the addition of non-moving illustration to take the place of the reader's image on the screen while the voice continues to add information.

The generic term *caption* is sometimes used to define all this material, although it may also fall into two separate categories: *graphics* for artwork and *stills* for anything photographic. The latter includes 35 mm colour slides, colour, black and white or computer-generated prints, or the self-developing pictures taken by Polaroid-style cameras.

At one time, the stock 'personality' pictures to be found in television news departments resembled the dull, full-face 'mug-shots' usually seen in police records or staring from the pages of passports. Fortunately, the spread of colour television in the late sixties and early seventies gave an opportunity for a complete re-think. As a result those ugly passport snaps gave way to bright, natural, frequently unposed pictures taken by photographers mindful of the television screen format, which is wider than it is high.

The bulk of these are 35 mm colour transparencies, although a percentage of colour prints, including instant pictures for speed, are also used. Government departments, embassies, specialist and trade libraries also provide a mixture of shapes, sizes and qualities, often without charge.

The international picture agencies, while remaining easily the most important source of black and white prints, particularly from abroad, are now also able to transmit colour pictures by wire through a tri-colour separation process. An original colour picture is re-photographed success-ively through red, green and blue filters, and the results sent over the wire. In the darkroom at the receiving end the original scene is reconstituted in full colour by application of the same process in reverse.

Rather less complicated and cheaper methods of acquiring stills include the re-photographing and enlarging of separate frames of 16 mm film, where it is still in use. Print size and quality are just about adequate for reproducing on television news programmes. Another way of using 16 mm film is to stop it at a pre-selected point on its way through telecine to give what is known as a *still* or *freeze frame*. Stills may also be made electronically by 'freezing' frames of videotape in a similar way, but both these methods have the disadvantage of engaging (for perhaps only brief and marginal benefit to a programme) equipment which may be in short supply and needed for other purposes.

The digital frame-store

Although these proven methods are still being used in many broadcasting centres, they are fast becoming superseded by the technological advances offered by the computer age. Nothing has done more to improve the 'look' of television news programmes over the past few years than these incredible pieces of equipment which have introduced almost limitless variety and versatility to stills and artwork.

Nearly all these depend on the concept of the frame-store, a bank of computer memory in which an entire (still) television picture is stored. Each *picture element* or *pixel* — and there will be more than 400 000 in a single frame — is converted into a digital representation of its brightness and its colour. That information is then stored in the memory — the digital frame-store. From there the picture can be redisplayed, recorded or modified, with virtually no detectable loss of quality (Fig. 2.2).

A typical system for recording and transmitting stills would have two frame-stores and a magnetic disc memory just like the Winchester disk machines used with larger computers.

STILLS AND COMPOSITES

Fig. 2.1. Old style 'mug shot' still could have been taken from a passport.

Modern style photograph, natural and unposed.

Split screen. Uneven composition looks untidy and is bound to create a distraction for the viewer.

Split screen. The two pictures should be of similar size and quality, with subjects looking in towards each other. Identify the characters left to right.

Three-way split. Names are printed on to avoid confusion, and the commentary must follow in the same order.

We must strive to achieve a better balance in the world

Split screen quotes. For long quotations a moving roller caption can be used.

Split screen using a still and a map.

THE DIGITAL FRAME STORE

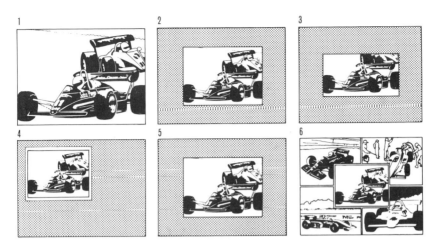

Fig. 2.2. Part of the electronic technology which has revolutionized the 'look' of television news. Pictures can be taken from any video source, stored, cropped, shaped or moved to fit into any background colour or montage. 1, full size picture; 2, picture size; 3, crop; 4, picture position and border; 5, matte; 6, montage.

In its simplest form, pictures are taken into a frame-store from a video source — a camera or videotape machine for example — and then transferred to the disk memory under an identifying number, a single disk holding perhaps between 250 and 300 frames.

Any still frame recorded on the disk may be called up by its number, transferred into the frame-store and offered as a picture source to the vision mixer in the studio control room, or direct to a videotape machine or even another frame-store.

The refinement offered by *two* frame-stores allows one to provide the picture for transmission while the other is being loaded with the next selection from the disk, a process of little more than one second. If two monitors are connected to the output of the frame-stores, one will show the 'on air' picture, the second a preview of the next available still. A video switch between the two frame-stores then makes it possible to cut directly from one to the other without the need to come back to 'vision'. The next logical step is to arrange for the 'off-air' frame-store to be loaded automatically, as soon as it is free, with the next picture from the disk. Thus a series of presses of a single button will transmit a sequence. A further facility may be provided to allow the change-over from one frame-store to the other to be an electronic mix or wipe as an alternative to the usual cut.

To take full advantage of these options it is necessary to have some way of putting the pictures into the order required for transmission. One way to achieve this is by what resembles the 'Polyphoto' technique, a sort of mosaic of 16 or more pictures from the disk displayed simultaneously at reduced size together with their catalogue numbers. Using a keyboard and cursor on the screen, the operator may then move, insert or delete pictures to obtain the sequence he/she requires.

(It's perhaps interesting to note that in operations of this kind the pictures are not actually transferred from one part of the disk to another. Instead the disk's directory system merely reorganizes the references to where they are to be found for retrieval in the desired order.)

Stacking and cropping

In yet another refinement, dozens of sequences of stills may be recorded by the machine as groups, or 'stacks', of perhaps as many as 80 pictures each. A stack may itself be one of the items (instead of a picture) within another stack. When the machine encounters one of these 'nested' stacks, it reproduces the pictures in it in order and then returns to its place in the original stack. This facility is also provided to modify previously prepared stacks at the time of transmission, so that items may be inserted or skipped to allow for late changes in the programme.

The frame-store principle also makes it possible to alter the framing and size of a picture. To 'crop' a picture, a rectangular outline is superimposed on the screen. This rectangle may be altered in size, proportion and position to frame any part of the image and that information is stored together with the picture to which it applies. Thereafter, when called upon to do so, the machine will offer that image cropped in the memorized format, if necessary reduced to fill the space allotted to it. (Usually magnification is not allowed since that would imply a reduced quality.)

A similar procedure allows the creation of composite pictures. A background may be formed by using an existing picture or one of a number of colours provided, and the cropped image then 'inserted' into it. If a composite picture is first stored and then used as the background for a subsequent composite and that process repeated, the resulting stored frames may be made into a stack.

The effect on being replayed in sequence will be that of an animation, adding one stage at a time. The precise working of the machine ensures each frame is in perfect register with its predecessor.

Storage and retrieval

The number of pictures it is possible to store will usually be limited only by the number of disks which can be afforded or accommodated. Even quite a big Winchester disk will contain only a thousand or two, and an eight inch floppy disc will hold only one still frame at broadcasting quality. Even at that sort of size a management system is needed to keep track of the contents. Dates and titles can be added and the pictures retrieved by number, name or category, but in the end the effectiveness of a library system such as this, particularly as it grows, will depend a great deal on methodical house-keeping — clear titling and cataloguing backed up by a ruthless weeding out of unwanted material.

The frame-store is therefore making everything else seem out of date, although there remains plenty of life in the modified projector-camera systems known as *slide scanners* or *tele-jectors*, the *micro-scanner*, a mounted camera which focuses on small photographic areas when moved up or down on the darkroom enlarger principle, and the simplest method of all — putting stills on the air by placing them on stands or pinning them on boards within sight of the electronic camera in the studio.

Making the choice

In many respects it is far easier to choose a still from a strictly limited range, for if a collection carries only one picture of a person or subject the decision comes down to a straight choice between using it or not. The headaches begin with the vast libraries. In mid 1986 the BBC Central Stills Department in West London carried approximately *one million* stills, 800 000 of them as 35 mm colour slides. Such luxury demands the newswriter's intimate knowledge of each subject as it arises, for no one else is in a position to decide which of the available selection most aptly matches the mood of the story. Judgements may be as basic as ensuring that an item about increased taxes does *not* show a broadly grinning finance minister who has just announced them to Parliament in the face of strong opposition. That decisions as simple as this are needed only goes to prove what traps exist for the unwary.

For while straightforward mistakes in identity could in some circumstances have legal implications (and have, on occasion), even where the matter of identity is not disputed a writer's preference for one still over another could lead to charges of distortion. Take the astonishing change of physical appearance from the confident, PR-man's Richard Nixon, fresh from re-election, to the hollow-cheeked President facing the immediate consequences of Watergate. In reporting matters connected with his memoirs, who could say authoritatively which picture from the library most accurately represented the *real* Nixon?

It may not be a case of simply choosing the most recent photograph, although constant attention must also be paid to such apparently trivial details as general appearance and changes in clothing or hair-style. George Best, at the height of his soccer-playing fame, seemed to be alternately bearded and clean-shaven week by week.

Even if the journalists had difficulty in keeping up to date, the aficionados of the game had no doubts, and were quick to pounce on British television programmes foolhardy enough to choose the wrong style for the wrong week.

Writing to stills

A news still should appear on the screen for no fewer than five seconds (15 words). Three seconds are about the absolute minimum, otherwise the image appears to flash in front of the viewer's eyes and disappear again before the information can be assimilated. The maximum time depends very much on the subject.

A fairly 'busy' action shot of casualties being carried by a stretcher away from a train crash needs longer to register than a library portrait of a well-known politician, but it is fairly safe to assume that a ten second shot is long enough in most cases. Economics add an exception to the rule; a photograph bought for a large sum because of its exclusivity or rarity value should be exploited fully even though the picture itself (say, the last one taken of someone now missing) might be unremarkable. To dismiss this valuable property in a brief five or six seconds of air-time would be wasteful.

However long it is held on the screen, every still should be used to its maximum advantage by introducing it into the narrative at a point which helps to add definite emphasis to the story. It must not be allowed to drift in, apparently at random, causing moments of confusion for the viewer:

Referring to the . . .
(up still of Prime Minister)
. . . latest trade deal, the Prime Minister said . . .

Bringing in the picture a few words later makes all the difference:

Referring to the latest trade deal, . . .
(up still of Prime Minister)
. . . the Prime Minister said . . .

The same principle applies to choosing the right moment at which to return to the reader in vision. It is not acceptable to whisk the picture from under the viewer's nose without good reason. Much better to wait until the end of a sentence.

Where events call for a sequence of pictures, it is important to maintain a rhythm by keeping each on the screen for approximately the same duration. Six, five and seven seconds would probably be reasonable for three successive stills referring to the same subject. Five, twelve and eight would not. The temptation to go back to the reader on camera for a few seconds between stills should be avoided, otherwise continuity is broken. In this context, a brief shot of the newsreader becomes *another*, but *unrelated* picture, interrupting the flow. If returning to the newsreader during the sequence is inevitable, it is far better to make the link a deliberately long one.

Writing to a series of stills can, and should be, extremely satisfying, particularly when action shots are involved. Unlike moving pictures, where the writer is sometimes a slave to editing grammar, stills may be arranged in any required order to suit the script, and even a fairly routine item is capable of being made to look and sound interesting:

Four men have been rescued from a small boat off the Kent coast. They'd been adrift for twenty four hours after the boat's engine failed during a storm. Their distress call was answered by . . .
(Still 1, helicopter landing)
. . . a Royal Air Force helicopter, which flew them forty miles to Dover for medical treatment.
(Still 2, man on stretcher)
The owner of the boat is now in hospital suffering from exposure; the three others have been allowed home.
(Still 3, boat in sea)
Attempts at salvage are thought unlikely before the weekend, when the forecasters say the weather will improve.

Apart from the opening news point, the story is told and the pictures shown in chronological order for ease of explanation. Note, too, that the basic rule of television scriptwriting is observed: the commentary *complements* what the pictures show and does not merely repeat what the viewer can see for himself. Still 1 says where the rescued men were taken and for what purpose. Still 2, while identifying the stretcher case and his condition, does not leave the viewer to wonder about the fate of the others, of whom there are no pictures. Still 3 completes the story by looking to the future.

From a production point of view it makes sense to go from one still to another in the same sequence by using the same technique — cutting or mixing. The use of an electronic wipe from one to another should be reserved for changes of subject. It is also easier on the eye to use either all colour or all monochrome pictures for the same sequence. If they have to be mixed for some reason, the two types should be shown in separate blocks.

Composites and split screens

Composite stills, or split screens, are effective if used sparingly. In their most common form these consist of two heads, each occupying one half of the screen. The effect is achieved electronically by the frame-store, by physically mounting separate pictures on one piece of card, or by copying them photographically.

For preference the faces should look slightly inwards towards each other and not out of the screen, and they should be matched in size, style and picture quality, even if it means copying one or both originals. The commentary should identify the characters from left to right.

A *three-way split* is also possible, but the screen inevitably looks crowded, so it is perhaps worthwhile to put the names clearly on the bottom of the picture. It scarcely seems worth the effort to show four or more pictures together for a few seconds. They tend to resemble postage stamps on most domestic screens, though the technique can be made to look effective if some means is used to focus on one image at a time.

Other versions of the split screen have one half of the picture occupied by a photograph, the other by some form of artwork. Written quotations and maps can be particularly striking illustrated in this way. A further variation is the *roller caption*. The photographic half of the still is retained on the screen while an extended quotation is printed on to the surface of a moving belt, its speed controlled to reveal the wording in step with the reader's speaking pace.

The opportunities which now exist to employ such a wide range of styles are undeniable advantages to television news as part of its job to make programmes visually attractive as well as informative, especially as it is now possible to achieve all these effects, and more, electronically as well as manually. Yet it is precisely because stills are available in such quantities that the danger of over-kill is ever present.

Writers must avoid the temptation to use them automatically, almost as a reflex action, without thinking whether they are actually adding anything to the viewer's comprehension.

Seeing the screen littered with the faces of the best-known politicians and royalty every time they are mentioned in a news programme quickly becomes irritating. The fact is that some stories are better told with no illustration other than the presenter's face.

David Frost had a cruel but accurate comment about the obsession of some television people to try to illustrate everything, however unsuitable. It has become known as the Lord Privy Seal syndrome (see Fig. 2.3) and stands as an awful warning to anyone lured into the use of pictures just for their own sake.

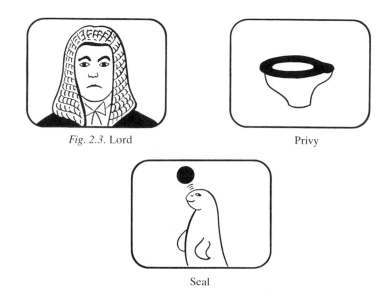

Fig. 2.3. Lord   Privy

Seal

Electronic graphics

Complementing the still photograph is the *caption*, the family name for television news artwork. Its use has clear advantages for journalists passing on information about events in a complicated modern world. Maps help the immediate identification of geographical locations and diagrams and charts allow sports results to be digested more quickly, and explain details not easily understood when given by the newsreader alone: budget proposals, the main conclusions of official reports, detailed timetables of events, the ups and downs of bank rates and trade figures.

How this artwork is prepared depends on available resources and the extent to which specialist staff and materials can be properly employed. Some local or very small national news services are able to get by perfectly adequately with part-time artists, either staff members spared briefly from other duties, or design students happy to earn small sums for an hour or two's extra labour of love. In each case the 'studio' usually consists of some handy corner not far from where the newsroom journalists are at work, plus a stock of basic raw materials including stacks of blank black card measuring 12 × 9 in (30.48 × 22.86 cm), an atlas, a number of previously used maps and charts outlined in white, pens, pencils, erasers, rulers, white paint, brushes, razor blades, scissors and sheets of rub-on instant lettering in a limited range of type faces and sizes.

News departments which have to take their artwork more seriously employ full-time, trained artists and designers. There are hot press machines to turn out clean, unfussy type in several sizes. Hundreds of stock maps, all carefully catalogued, are painted on to card, the place names printed on to removable plastic cells so that the original outlines underneath remain untouched for re-use. Sketched figures and symbols are stockpiled as backgrounds for the charts and diagrams in most frequent demand.

But these 'cardboard' graphics are now on their way out, replaced by new, powerful tools for the creative artist. These, the brothers and sisters of the electronic frame-stores, have added an extra dimension to television programmes of all kinds, but have given news in particular the opportunity to display much more sophisticated artwork more quickly than was possible using manual methods.

Perhaps the best-known version of this equipment is the Quantel *Paint Box*. This, as its name implies, allows the graphics designer to 'paint' coloured artwork directly on to the screen, though that description does not do justice to the range of facilities available. It is not necessary to know anything about electronics or computers to use it to the full extent of its considerable capabilities, because it has been designed for use by a trained artist, not a graduate engineer, and the terms used are deliberately those with which an artist would be familiar.

The artist sits in front of a tablet resembling a smooth, blank drawing-board, and draws on it with an electronic pen which leaves no

Fig. 2.4. Artwork plays a large part in helping to explain complicated issues. Before the introduction of electronic graphics, some news organizations had their own departments to produce hand-drawn designs for maps, charts and diagrams. (*BBC Central Stills*)

Fig. 2.5. Computer-generated artwork. A combination of speed, clarity and versatility.

mark. Instead its movements are reproduced on a colour monitor screen in front of him, its position indicated by a small cross.

By moving the pen to the bottom edge of the tablet, he displays on the screen a palette of colours contained in small square 'paint pots', together with an area for mixing other shades and colours. When the cursor is positioned over one of these pots, a sharp tap of the pen lets the artist charge his 'brush' with the chosen colour which he may then use to 'paint' on his 'canvas'. Blends are achieved by applying pen pressure on the mixing area to deposit one colour, then re-charging the brush with a new one and depositing that in the same way. If the artist wishes, he can leave an inexhaustible supply of the newly mixed colour in one of the 'paint pots' and the whole palette can be stored electronically in the memory to be recalled later.

A panel to the right of the palette allows the selection of one of five brush thicknesses, again by tapping down on the appropriate square. Calling up a menu of other options lets the brush be changed to an airbrush, for example, a faithful reproduction of its texture being shown on the screen.

Another menu option selects 'graphics' which provides for the drawing of separate or connected straight lines by 'rubber-banding'; one tap of the pen positions the start and a second tap the finish, the line being 'stretched' between the two points. Using the same method, shapes can be drawn to any size, outlined or filled, anywhere on the screen, in any colour, thickness or texture.

Fig. 2.6. Artist at work with *Paint Box* electronic graphics system. The image is 'drawn' on the tablet with an electronic pen which leaves no mark. (*BBC Central Stills*)

The Paint Box also provides electronic versions of stencilling, cutting-out and pasting used in conventional graphics. In stencil mode, a mask is made to protect one part of the picture while work is carried out on the rest using all of the machine's facilities.

Further stencils can be generated within the area being worked on, and any part of the picture covered by the stencil can be revealed and the remainder protected. Every stage can be stored in the memory so that if the next process does not give the desired effect nothing is lost, as a perfect copy of the previous artwork is instantly available.

The artist can start from a blank canvas primed to any chosen colour, a background shaded from one colour to any other. A still picture or a frozen video frame can be worked on. Blemishes on faces can be painted out using an exactly matching colour picked up on the brush from elsewhere on the 'skin'.

Any part of the picture can be 'cut out' electronically without destroying the original and then enlarged, reduced, turned over top to bottom, reversed left to right and 'pasted' anywhere on the screen, processes which can be repeated as often as required. The same effect can be achieved with different styles of type, which can be cut, manipulated and then pasted into any position in any colour, outline or solid, plain, embossed or with drop-shadow (of any depth in any direction).

Library storage and retrieval, with comprehensive searching and browsing facilities, represent only some of the capabilities of the Paint Box, and new features are being added all the time. It is a way of producing graphic work for television of a high technical picture quality and at the same time giving the artist freedom of expression. Probably the only drawback is that the cost of the equipment is likely to mean that few television news graphics departments can afford to buy one Paint Box for each member of the team.

The artist and the writer

In the past news-writers did not necessarily expect to be overly concerned with the fundamentals of graphic design of any sort.

But now the electronic age has added this new dimension to television art, interest in and knowledge of what is possible should be encouraged, because the opportunity exists to create *exactly* the illustration necessary to accompany a news story.

Not surprisingly, the designers often develop love-affairs with their exceptional new toys and the images they create, and it is up to the journalist to ensure that their enthusiasm does not carry them away. Most artwork for television news, whether created electronically or on card-board, has a screen life of no more than a few seconds, and for that reason if nothing else, it must be clear and easy to follow, with bold strokes on unambiguous backgrounds.

An awareness of the dimensional limitations also helps. Among the most important of these is the amount of information that can be squeezed in, bearing in mind that unnecessary clutter reduces visual impact and that 'cut-off' (the edge of the television picture automatically lost in the process of transmission) reduces the area the artist has to work on. The effect is exaggerated on old or mis-aligned receivers, so losing some of the information intended for the viewer. All this adds to the journalist's problem in deciding the wording to go on charts, and particularly affects the name and title superimpositions which occupy the bottom third of the screen, these being the most common forms of artwork used in television news.

Not only is it a matter of sometimes trying to squash too much into a limited width so that exaggerated cut-off mutilates each end of the lettering, the information occupies so much room part of the background illustration is itself obscured (Fig. 2.7). Smaller lettering would be difficult to read, so the alternative solution is much better as it occupies only two lines, one an abbreviation of the title.

Above all, using the artist's skill to illustrate a story must anticipate how the accompanying commentary will be structured. There is little point in commissioning good-looking charts full of important details to which no reference is made, or in cramming beautifully scaled maps with place names which the script ignores, to the confusion of the viewer, who is then left wondering why they were put there in the first place.

The temptation to add anything except the strictly relevant must be resisted. In the report of our Pitkin's Bank raid, a map illustrating the location of Luton needs only the additional reference points of London and the most important trunk road, the M1, to give a clear idea of the town's position in southern England (Fig. 2.7). The arbitrary addition of several other big cities and county names may make the map look more attractive to some eyes, but would do nothing for the viewer during its few seconds on the screen. At the other extreme, a large-scale map isolating Luton from everywhere else in the country is equally valueless.

The key to success in writing to graphics lies in the assembly of words in sequences which lead the viewer's eyes progressively across the screen from left to right, top to bottom (see Fig. 2.9). It is not enough for the programme presenter to repeat what the viewer is seeing. Some complementary information must be fed in as well, but if, through carelessness, too wide a difference is allowed to develop between what the audience is being told and being shown, the effect that writer and artists have been at pains to create will be destroyed.

Fig. 2.7. Too much lettering obscures part of the picture.

Abbreviate the title. Smaller lettering would be hard to read.

MAPS

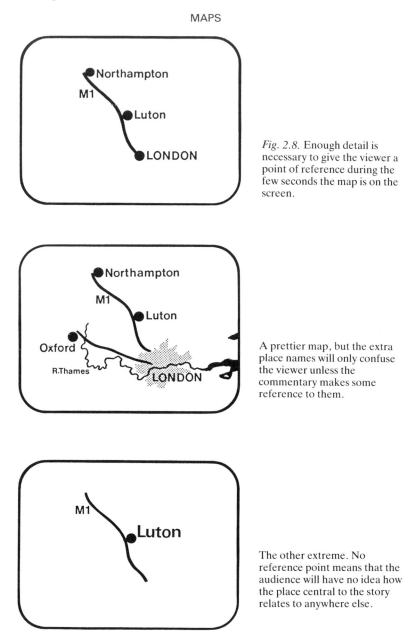

Fig. 2.8. Enough detail is necessary to give the viewer a point of reference during the few seconds the map is on the screen.

A prettier map, but the extra place names will only confuse the viewer unless the commentary makes some reference to them.

The other extreme. No reference point means that the audience will have no idea how the place central to the story relates to anywhere else.

CHARTS AND DIAGRAMS

DEFENCE SPENDING

	Then	Now
Tanks	£30M	£56M
Guns	£26M	£38M
Planes	£21M	£85M

Fig. 2.9. Simple charts help to get figures across. Accompanying commentary must lead the viewer's eye from left to right, top to bottom. (See also the following illustrations.)

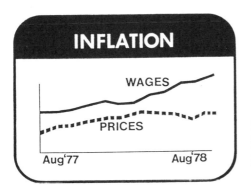

INFLATION

WAGES

PRICES

Aug'77   Aug'78

Diagrams and graphs follow the same pattern of simplicity. Extra information can be given in the script.

That is likely with even the most simple illustrations:

TRAIN FARES

Glasgow UP £1.75

Brighton UP £1.00

'One pound goes on a day return to Brighton, making it six pounds forty. One pound seventy five is put on a single to Glasgow to make it forty two pounds.'

By transposing the two sentences of commentary, some improvement is achieved, but not a complete cure:

TRAIN FARES

Glasgow UP £1.75

Brighton UP £1.00

'One pound seventy five is put on a single to Glasgow to make it forty two pounds. One pound goes on a day return to Brighton, making it six pounds forty.'

It is far better to use the same phraseology as the chart, and in the same order, so that there is no conflict between words and picture:

TRAIN FARES

Glasgow UP £1.75

Brighton UP £1.00

'The Glasgow single fare rises by one pound seventy five to forty two pounds. The Brighton day return goes up by one pound to six pounds forty.'

Probably the most admired exponents of the art are the makers and writers of television commercials, who have very similar periods of screen time in which to get across their message, and need to establish immediate unambiguous links between what the viewer is seeing and hearing.

The technique is all the more important where information is added one stage at a time. This, always a popular way of emphasising facts or figures, has become even more common since the introduction of electronic equipment. The effect is achieved either by a superimposition (mixing two sources electronically to produce a single picture) or by animation (revealing extra information mechanically) by moving flaps or tabs which are slid back at the appropriate moment during transmission. In either case, in the example of higher train fares, the first sentence spoken would accompany one fact on the chart:

TRAIN FARES

Glasgow UP £1.75

'The Glasgow single fare rises by one pound seventy five to forty two pounds . . .'

The next part of the commentary would be spoken simultaneously with the introduction of the stage completing the picture:

TRAIN FARES

Glasgow UP £1.75

Brighton UP £1.00

. . . The Brighton day return goes up by one pound to six pounds forty.

The news-writer's responsibilities do not end with the written commentary. Completed artwork must be checked carefully against any original plans, however sketchy. Where sequences of captions are involved, no doubts must be left about the exact order in which they are to be transmitted. To have one illustration on the screen while the commentary is clearly referring to another is hardly likely to inspire the audience's confidence. Mis-spellings, which somehow seem to occur in only the most simple, everyday words, have a tendency to harvest bulging post-bags of complaint.

It is true that genuine variations do exist in the spelling of certain place-names, particularly where they are transliterations, and news agency reports frequently contain spellings which differ widely from those in atlases or gazetteers. To the domestic audience it may scarcely matter which is used as long as there is consistency. The solution to all these problems is to adopt certain standard reference books (the Times Atlas, the Oxford Dictionary, etc.) as the arbiters and ignore everything else.

For the sake of speed and simplicity, most television news artwork has always been very basic, with specially designed animated drawings, one-off street maps, cartoons and models considered to be extremely advanced, daring and time-consuming compared with the volume of maps and diagrams quickly made and stock-piled. But, like every other area of the business, the art departments have begun to learn that their work is being changed radically by the new technology, and in every way.

Character generators

Character/caption generators have arrived alongside the frame-stores and paint boxes, coming to the aid of those used to the laborious process of lettering by hand.

This equipment consists of a typewriter-like keyboard (with extra keys to control special functions) and a display monitor. A cursor indicates to the operator where the next character he types will appear on the screen.

Depending on the complexity of the particular machine, several type-faces or fonts in different sizes may be available, with complex arrangements for deciding the spacing between pairs of characters in different fonts. Often three fonts are provided as standard, with others called up from a library held on disk.

It may be possible to use the lettering in one of a number of colours, or in outline, or in one colour outline filled with a second colour on a background of a third, or with a relief shadow effect, and so on. Provision is usually made for the lettering to be prepared in advance and stored on disk to be called up as required, but it may have to be prepared as the programme proceeds. Some systems also allow the creation of charts, histograms and block diagrams and a degree of animation including scrolling (vertically) or wiping (horizontally).

Many machines provide an alternative output in the form of a 'key' to be used in other effects.

On the screen the letters appear crisp and clean against virtually any background, an advantage to those engaged in the subtitling of programmes.

Alongside all these advances, a subtle change is taking place in the convention that whatever the shapes the images may take within them, all artwork and stills must conform to the overall 4 × 3 ratio. At one time

CHARACTER GENERATORS

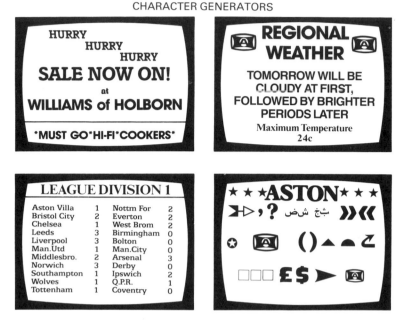

Fig. 2.10. A wide range of type faces can be created electronically in several sizes as text on charts, and for sub-titling. Foreign-language versions are also available.

some news organizations simply refused to use pictures which were in the wrong format to fill the screen.

An interesting theory has been put forward by Bertil Allander of the Swedish Broadcasting Corporation. Discussing the whole question of perspective he suggests[1] that there is positive value in breaking with tradition. The television screen, he believes, is capable of accepting all kinds of formats, and there must be times 'when one will cheerfully accept a smaller picture in order to get a neater composition or add to the expressiveness of the format'. At all events, says Allander, 'it must surely be unnecessary to fill up a picture with uninteresting material for the sake of the format and, into the bargain, run the risk of leading the viewer's eye astray'.

The application of that principle has already begun to make way for a whole new range of shapes once considered unacceptable. (See Fig. 2.11).

It is worthwhile remembering, in connection with all artwork, that any illustration is also an extremely useful means of 'punctuating' a programme. Ending an item with a still picture, map or chart presents the ideal opportunity to return to the presenter for an entirely fresh subject, while sequences offer excellent variety.

Pictures with tape sound

So far the emphasis has been on the addition of visual material to

[1] . . . *it's not reality any more* (Swedish Broadcasting Corporation, 1974).

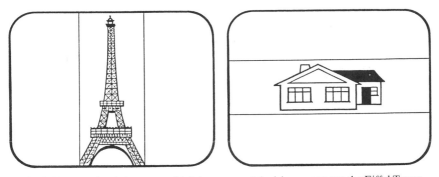

Fig. 2.11. Two previously 'unacceptable' shapes on a television screen are the Eiffel Tower and a bungalow.

accompany words spoken by the presenter in the studio. Now comes the moment to create a temporary but complete replacement for the reader by the use of sound-only reports.

These are the blood-brothers of the dispatches which have become the stock-in trade of radio news programmes all over the world. For use on television, telephoned or radioed sound reports, whether 'live' or recorded on to magnetic tape, come a poor second to moving pictures or other forms of illustration. But the nature of world news demands that the voice of the reporter on the spot is, on many occasions, infinitely preferable to the alternative of nothing at all.

That said, the news-writer's main considerations in dealing with such material centre on three main factors: quality, duration and illustration.

Where sound *quality* is concerned, high standards of intelligibility are required, and technical staff are usually on hand to say at once whether atmospherics or other forms of interference make a report technically usable. But there are times when sound of *any* quality merits inclusion. Those reports from the early manned space missions, for example, were scarcely intelligible, but this did not detract in the least from their news value.

Even now, where reports are themselves of intrinsic worth, despite lack of clarity, the answer is not to discard them but to assist the viewer by 'translating' the spoken words into captions for displaying simultaneously on the screen.

Bigger problems arise on those occasions when the voice quality is just on the borderline of being acceptable. Here the trap, into which it is all too easy to fall, is for the news-writer to convince himself that the recorded dispatch he has heard several times (usually through top-quality equipment under ideal conditions) is good enough for the audience to understand, even though their receiving equipment may be inferior and they have the opportunity of hearing it only once. In these cases the long-established journalistic test of 'when in doubt, leave out', should be even more rigorously applied, and the dispatch used as a source of information for quotation by the programme presenter.

The question of *duration* must be left open for individuals to decide for themselves in the light of the significance of each report. But, in drawing up broad guidelines, it is important to remember that sound reports, if

PICTURES WITH TAPE SOUND

Fig. 2.12. A composite still to cover a voice-only report usually identifies correspondent and location. The main difficulty arises when a dispatch is made from one place about events occurring in another.

intended mainly for radio news outlets, are invariably lengthy, and it is desirable to go only so far in adopting, intact, techniques of one medium for use in another. One way out is to encourage radio reporters to send extra, shorter pieces especially for use in television programmes, constructing them so that they cover any visual material likely to be available at a later stage. Where this is not possible, intelligent editing can make a dispatch more suitable. Straightforward factual material is omitted and then condensed for the presenter introduction; what remain are the descriptive passages conveying atmosphere.

This leads to the final difficulty of finding relevant *illustration* to accompany the sound.

As it is considered unacceptable to put either a blank screen or the presenter's face in front of the viewer while the report is being heard, an attempt must be made to offer something else visually relevant. Fashions change, but current thinking envisages a specially created composite caption identifying the location from which the report is being made, and the person who is making it (see Fig. 2.12).

This is an apparently ideal solution, but it does pose its own problems, particularly when, as often happens, reporters are calling from one place with information they have gathered about events occurring in another. How individual news-writers deal with that depends on a straight choice between what is accurate and what will help the viewer's comprehension.

3
Words and moving pictures

The power to transmit moving pictures, whether in colour or black and white, live or recorded, through film or electronic means, sets television apart from all its rivals in the business of disseminating news about world events.

For the newcomer embarking on the acquisition of the basic skills to cope with this extra dimension, two major hurdles bar the way. First, and most important, is the need to develop an instinct for the construction of written commentaries in a way which allows the viewer to draw full value from both words and pictures. Second comes the requirement for at least a rudimentary knowledge of how film or videotape works. Each has its own mystique, particularly film about which enough has been written to sink a whole fleet of proverbial battleships. In every library, shelves groan under a weight of material (much of it by masters of feature and documentary work) sufficient to occupy the keen student for years. Videotape may never need to catch up, for while each medium uses a different method of storing the image, the *art* of picture-making is common to both.

It is not necessary for every news-writer to make a full-time study of either, but it clearly *is* important to know that, with ingenuity and imagination, film and videotape are tools which are capable of being wielded with great delicacy, even within the large blunt instrument which is the routine television news programme. Many television journalists who have developed a naturally high level of these skills have gone on to find success in other areas of television which demand the subtle use of pictures on the one hand with qualities of journalistic hard-headedness on the other.

The lightweight revolution

What has surprised many is the speed at which film, once undisputed king, has been overthrown in favour of the newer master, videotape. Those who forecast that film would continue indefinitely to claim at least a part of news-gathering have been proved wrong. Except in those outposts where for purely local reasons film is still retained, the electronic camera — or more specifically the system commonly called *ENG* (Electronic News

Gathering) — has shouldered the whole burden of providing the means by which world audiences for television news have come to be able to witness history as it is being made.

This 'lightweight revolution', as it is called, was completed well within ten years. In hindsight it is now possible to say that it was inevitable from the moment film and videotape development began marching side by side towards the news programme makers' goal of mobility and miniaturization.

The first breakthrough came in the 1950s. Until that time the experts were dismissive of anything smaller than the 35 mm film format used for cinema features and newsreels. The quality of the image was undoubtedly superb, but the equipment for sound filming was cumbersome and virtually impossible to use without a sturdy tripod. This partly explains why in those historic film interviews which are shown on television from time to time, the *subject* has clearly been brought *to* the camera and microphone, underlining the air of stiff formality and self-consciousness which is always so apparent.

The introduction of 16 mm — it is said by American television news executives who wanted to find a better way of covering the Korean war — at last made it possible to take the camera to the subject. Sixteen millimetre was a format familiar mostly to amateur film-makers. The camera was still heavy, but at least it could be held with reasonable comfort on a shoulder or screwed to a monopod and carried into action, the sound recorded on to a thin strip of magnetic tape attached to one edge of the film during manufacture.

One award-winning veteran cameraman used to like recalling how the makers of the first 16 mm camera he was issued with were so sure it would be used by an amateur that the instruction booklet included something along the following lines: 'Having placed the camera on the tripod, seat the subject at the piano, making sure you are at least five feet away and that sufficient light is available from the window'. So equipped, he and the rest of the world's television news camera teams went to war to bring back vivid pictures which made the viewer feel personally involved as never before. He survived Vietnam, Biafra, Aden, Cyprus, the Middle East, Belfast and many other trouble spots, only to be killed one night as he crossed the road near his home.

For about 20 years there was nothing to touch 16 mm. The cameras were reliable and impervious to most of the knocks and other ill-treatment they inevitably suffered in the field. The film they consumed — first monochrome, then colour — was fast and versatile.

Some news organizations did experiment with Super 8, commonly used for home movies, as a way of avoiding problems at foreign airports, where the arrival of news camera teams and their unmistakable silver boxes often led to frustrating bureaucratic delay or the impounding of equipment. So there were some occasions when a cameraman who would have been denied entry with his Arriflex or Cine-Voice was allowed in on a tourist passport and contrived to shoot a story on his 'toy' camera.

But even if no serious attempt was ever made to replace 16 mm with 8 mm, a complete alternative to the use of any film for straight news work was becoming both an attractive and practical proposition.

Film had its limitations. Until processing was completed, not even the world's greatest cameraman could guarantee that he had measured the light correctly, that there was not some other fault, or that the images he believed he had captured were indeed on the film in the way he had intended. And since news by its nature happens only once, there was never the possibility of going back to re-shoot it, unlike feature film work, where expensively assembled casts and technicians are kept together until the cameraman's work has been seen and approved. To add to these hazards, despite the best endeavours of the news laboratory workers and their increasingly sophisticated developing equipment, film did sometimes 'go down in soup' (chemical processing bath) to be lost for ever.

The biggest drawback of all was that even though processing time was being reduced to the point where it took no more than a few minutes to develop each hundred feet of film, it was still comparatively slow, and in news, time is a luxury which can rarely be afforded.

It was for that single reason television news and some other topical television programmes had already cut out many of the intermediate stages in conventional film-making, so that progress from camera to screen would be as short as possible. Instead of first making prints from an original negative, they took the developed negative material and transmitted that.

In adopting this method, television news people had to accept the very real risk that a careless or unlucky film editor, working under deadline pressure with much-used equipment, might do irreparable harm to precious material, and that in some circumstances an edit once made might be impossible to restore. That in turn put greater responsibility on the editorial staff to ensure that the right decisions about editing the film were made first time.

To compound the difficulties, film editors and news-writers working for stations transmitting only black and white pictures had to make their decisions based on the identification of people and events from film viewed in negative, as delivered by the processing department. After a while, experience taught that it was possible to recognize the better known public figures. But all too often a certain amount of guesswork was involved. Fortunately, the viewer was spared such mysteries. During the film's transmission stage all was put right by the use of 'phase reversal', an electronic means of changing the blacks to white and the whites to black, thus producing a normal positive image.

Much to the relief of every writer, the problem disappeared during the switch from monochrome to colour filming, which began in the sixties. After much discussion and experiment many news services opted for a particular 'reversal' film stock, which meant that once it had been through the processing bath it appeared in the same form as the amateur photographer's 35 mm colour transparency, as a positive which was taken directly to the cutting room for editing before transmission.

During the same period developments in recording pictures and sound on to magnetic tape were taking place almost in parallel. The system may not have been originally conceived as one which would necessarily benefit television news, but it seems significant now that the very first broadcast using videotape, on November 30, 1956, was that of *Douglas Edwards and the news*, which was transmitted by CBS from New York, recorded in Los

Angeles, and replayed three hours later for viewers on the west coast of the United States.

It had long been recognized that some form of recording system for television was desirable, if only to give studios the flexibility to create their productions at times which suited them and their participants rather than forcing them to continue taking all the risks associated with transmitting programmes live. One step towards that end was *tele-recording*, a way of filming productions or production segments off high-quality monitors. Despite its success, this system had to rely on the conventional photographic technique of chemical processing with the inevitable delay before recordings could be examined.

The main snag in developing instant playback along the lines of quarter-inch tape sound recordings lay in the very high speed and consequent amount of tape expended to reproduce pictures of sufficiently high quality for broadcasting. The problem was eventually solved by Ampex, an American company which had begun its research into magnetic tape recording for television in 1951. By early 1956 the company's pioneers were able to demonstrate a machine on which the speed of a 2 in (51 mm) wide tape was kept down to 15 in (38 mm) a second as it was moved past four recording heads rotating about a hundred times faster.

The end result of this *quadruplex* technique was picture reproduction which most laymen found indistinguishable from the original, and for the name of Ampex a permanent place in the language of television (see Fig. 3.1a).

Television news, for which perfect picture quality has never been the priority where important news stories are concerned, believed the biggest advantage of video to be that it could be replayed in no greater time than it took to rewind the tape, opening up previously undreamt of possibilities for flexibility within programmes. Many news items which began their lives in the 16 mm sound camera now ended them on the screen as videotape recordings, for film which could be processed and edited at regional or other television stations was then available to be pumped along public telecommunications cables to headquarters. In addition, anything photographed by the electronic cameras in the studio or outside could easily be linked to a videotape recorder. Coupled with the strides then being made in intercontinental communications systems, the development of videotape suddenly opened a new era for the gathering of foreign news in particular, and the whole effect was to extend deadlines until the end of programmes.

The equipment remained expensive to buy and install, particularly when colour came in. The cost was only partly offset by the fact that recordings could be erased and the same 90 min tape used over and over again until 'pile-up' (thick horizontal lines of interference) showed that its useful life was over. Another disadvantage was the size of the machinery. Each quadruplex resembled an overgrown reel-to-reel audio recorder, and together with its ancillary equipment took up the space of a small room. Studio and outside broadcast cameras were even less manoeuvrable than the old 35 mm film equipment.

It was not until the seventies that real progress was made towards producing a tape which was smaller yet still of a standard high enough to satisfy the exacting requirements of the broadcast engineers. When it came

THE SHRINKING SIZE OF VIDEOTAPE EQUIPMENT

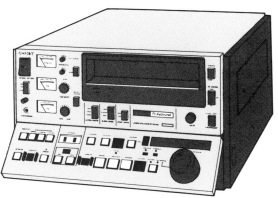

(a)

(b)

(c)

Fig. 3.1.(a) Quadruplex videotape recorder using two-inch wide tape, developed by Ampex in the fifties.
(b) One-inch . . . high quality in a smaller package.
(c) U-matic. Three-quarter inch tape cassette machine at the heart of the lightweight revolution. Half-inch is gaining popularity.

it was of a single size, one-inch, and in two technical specifications, because two solutions had been found to the problem of cramming the same amount of audio and video information on to a tape surface half that of the original Ampex (Fig. 3.1b).

The appearance of one-inch for studio-based work was swiftly followed by recorders and cameras which allowed more than a degree of portability, but the start of the true lightweight revolution probably dates from the time American broadcasters began experimenting with Sony *U-matic*, a Japanese system which had originally been designed for industrial use (Fig. 3.1c).

The biggest single advantage of this format was that it did not use the tape spools needed for one inch; instead sound and picture were recorded on to a three-quarter inch (19 mm) tape safely enclosed inside a strong plastic cassette. No handling of the tape was necessary. In the field the cassette was automatically threaded when inserted into a recorder which was carried in a leather case and simply slung over a shoulder.

The rest, as they say, is history. Once Sony had produced a new specification to satisfy the 625-line television picture standard used by most of Europe, the way was clear — technically, anyway — for the biggest advance in news gathering television had seen for 20 years.

The rise of ENG

The first television station to take the plunge and replace its entire film equipment with ENG is believed to be KMOX-TV in St. Louis, Missouri.

Cameras, processing, viewing and editing facilities were all disposed of in one grand gesture in September, 1974. Interest in the system was already spreading among other local American stations which were beginning to appreciate how ideally electronic cameras were suited to their needs for early-evening news programmes.

By 1976, ENG had dominated television reporting of the Democratic and Republican party conventions and the Presidential election campaign. It was also being used in Europe; Japanese coverage of the London economic summit of May, 1977, included ENG pictures which were beamed back to Tokyo by satellite and, as a bonus, transmitted by the BBC as part of their domestic output. But the European services themselves were moving more cautiously, opting for trial periods in which to evaluate the technical and editorial problems, while managements sorted out the changes in staffing and re-training necessary if ENG were to become permanent. NOS of Holland started their experiment using film as a back-up if anything went wrong. The BBC opened their 12-month trial on October 10, 1977, when an interview with Margaret Thatcher, then leader of the Conservative opposition, was recorded at the House of Commons and shown on the lunch-time news. ITN, their British television news rivals, began their experiment during the general election campaign of April–May, 1979, a year during which it was reckoned that more than half the television stations in the United States already had some ENG capability and more than 300 had followed KMOX-TV and gone all-electronic.

The final adoption of ENG elsewhere was still by no means automatic.

Negotiations with the broadcasting unions were proving particularly difficult and long drawn-out.

The networks had no doubts about ENG and committed themselves heavily. Within the United States, it meant that facilities for processing 16 mm film were rapidly becoming so scarce, foreign-based news services faced the unattractive alternative of either air-freighting their undeveloped material home (with the obvious risk of it being well out of date before it reached the other side of the Atlantic) or buying American electronic coverage off the shelf. Abroad, ENG was being used to the extent that the editor of one British television news organization complained that he would be able to use material satellited from London and back by an American crew many minutes before film of the same story shot by his own team on their own territory was out of the processing bath. That, he believed, was unacceptable. His argument may not have been the clincher, but by 1980 any remaining opposition was disintegrating, and the switch from film to ENG was going ahead at full speed.

How ENG works

The basis of electronic news gathering, also known as EJ (*Electronic Journalism*) or ECC (*Electronic Camera Coverage*) is a camera weighing only a few pounds and an equally portable videocassette machine on which both picture and sound are recorded. The two pieces of equipment, usually linked together by a cable, are invariably operated separately by a cameraman and recordist working as a team.

Compatibility is essential between recorder and tape size. In the mid eighties the most popular was still three-quarter inch (19 mm), the cassettes containing enough tape for 20 minutes of material. But so rapid

COMBINED CAMERA-RECORDER

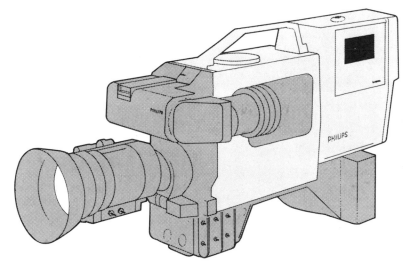

Fig. 3.2. Quarter-inch video systems allow for the camera and recorder to be operated separately or as one piece of equipment.

have been the advances in the technology that half-inch (12.5 mm) and even quarter-inch (6 mm) systems are also in use, the main advantage of both being that they are small enough to allow for the development of camera and recorder as one piece of equipment, by one person.

The first professional half-inch system, *Sony Betacam*, has already proved so successful some broadcasting organizations contemplating the change from film have been able to leap-frog the three-quarter inch format altogether. Those others who have invested heavily in U-matic type systems may regard with dismay the prospect of changing to yet another new format, and so the economic facts of life seem likely to have a slowing down effect on the universal acceptance of half-inch.

The reduced weights and sizes of cameras are not in themselves considered to offer the main operational benefits of the electronic medium. ENG scores in other ways. The main advantage is its ability to cut out that wasteful, frustrating period between the moment the film is shot to when it appears on the screen — the time spent going through the processing bath. It means that crews, who once had to judge to a nicety the point at which it became too late to shoot film for their programme, are now aware that deadlines have been extended, so they are freer to produce late material for a story they have already covered or, better still, to cover more stories.

The financial savings are obvious. For although the cost of a fully equipped ENG unit is many times that of a film camera, processing departments are no longer necessary, staff can be retrained for other duties, and tape (about ten times cheaper than film) can be re-used time and again. If these were not compelling enough reasons for news

Fig. 3.3. Three-quarter inch Electronic News Gathering (ENG), the system that has revolutionized television news coverage since the end of the seventies. Here one member of the ENG crew operates the camera while the other carries the portable videocassette machine which records sound and picture. The lighting assistant — not always a permanent part of the team — is called in to supply extra illumination for an interview in an industrial setting on a dull day. (*Ivor Yorke*).

organizations to turn to ENG, then the case is surely proven by the flexibility of the system to meet a wide variety of requirements for news (Fig. 3.4).

At its most fundamental, the ENG camera is used on location to record pictures which (with the appropriate recorder model) can be played back through the viewfinder for content and quality checking on site before the tape is returned to base by hand for editing and transmission. These procedures, with the one obvious exception, are identical to those traditionally used for film.

Where ENG really comes into its own is when pictures and sound from the unit are fed back to news headquarters by microwave link — live or already recorded on to cassette. Some ENG teams, especially in the United States, travel in customized vans (*Minicams*) carrying their own equipment to transmit the signals home. Other countries use unmarked camera cars and have their transmitters installed in separate vehicles (sometimes called *Facilities Units*) with which they can rendezvous at some convenient time and place. The tape is replayed to base by the unit's own cassette recorder.

THE VERSATILITY OF ENG

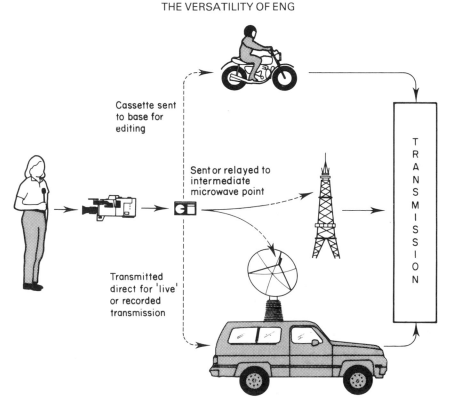

Cassette sent to base for editing

Sent or relayed to intermediate microwave point

Transmitted direct for 'live' or recorded transmission

TRANSMISSION

Fig. 3.4. One of the main advantages of electronic news gathering over film is its versatility. Material can be recorded on to a cassette which can then be sent or delivered by hand; it can be transmitted back to base directly or from an intermediate microwave point; it can also be transmitted live and recorded at the same time.

Fig. 3.5. Satellite News Gathering. This compact terminal is small enough to be carried aboard a private jet aircraft. Picture and sound signals from ENG cameras are transmitted via the dish to a communications satellite for linking back to base for broadcasting. Some television stations with SNG capability have joined forces to share and broaden their news coverage. (*GEC-McMichael*)

As a much-used alternative, the camera signal is relayed from location to the Facilities Unit over a short-range radio link. Here again the pictures are recorded on the spot or simply bounced onwards using the aerial on the vehicle roof. (If the location is close by, the short-range link is itself powerful enough to transmit the signal to base.) The aerial is aligned with microwave link dishes sited on the tops of tall buildings or masts which in turn pass the signal to receivers at news headquarters. Another option is to play the tape direct from the telecommunications points dotted around the country.

Permanent circuits are also installed in some urban areas. London, for example, has a sound and vision ring-main system which was originally established to feed outside broadcast pictures of the coronation of Queen Elizabeth II in 1953. These metal boxes are sited near buildings at various convenient places throughout the capital. When they are needed, the engineers open them, plug in sound and video leads, and route the pictures by coaxial cable to the studio.

In very remote areas where none of these systems exist or are near enough to be useful, an ENG team carrying its own mobile antenna and other equipment in a van, towing it behind in a trailer or packing it into a private aircraft, is able to transmit its material by bouncing the signal off a communications satellite. This *Satellite News Gathering* is already being operated successfully by a number of news services, some of whom, particularly in the United States, have seen the value of pooling their resources to provide state-wide coverage by satellite.

In the editing suite

In an ideal situation, every television news-writer would be able to sit at ease and watch the 'rushes' (the raw material recorded or fed direct from the camera) on a screen big enough to appreciate all that the ENG team has accomplished. Unfortunately, on most occasions, news-writer and picture editor go straight into an editing booth with their cassettes and find themselves working against the clock, able only to make instinctive decisions about material they may have time to see once — and that at faster than normal speed.

What they select depends on the nature of the subject, its interest, importance, and nominated position and duration within the programme they are working towards. Equally important on occasion is the extent to which the two have briefed themselves, so that by the time the tapes reach them they are already aware of the contents and have planned a rough scheme for editing.

At this stage there is no room for clashes of interest or temperament — only teamwork to ensure that what appears on the screen, perhaps only a few minutes later, reflects the successful fusion of separate professional skills. In recent years this has become more possible than ever before, as relationships between picture editors and writers are less strained than they once were.

Most of the old-style cutters who originally left the film industry newsreels to join the pioneers of television news have now departed. With them has gone much of the friction which arose with writers who felt that getting the story across was always more important than sticking to some of the more rigid rules of film editing grammar.

The old school has been replaced by a new breed of young editors who acknowledge that they and the news-writers share one common aim: to tell the story, in pictures and words, as coherently as possible. The result is modern, streamlined and effective. Not that the younger picture editors are any more keen than their predecessors to break the rules. It is just that for the sake of simplicity they are prepared to dispense with the irrelevant.

It can also be considered fortunate that many of today's editors were still in the early stages of their careers as videotape began to take its hold, and so they have retained a precious knowledge of film techniques. Others who once spent their time working with two-inch videotape have brought with them into the ENG editing suites hard-won technical experience which has made it easier for them to make the transition to smaller format working.

Much of the negotiation which was necessary at the time of change to three-quarter inch tape concerned film and videotape editors, whose skills and status were reflected in the different ways recruitment, training and careers were structured. The outcome in some news departments has been the creation of a single *Picture Editor* category which recognizes the need for the practitioners to be able to handle the entire range of material in any format. All this has helped to increase the flow of expertize in unexpected directions, and those writers with a developed sense of things visual need no longer feel surprised or upset when an enthusiastic picture editor with a feeling for words suggests a possible line for the commentary.

So, in many ways, it has blossomed into a genuine, two-way relationship, in which more is expected of the editor than the slavish matching of tape to editorial orders. And it remains significant that in the best-ordered news services the commentary is planned around the pictures and not vice versa. None of these valuable relationships can exist where journalists edit their own pictures or where news is merely one 'customer' for picture editors handling all types of programme material. In these case, editorial staff may be required to view the rushes on 'off-line' home video type recorders, noting the length and placing of each shot to construct a cutting order which is given to the editor to follow.

Where the two skills are practised alongside each other, the picture editor is able to understand how his main problems are identical to those of his editorial counterpart — lack of programme space in which to tell the story and lack of time in which to meet an approaching deadline.

In these days of longer newscasts, an editor is probably asked to assemble reporter packages much more often than the bread-and-butter items which news-writers used to script regularly as an everyday part of their work. But the principles have not changed, and any editor aspiring to the more challenging work first has to master the techniques on which all editing is based. Because it really is remarkable how much can be told in 30 seconds of screen time. This represents probably no more than six or seven shots, yet if they are put together skilfully the item will make just as much sense visually if dug out of the archives next year as when viewed on the air in an hour's time.

Sometimes the choice of material to edit may be so limited as to make the picture editor's task a matter of simple assembly. On other occasions he will be overwhelmed. Much depends on the cameraman who, given a reasonable amount of time on location, aims to provide a series of shots for selection without falling into the temptation of recording everything in sight just because it costs no extra to fill up an entire cassette, which is re-usable anyway.

Editing usually takes place in any one of a number of special cubicles, the nearer the newsroom and transmission point the better. As a reminder that these were probably once film cutting rooms, an old Steenbeck editing machine and a cloth-covered bin may lurk in an odd corner, to be brought out of retirement on the rare occasion the editor is asked to cut 16 mm film. It is only then that the lights are turned off and the editor has to work in semi-darkness, as one advantage of video is that it provides an image easily bright enough to be viewed in daylight.

There is probably no such thing as a typical editing suite for three-quarter inch video, as so many news services change from one piece of newly developed equipment to the next. There are, though, a few common important features, because whatever system is in use the fundamentals of editing remain the same: the raw material from the camera — the master tape — is never actually 'cut'.

News *film* was viewed and then broken out by hand into individual shots which were joined together in sequence with clear sticky tape or liquid cement. Sound tracks were edited separately in the same way. *Electronic* images and sound from videotape are re-recorded — to the layman with scarcely noticeable loss of quality — on to fresh tape, leaving the original intact.

To do this, every editing area needs to be equipped with two linked video cassette players and monitors (television screens), one set to display the rushes, the other on which to build up the edited story. See Fig. 3.6.

There may also be a *time code generator/reader* displaying in digital clock form the elapsed time as recorded on to the tape during shooting (making it quicker and easier to locate specific shots) and a *time base corrector*, a device to even out the electronic pulses from master tape to new recording during editing.

All this equipment can be housed comfortably on a single workbench. One of the most popular cassette players in professional use is the Sony BVU (*Broadcast Video Unit*) 800/820 series, a metal box measuring 454 mm (17.8 in) in width, 283 mm (11.1 in) in height and 550 mm (21.7 in) in depth. It weighs approximately 37 kg (81 lb 9 oz).

Although the news-writer may not be present during the entire editing process, he will invariably try to be there when the picture editor starts work. The story may be spread over several cassettes for which there may or may not be accompanying paperwork to help with identification.

The first step is always to view the pictures. The editor will make sure the power is on before inserting a cassette (tape first) into the horizontal slot in the front of the player. Within a few seconds the tape is automatically threaded and a still picture appears on the monitor. From there the tape is viewed at normal speed, seen 'shuttled' up to ten times faster, 'jogged' gently in either direction using the search dial, or simply fast-forwarded or rewound. A time counter indicates the position of the tape in hours, minutes, seconds and frames. When it is necessary to view

ENG EDITING

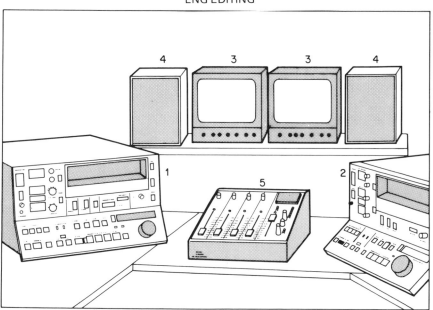

Fig. 3.6. Lay-out of typical editing suite showing (1) cassette player for 'rushes', (2) recorder on which edited story is built up, (3) monitors for viewing the pictures, (4) linked loudspeakers, (5) fader box for controlling sound volume and tracks.

another tape the eject button is pressed and the cassette automatically disengages.

The sound from the tape's two tracks comes from a monitor or a loudspeaker controlled by a central fader box which allows the volume to be adjusted to any desired level. As the news-writer watches, the editor goes through all the picture and sound material, checking for quality and content.

Together they discuss the general outline and duration, building up a mental picture of the sequence of events and how they will eventually appear on the screen. Once this first viewing of the rushes is completed and the decisions taken about the rough shape the item will take, editing proper can begin.

The second machine, the recorder, is now brought into use. A fresh tape is loaded and the 'insert' editing mode selected. Volume controls are checked on both machines. The picture editor again presses 'play' on the player, then pushes in the 'search' dial, twisting it into the forward or reverse position to control the direction and speed of the tape containing the rushes. He watches the monitor carefully until his first chosen shot appears. As soon as it does, he stops turning the search dial, and the moving pictures are frozen into a single still frame. From that position, he inches the tape forwards or backwards using the search dial in the 'jog' mode until it reaches the exact point at which the edit is to be made. Pressing the 'in' and 'entry' buttons on the front panel at the same time automatically memorizes the start time of the shot on the player's digital tape counter. When the end of it is reached the picture editor presses the

Fig. 3.7. Editing suite for ENG. Picture editors and journalists work together to assemble news items as they did in the days of 16 mm film, but now the raw material from the camera is magnetic tape which is never 'cut'. (*BBC Central Stills*)

'out' and 'entry' buttons to memorize completion of the edit, or simply presses 'stop'.

The editor now turns his attention to the recording machine, using the 'in', 'out', and 'entry/stop' buttons in much the same way. He then selects 'preview' which allows him to rehearse the edit. Although the pictures are displayed on both screens, the actual checking is being made on the recorder monitor only. If the picture editor is unhappy with what he sees he can go through the whole procedure all over again, selecting new editing points. If fine adjustment by a few frames is needed he does this with the 'trim' button.

If he is merely uncertain, he can use 'preview' to rehearse the scene once more. But if he is completely satisfied, he records the shot from the rushes to the new tape in what is sometimes known as 'electronic splicing', by pressing 'auto edit'. When this mode is engaged both tapes roll back three, five, seven or ten seconds from the start of the shot and automatically move forward again to make the edit.

The first scene should now be safely recorded, but it is possible to check it on the monitor by means of the 'review' button. Once that is accomplished, the picture editor goes on to find his chosen second shot from the rushes, lines up the end of the first shot already on the recorder and plays it across in the same way as before. The process is then repeated each time with succeeding shots until the whole story is successfully assembled. At any stage the editor may replace a shot or add sound (possibly the commentary already recorded on to another cassette). A prepared 'leader', 10–15 seconds of spacing marked in numbers which count down to zero, precedes the opening shot and is a way of enabling the studio director to count the edited tape into the programme at exactly the right moment after it has been introduced.

There are many picture editors who are nostalgic about the old days when there was a pleasurable feel to the material they were cutting. But although it is something they miss, most admit that editing video is equally enjoyable. It chiefly comes down to the ability to preview any edit before it is finalized, and then to watch it being executed automatically.

In the past editing had to be carried out by hand, and however skilful editors were it was always likely that some slight adjustment would be necessary. That meant unpicking the taped join, snipping perhaps a few frames of picture and sound from each track, rejoining them carefully to ensure exact synchronism, and then going through the whole viewing process all over again. At times edits might have to be restored, always assuming that the originally unwanted bits had not been thrown away. The arrival of the video age has at least spared picture editors that embarrassment.

Long and complicated news stories, especially those where sound or the overlay technique are involved, may take several hours to put together, and the news-writer will probably leave the picture editor and return to the newsroom for other chores. At some stage the writer may be called back to give an opinion as editing progresses, but, as often as not, there is no further contact between the two until the editor's work is completed. Then, after running the story through, a decision is taken at once about whether the cut version comes up to expectations or whether changes are necessary.

Shot-listing

Once he is satisfied, the news-writer's next step represents what is undoubtedly the most critical point in the entire operation to ensure that, on transmission, the written commentary matches the edited pictures.

This is called shot-listing, which consists of noting details of the length, picture and sound content of every separate scene in the edited sequence, at this stage usually referred to as a *cut story*. What makes this process even more important is, as we shall see at a later stage, that news programmes are among the very few still transmitted live, and that there is usually only one chance for the news-writer to find out whether his script is accurate, and that is when it goes on the air.

Shot-listing procedure is simplicity itself, however long the edited tape, although for this example we shall take an imaginary, typical 30 second story about the arrival of a party leader for a political conference.

The picture editor sets the counter to zero on his cassette player. At the end of the first edit the machine is stopped so that the writer can put down on paper everything the scene contains, together with the clock time at the end of the first shot, say, three seconds:

GV (general view) exterior of conference hall   . . . 3 sec.

The machine is restarted and the pictures run on until the next shot, which lasts four seconds. The news-writer makes a note of the details and the *cumulative* time:

MS (medium shot) delegates arriving on foot   . . . 7 sec.

This operation is repeated until the end of the edited story and the news-writer's shot-list looks like this:

GV exterior of conference hall	. . . 3 sec.
MS delegates arriving on foot	. . . 7 sec.
CU (close up) crowds waiting	. . . 10 sec.
LS (long shot) leader's car turns corner	. . . 15 sec.
MS motorcycle escort dismounts	. . . 18 sec.
CU car door opens, leader gets out	. . . 24 sec.
GV leader walks up steps into building	. . . 30 sec.

Armed with those details back in the newsroom, the news-writer will be able to time a reference to the party leader to the precise moment, 18 seconds from the start, when the car door opens and that familiar figure appears. Without that information to hand, accurate scripting would be impossible.

Often, when time is pressing, the temptation is to skip shot-listing and rely on the memory. It never works. Even if it means nagging the picture editor into more viewings, the news-writer must be absolutely certain that, before leaving the editing suite for the newsroom, the shot-list is complete down to the last detail. Going back to see the pictures again later before transmission is at best difficult, at worst impossible.

4

Writing to pictures

The mechanics of writing any sort of commentary to pictures can be explained and understood in about an hour. To apply them well requires a special ability to appreciate the value that moving images have in relation to the words necessary to complement them. Writing to news pictures is a distillation of that special skill which some journalists, despite a genuine feeling for words and empathy with pictures, never quite develop.

Basic commentary construction

Exactly what it is that distinguishes the excellent from the merely acceptable is virtually impossible to explain without the impact of the pictures themselves. Looking at the written script by itself will provide no clue. The purists would shudder at the use of the two-word, verbless, inverted sentences and the apparently casual regard for punctuation. The test is to ignore the printed script and to sit back, listen and watch as the commentary adds a delicate counterpoint to the pictures.

Probably the first mistake the novice news-writer makes is to try to cram into 30 seconds of screen time the maximum number of facts that previous journalistic experience taught was essential. The result will be total chaos. The script takes little or no notice of the pictures they were meant to accompany; the style is heavy, as written for the printed page and, most likely, the reader will come a poor second in the oral sprint to finish the commentary before the tape runs out.

At three words to the second, a 30 second story gives the writer a maximum of 90 words to play with. No matter how cleverly they are used, there is no way in which it is possible to squeeze in more and still expect the commentary to make sense to those hearing it. From the outset, the news-writer must learn to exercise a ruthless economy of words, first so that the pictures are able to do their work properly and, secondly, to avoid the ultimate sin of having them finish while the reader is still speaking. It is far safer to under-write and leave a few seconds of picture unscripted.

Most beginners' commentaries tend to refer in great detail to people, places or events which do not appear at all. This, in many ways, is an understandable fault, but one which must be corrected at once. Over the years the viewer has come to recognize such references as signposts leading to whatever he is about to see, and he is bound to feel cheated if, in the end, those signs lead nowhere.

Too much detail has, equally, the effect of drawing attention to what may be missing from news coverage. A blow-by-blow account of cars screaming to a halt, armed men tumbling out and shots being fired during a jewel robbery should be avoided when all the camera is able to record in the aftermath is a solitary policeman walking over broken glass from a window, a few specks of blood on the floor and tyre marks on the road. The atmosphere can be conveyed just as effectively without using words which make the viewer feel let down that the action is not taking place on the screen.

Similarly with sound: 'cheering' crowds, 'screaming' jet engines, the 'crackle' of small arms fire — all conjure up definite mental pictures.

If the viewer does not hear what is generally accepted as a cheer, scream or crackle, the suspicion may arise that the television people do not really know what they are about. Exactly the same response will be evoked by talk of the 'booming' of artillery when what can be heard quite clearly on the sound track is, indeed, the authentic crackle of small-arms fire. In such cases, the news-writer is well advised to use general words less liable to misinterpretation. After all, 'gunfire' is a term capable of being applied to virtually anything between a few pistol shots and a full-scale battle.

Having learned these early lessons, the new news-writer's next mistake will be to write a commentary which reads like a series of newspaper captions. With every change of shot, the viewer is treated to nothing more or less than a verbal repetition of the sights and sounds unfolding on the television screen a few feet away. Thus the news-writer's influence is as good as meaningless, especially where the script includes clumsy phrases to ensure that the viewer does not escape even the most obvious:

'As you can see here . . .'

'The Prime Minister, on the right . . .'

True, there are occasions when it is necessary to take the viewer metaphorically by the scruff of the neck:

'The Smiths knew nothing of the explosion until they returned home a week later. Then, all they found . . . was *this*.'

But this is a technique to be used sparingly.

In most cases, to recite what is happening on the screen is to lose a great opportunity of telling the viewer something worthwhile. The news-writer's skill lies in being able to convey what is *not* clear from the pictures.

Take almost any international conference. Ten minutes after the routine photocall, during which delegates are seen talking and joking, a furious row breaks out in the privacy of the closed session. Probably all the news-writer will ever have to work with are pictures suggesting that all was sweetness and light. Instead of throwing away the apparently irrelevant, the news-writer should be able to make almost a virtue of the scenes of accord, using them to pinpoint the contrast between events occurring before and during the conference:

'. . . but the spirit of co-operation didn't last long. Almost as soon as the conference got under way . . .'

The use of archive material when no other illustration is available poses a similar test of ingenuity. Then the news-writer may be faced with the daunting prospect of matching the apparently unmatchable — out-of-date pictures with up-to-date facts. The temptation here is probably to 'talk against picture', to ignore what the film or tape contains in order to get the story across. This can be done for very brief periods in a commentary, but the technique needs careful judgement to ensure that words and pictures do meet often enough to avoid confusion.

Here's a possible treatment. News breaks that the leader of an important South American country has been overthrown in a military coup.

No pictures are expected until the next day, and the only material available in the archives consists of a few (unused) shots of the President reviewing troops when he took office on Independence Day a few months earlier.

Armed with the latest agency tape, a few background cuttings and a carefully made shot-list, the news-writer should be able to make those pictures work for him and the audience. The story is told simply enough, even though the pictures and the words accompanying them need be nothing special. Imagine that some of the details of the coup, together with a map and the first political reactions at home have already been given in the vision intro: the words 'library pictures' will be superimposed on the screen so the viewer is not misled.

Shot-list	Cumulative time	Commentary
Long shot, troops marching through city centre	0 sec.	It's not even a year since army leaders pledged their loyalty to the civilian government.
Medium shot infantry passing	6 sec.	Then they promised to stay out of domestic politics, whatever the result of the elections.
Medium shot tank column	13 sec.	But in the capital today the tanks were out to enforce a curfew and people were
Long shot crowds waving	17 sec.	ordered to listen to the state radio for an official announcement.
General view government ministers on saluting base	20 sec.	Most of the leading politicians are now under house arrest, although what's happened to
Close up President on platform	25 sec.	the President isn't clear. He's reported to have had warning
General view reverse angle President salutes as men	29 sec.	of the coup and taken his family out of the country at
past	32 sec.	the weekend.

One of the best tips about scripting good pictures is *don't*. The greater the action, the greater the need to say less. The same principle applies to good sound: let the band play, the cheers ring out. When words are needed in quantity it is important to use them to their best advantage. Too many inexperienced writers use up all their most interesting facts to cover the early shots and leave themselves short of anything else to say at the finish. Even the commentary to cover a routine 30 second item can be structured to ensure a proper opening, middle and end instead of being allowed to dribble weakly to a close.

Building in the pauses

As has already been made clear, the shot-list is the only sure method by which the writer is able to identify separate scenes in an edited news-story with any real accuracy.

Applying the formula of three words a second to the example on page 68, it would take 54 words to reach the beginning of the shot where the party leader emerges from his car. But this does not allow for the fact that there may be some good 'natural' sound to be heard, that the writer may not wish to cover all 18 seconds with commentary or, indeed, that there may not be enough to say that is relevant or worthwhile.

Added to those factors is the possibility that a hesitation or 'fluff' may make the reader's speed vary, so that by the time 18 seconds have elapsed he may be significantly out of step with the pictures. What is needed, therefore, is some measure of control over the reader while the item is being transmitted live.

The item that follows is a variation on The Party Leader Arrives. This time it is the foreign minister of a friendly country.

He is about to conclude a big trade deal which includes the sale of military equipment. Others fear it may be used to quell internal unrest. Outside the building where the signing ceremony is to take place, police struggle to hold back a group of demonstrators who are waving banners and shouting loudly: 'Butter not guns!' As he arrives, the minister ignores the crowd and goes straight in to his meeting.

Shot-list

General view minister's car and escort	. . . 3 sec.
Medium shot police link arms to restrain crowd	. . . 7 sec.
Close-up minister out of car, waving	. . . 11 sec.
Medium shot group with banners shouting 'Butter not guns'	. . . 16 sec.
Minister walks straight past, up stairs into building	. . . 22 sec.

Consulting this shot-list back in the newsroom, the writer decides that the most interesting point is the brief confrontation between demonstrators and politician, and that the chants of 'Butter not guns' should be heard without the accompanying distraction of the newsreader's voice. The aim, then, is to hold the reader back for the five seconds of the chanting, and then to give a signal to restart the commentary immediately afterwards.

The secret lies in part in the lay-out of the written script on the newsreader's desk. As the story is transmitted, the reader speaks the commentary until the point is reached where the production instruction 'cue' appears in the left-hand margin. This is the signal to treat the *preceding* full-stop as an invisible barrier which must not be passed until a signal, possibly a coloured light out of the sight of the camera, is given to carry on. The gap between the two may be a few seconds or considerably longer, but the reader must wait for the signal.

Usually the word 'cue' is accompanied by a definite time, to indicate when the reader is to be signalled to restart the commentary. More often than not it is the news-writer who does the cueing, using the tape leader countdown from the control room as a guide for starting a stop watch:

'As the Minister arrived, large numbers of police were kept busy holding back groups of left-wing demonstrators determined to make it known what *they* thought of the arms deal.'

In this case the reader will have reached the words '. . . thought of the arms deal' in exactly ten seconds. Seeing the instruction 'Cue 16 seconds', he pauses. At 11 seconds the point is reached where demonstrators begin chanting. As the second hand on the watch reaches 16, the writer presses the button operating the cue light, and the reader smoothly picks up the thread of the commentary:

'But even if he heard them, the Minister didn't appear to notice the protests'.

For sheer professional results every time, the stopwatch and cue light method is difficult to beat, despite the danger that in occasional moments of stress the writer is likely to press the wrong button and stop the watch too soon. Nevertheless, it is generally recognized that only the writer knows intimately what the pictures contain and is in a position to make minor adjustments to cue times, even during transmission. In any case, most writers are obsessively protective towards their precious scripts and are uneasy about leaving the cueing of them in the care of anyone else.

Where there are no arrangements for cue lights to be worked by editorial staff, the operation is usually carried out from the control room by the production assistant, although this would appear to be putting an unfair additional burden on someone already occupied with other responsible duties during transmission.

Hand signals relayed by the floor manager on instruction from the control room seem likely to increase the time-lag between cue and reader reaction. The same objection may be made about another widely used system where the reader is expected to pick up his own cues from the studio monitor at some recognizable point in the story. This invariably means waiting for a shot-change, and by the time the reader has reacted, the viewer may have spent two, maybe three, seconds looking at some new and unexplained scene.

From the reader's point of view, too, it is unsatisfactory, as it is all too easy to fall behind if the script is tightly written. This self-cueing system should be discouraged almost as much as the one where the newsreader is given such imprecise written instructions as 'pause for three seconds' and is then expected to hit every shot with unfailing accuracy.

Of course every reader needs some time to react, whatever cueing system is employed, and in planning the script it is essential that the writer builds in a nominal one second between every cue and the expected resumption of commentary. Experience will tell whether that is long enough.

Getting started

Writers vary in the way they set out to construct their scripts. The method favoured by many is to begin by writing the words around one key shot, not always at the start of the story, and then building up the commentary before and after it, fitting in the cues as necessary.

At this stage, unless pressure of time is great, it is wise to put down more or less anything which sounds right, leaving any 'polishing' of words and phrases until the first draft is complete. This method is further helped by writing only three words to a line, preferably on a ruled pad, so making it simple to add up the number of seconds of commentary already written. It is surprisingly easy to lose count if the words for a 40-second script are strung out across the page, and minor adjustments may take far longer than expected. The introduction of computer systems does not mean the end of this approach; the words can be typed three to a line on a blank screen and 'justified' into script format later on.

No matter whether a script is being written on a brand new VDT or a scruffy pad, the rule remains the same — accurate identification of shots can be achieved consistently *only as a result of careful writing and cueing from the shot-list*, and it is disappointing to discover newsrooms where no demands at all are made on writers to 'hit the shots' as a matter of course. Pictures are allowed to run their course while the words simply wash over them, meeting, if they ever do, more by luck than judgement. What the poor viewer is supposed to make of it all is hard to tell. 'Block' scripts, those written over the entire length of a story without pause, should be reserved for those infrequent occasions where clear identification is not necessary. It is also leaving too much to chance to allow more than 20 seconds without a cue, far less when individuals need accurate identification.

At the other extreme lies the temptation to insert a cue for every sentence of script. This soon becomes boring and predictable; the target should be a reasonable variation in the length of cues so that sometimes a single paragraph straddles a sequence of shots. It may mean padding out where there is too little to say, cutting out words when there is too much, or achieving the desired effect by 'borrowing' a phrase intended for one shot to say over another. In that way, one neatly constructed sentence cued to coincide with, say, the first in a series of personalities arriving for a political conference, should ensure perfect synchronism between words and pictures.

Finally, if things do go awry, it is far better that the script should anticipate what is about to happen rather than follow what has already taken place. The viewer ought never to be left in limbo, staring at a brand new shot and wondering for a few uncomfortable moments whether he is being prevented from hearing the commentary because something has gone wrong with the television set.

Scripting sports news

It really is quite surprising how many experienced television news-writers who have no difficulty explaining the most complicated or abstract issues are completely lost when scripting news about sport.

This has nothing to do with the live broadcasts or other sports programmes which are usually the preserve of specialist departments; what we are considering here are the brief edits for inclusion as part of routine news programmes, for there are times when sport is news and has to be treated as such.

Every sport is a subject in its own right, but unless a television news service enjoys the luxury of having its own resident experts, there are bound to be occasions when the writer who is happiest dealing with international crises suddenly finds himself having to script a tennis final or a soccer match. Sport has a language of its own, with accepted terms and phrases that are recognized by the afficionados but which are inapplicable, unintelligible even, out of their own context.

Simple things: teams take the collective noun. It may be more grammatically correct to say: 'England *is* . . .', but the knowledgeable sports enthusiasts among the audience will pour scorn on any organization which permits that to be broadcast in place of the accepted: 'England *are* . . .'.

The second, and much more difficult problem, concerns the construction of the script itself, because the action in most sport is telescoped into a very short space of time. Long before any accompanying script can explain what has happened, the golfer has sunk his putt, the tennis player has served an ace, the batsman has been clean-bowled. So the most sensible approach to scripting virtually any sport is to remember that the action is far better 'set up' *before* it takes place, with any additional information added immediately a suitable pause occurs — as the golfer picks the ball out of the hole, the tennis player winds up for the next service, the batsman starts to walk back to the pavilion.

The edited opening 15 seconds of a report on an England soccer match should give the idea. The script is simple, straightforward and economical. The opening words set the scene and at the same time warn the audience that something important is about to happen. They also cover the second shot, identifying the player who has been tackled illegally, and there is still enough time to squeeze in the information about the free-kick before the commentary pauses at nine seconds to let the action take place.

During the next four seconds the free-kick is taken, Lineker leaps in the air and heads the ball past the goalkeeper. It is only after that, at 11 seconds, as the scorer turns to celebrate, that the commentary is allowed to resume, confirming what has happened and completing the sequence.

Note how the shot-list splits the action into very short scenes to ensure maximum accuracy in the commentary writing:

Picture details	Cumulative Time	Commentary
GV Stadium and spectators	0 sec.	A capacity crowd of fifty thousand saw England take an
MS Robson, no. 7 tripped	5 sec.	early lead after Robson, number seven, was brought down. The free kick, by
WS Barnes takes free-kick	9 sec.	Barnes, was perfectly placed.
MS Lineker leaps	10 sec.	Cue 10 sec.
MS Goalkeeper is beaten	11 sec.	Lineker the scorer after six
CU Lineker celebrates	15 sec.	minutes.

It is a treatment which probably works equally as efficiently with other sports, the essential point being that the script always helps to build up the expectation of important action, and does not spoil it by swamping it with unnecessary words.

Cueing into speech

Some of the problems involved in cueing sound effects within a news story have already been touched on. A whole new set of difficulties present themselves when the sound is that of human speech.

Much of what is spoken within television news reports comes from two categories of people — reporters or those being interviewed by them. In either case, the aim of the news-writer must be to construct any additional commentary for transmission in a way which links most naturally into the words already recorded on to the sound track.

Where this comes within the body of the item rather than at the beginning, the onus rests even more heavily on the editorial team to ensure that the speech arrives a decent breath's pause after the commentary introducing it. Failure results in either an embarrassingly long delay between the two or, worse, what in the United States is called 'upcutting', the ugly overlap of live commentary and recorded sound.

Accuracy is achieved fairly easily, by positioning a cue paragraph immediately before the sound extract. The wording itself is of importance, and the writer is taking unnecessary risks if a planned lead-in to a speech demands timing to the split second:

'Reporting on the latest round of pay talks, the general secretary told the conference . . .'
(General secretary speaks)

will be impressive if the sound is heard without delay, but

'The general secretary reported on the latest round of pay talks . . .'
(General secretary speaks)

would be much safer, for it would still make sense if the recorded speech were delayed for a few seconds or did not arrive at all because of some technical fault. The whole principle is based on the fact that flexibility rests with the writer's words and not on the speech placed at an immovable point on the edited sound track.

With interviews in which the reporter's first or only question has been edited out, the words leading up to the answer must be carefully phrased to produce a response which matches, otherwise there is a clear danger that the writer will be guilty of putting words into the interviewee's mouth. It is equally important to ensure that if the viewer is about to be shown an interviewee in close-up as he prepares to answer a question, the commentary leading up to it should leave no doubt about who is to speak. This is achieved by referring to the first speaker last. So it is:

'Tom Bailey asked the Foreign Minister for his reaction . . .'
(Foreign Minister answers)

and not

'The Foreign Minister talked to Tom Bailey . . .'
(Foreign Minister answers)

Vision introductions to items should follow similar principles.

'We've just received this report from Tom Bailey . . .'

suggests Our Man will be audible or visible at once. The introduction which ends lamely with the words

'Our Bogshire newsroom reports . . .'

suggests a scene of newsroomers busily at work, and the viewer is likely to be confused by an opening shot which shows, instead, an exterior dominated by an un-named reporter. In any event, the flat statement

'Our Bogshire newsroom reports . . .'

makes listening which, by any standards, is less than riveting. Far more worthwhile is an introduction which passes on some information, at the same time as preparing the viewer for what is coming next.

'Tom Bailey has been finding out why exporting has suddenly become so much more difficult for the motor industry . . .'

has, at least, the merit of suggesting to the viewer that it might be worth keeping awake for the report about to follow.

Sound extracts

The selection of one or more extracts from a lengthy interview obviously depends on the amount of space the item has been allocated within a news programme. As it is fairly unusual for any interview to be shot to its exactly prescribed duration, however experienced the principals taking part, a certain amount of choice will inevitably be necessary. Given time, the programme editor may wish to make this a personal choice, but just as frequently it is the newsroom-based news-writer who will be faced with the task.

As every interview is unique, it is impossible to set down rigid rules. On some occasions, the single one-minute answer out of six will stand out. On others, the reporter concerned may have strong views about the merits of a particular section and offer guidance; in some news organizations, the reporter is expected to 'cut' his/her own interviews as a matter of course. The firmest general guideline to any selector probably goes no further than a suggestion that the ultimate value of any news interview rests in the opinion and interpretation of facts given by the interviewee. The facts themselves are best left for the presenter's introduction.

In making the choice, there should also be awareness that much more is involved than suitability of duration and content, important though they might be. The editing into, or out of, any recorded speech at precisely the required point *editorially* may, at the same time, not be feasible *technically*. So even at the expense of a few extra, unwanted seconds of screen time, the aim should always be to cut at the most natural points: ends of answers, or, where the selection consists of only part of a sound passage, a stop or breath pause during which the inflection of the voice is downwards. Although most people are well aware that editing takes place, it is always much better to avoid any cut which will appear both ugly and obvious.

Videotape writing without pains

Evidence of one of the most important side-effects of the introduction of ENG can now be seen in television news videotape departments across the world. Areas which once housed those imposing quadruplex machines running reels of two-inch tape have been giving way to the smaller, broadcast quality videocassette players, backed up, perhaps, by a few one-inch machines.

For the writer, the process of writing to larger-format videotape presents no more difficulty than writing to ENG and the mechanics are therefore the same.

The biggest technical limitation of two-inch tape used to be that when the machine stopped, sound and picture disappeared. This in no way restricted editing, but it made a hazardous hit-or-miss affair of shot-listing. Modern videotape equipment is now so advanced that the tape can be halted on any chosen frame for details to be noted. Integrated time-coding has made the use of the old-fashioned stop watch all but unnecessary, and the ability to 'freeze' picture frames (usually at the beginning or the end) has helped reduce the possibility of the words in a tightly written script running beyond the pictures.

The general all-round improvement of videotape equipment has also made it easier for writers to construct their opening paragraphs. At one time it took about ten seconds for a videotape machine to reach its correct operating speed, so studio directors encouraged their editorial colleagues to provide them with at least 30 words of script from which to calculate a run-up accurate enough to ensure that the first picture appeared on the screen as the reader completed the introduction to it. (This compared with three seconds usually needed for telecine machines transmitting film.)

Nowadays it is quite possible to run all videotape and film from a standing start, but as most studio directors seem to prefer to see moving leader numbers on their preview monitors when programmes are being transmitted, white numbers, calibrated in seconds, are added to black background leaders during the editing stage. By linking the videotape machine to an electronic keyboard, story identification or any other information can also be typed in. The advantage for the members of the production department is that they are able to decide for themselves the length of run up time most suitable for their particular needs, and can settle on a standard of, say, five seconds for all moving pictures.

Advances in editing technique

In the pioneering days, a videotape edit was carried out by hand. This was a slow process that required the physical cutting and joining of tape after a (literally) microscopic examination of the magnetic surface. Besides taking approximately 15 minutes to accomplish, each edit also ruined that particular portion of tape. This laborious method was eventually made obsolete by the technique of 'invisible' electronic editing which not only left the tape unimpaired for re-use, but was capable of being carried out extremely quickly by trained operators. Two machines were needed, as the chosen sections from the original tape were played from one to another which re-recorded them in sequence until a complete story was built up — exactly the same principle on which modern three-quarter and smaller format editing is based.

Later developments in two-inch and one-inch videotape technology resulted in machines being installed in pairs, so that one operator could undertake his own editing instead of having to carry it out in tandem with a colleague.

Another advance was that each machine in the pair could be used independently, allowing, for example, half the system to record one item while the other half re-played a second into the programme.

In some cases, videotape pairs of one inch machines are in use alongside ENG, one reason being that the larger tape sizes are believed by engineers to offer better broadcasting quality. Some organizations make it a rule to record electronic graphics on nothing smaller than one-inch, while those using the non-news equivalent of ENG (sometimes known as EFP (*Electronic Field Production*) or PSC (*Portable Single Camera*)) often treat their output in the same way.

If film editing is an art, then videotape editing becomes a science when practised by skilful operators capable of achieving a coherent pictorial precis from many hours of recorded material. So adept have they become at this, videotape editors in general sometimes share criticism with producers for helping to highlight interest, movement or action out of recorded events (particularly sport) which in reality were fairly dull. As far as news is concerned, there are circumstances in which too smooth an edit would create the wrong impression, and it would be more ethical to make the cut in a way which deliberately avoids giving the impression that particular portions of speech or action are continuous.

There is also a cautionary tale of how a videotape editor attempting to create a seamless two-minute robe out of a half-hour political speech inadvertently inserted a shot of the audience which overlooked the fact that one of those pictured applauding vigorously was, in the next shot of the podium, seen to be the person making the speech.

It is certainly true to say that, the greater the volume of material, the greater the difficulty in making editorial judgements about content.

A news-writer who spends a whole day sitting by a videotape machine watching an important state occasion or a cricket Test match may then be expected to condense the contents of several tapes into a maximum two minutes of air time.

The secret lies in the methodical, accurate logging of events as they occur and, wherever possible, the building up of an edited story during the longest natural breaks in action. This is sometimes inclined to force writers into making hasty or perhaps wrong decisions about what to include, especially in the light of later developments. But it remains the lesser of two evils. For even with time-coding to help him locate each shot accurately, even the most expert and willing videotape editor might be hard-pressed to make a swift compilation of half a dozen incidents spread over an equal number of tapes, since loading and unloading can still be a time-consuming business.

'Clean-feed' editing

On some occasions the recording may be of an event being broadcast live, and the news-writer may be asked to stipulate whether it is proposed to use the accompanying commentary or merely the natural sound effects when a shortened version is edited for inclusion in a news programme. The one question to be answered here is whether a commentary recorded at the time would inhibit the choice of pictorial edits made at a later stage. The usual answer will be 'yes', for the combination of picture, commentary sound and natural sound is technically impossible to unravel. Therefore the news-writer should invariably settle for the 'clean', natural sound obtained by by-passing the sound circuit carrying the commentary. There is nothing to stop this being recorded on to a second audio track on the videotape for guidance and, if required, it can be transferred to the edited version later.

One other point is worth making about videotape of any format. Faced with the somewhat overpowering technology and engineering jargon which pervade this particular area of television, many a newcomer to news-writing is understandably apprehensive. All the same it need not take too long to appreciate that videotape is just another tool which is quite capable of being mastered, especially if help is sought from those who spend their lives working with it. They are, after all, members of the same team.

Last words about pictures

Two temptations to avoid are puns and clichés.

Experienced writers usually consider that a really important, well-shot news story virtually tells itself, the task becoming one of assembling facts in an order dictated by the quality and sequence of the accompanying pictures. Much more testing are the down-bulletins items, often week-end fillers or 'soft' stories for which little information is readily available. With these, the temptation is for the writer to produce a stream of glib generalities or a series of puns, the aim in either case being to lower a curtain of words through which the lack of facts will not be noticed. There are occasions when, used sparingly, this technique does work. But, for example, a balloon race which wrings out such lines as 'soaring reputations' or 'rising hopes' will have the discerning viewer reaching for the 'off' switch in disgust.

For any unwary writer, the cliché presents another booby trap, and in television news it is a double-edged one at that, since trite pictures are just as likely to find their way on to the air as are trite phrases. Probably every viewer of every television news programme in the world has had to suffer the local equivalent of the following British examples:

● Trade union leaders arriving for or leaving from talks about pay.
● The Chancellor of the Exchequer holding aloft the despatch box containing secrets of the annual budget.
● Government ministers filing through the open door of No. 10 Downing Street for a cabinet meeting.
● Any VIP descending any aircraft steps anywhere.
● Shots of camera crews or security men on rooftops, used to telescope the action between aircraft steps and official car.
● Crowd 'reaction' shots.

As for the words, it seems almost impossible for some writers to avoid trotting out the stock phrase to satisfy the stock situation:

● The Big Fire.
  'Fifty/a hundred firemen fought/battled the blaze/flames.'
  'Smoke could be seen five/ten/fifty miles away.'
  'Firemen/ambulances rushed . . .' (what else would they do?)

● The Air Disaster.
  'Wreckage was scattered over a wide area.'
  'Rescuers tore at the wreckage with their bare hands.'

● The Great Escape.
  'Police with tracker dogs combed the area.'
  'A massive manhunt/search has begun.'
  'Road blocks have been set up.'

● The VIP Visit.
  'Security was strict/tight.'

● The Holiday Snarl-up.
  'Traffic was bumper-to-bumper.'

● The Appeal.
  'Unless the Government provides more money/changes its mind/a donor is found/comes forward, the department/hospital/exhibition/child will close/have to move/die.'

and that is not to forget my own personal favourite, usually attributed to a middle-aged eye-witness to any violent incident in the south of England.

  'It was just like the blitz.'

To be fair, it is perfectly understandable that when time is short and the pressure great, it is the familiar line rather than the elegant phrase which will suggest itself to the writer, besides which the over-riding priority must always be to get the commentary on the air, however much it might lack in originality.

But that ought to be reserved for the last resort. Where second thoughts are possible, the tired old standby must be shunned. As experienced journalists like to put it: 'Avoid clichés . . . like the plague.'

The golden rules of news-writing

Writing to moving pictures presents the news-writer with a genuine opportunity to extend journalistic experience into a completely new area. Yet, paradoxically, it remains one with limits which some regard as too restrictive. In accepting the first principle that there can be no place for scripted words totally unrelated to the pictures accompanying them, the news-writer may feel that a straitjacket is being fashioned from the very material it was believed would lead the viewer to new heights of understanding.

Among some professional news-writers this feeling is sincere, the gap seemingly unbridgeable. It need not be, provided what is an apparent weakness in the whole foundation of television news is seen as a means of refining news senses to a point where every single word is carefully chosen before being put to work.

As confidence improves, the dedicated convert to television news discovers that within the boundaries of content and duration, the treatment of words and pictures as complementary in character makes it possible to convey deeper understanding of both.

To begin moving towards that goal, the writer must take time and care to apply, ultimately by instinct, what can only be described as the Golden Rules of News-writing:

1. Words and pictures must go together.
2. The commentary must not repeat in detail what viewers are able to see and hear for themselves.
3. The commentary must not describe in detail what viewers are *not able* to see or hear for themselves.
4. The commentary must not be over-written. Or to put it another way, the best script is often the one with the fewest words.

5

Television news reporting

Despite the enormous satisfaction it is quite possible to derive from the business of putting together complicated news stories for transmission in a very short time, there is not much doubt that the glamour image of the average newsroom journalist lags far behind that of those who appear in front of the camera. For while no viewer would be expected to name any member of the back-room team, descriptions of nationally known news performers — the 'talent' as they are quaintly described in the United States — trip easily off the tongue. So it is hardly surprising that, sooner or later, many a starry-eyed newcomer to television news begins itching to achieve what is believed to be the ideal — to be seen by an audience of millions through a news report made in some exotic, relatively troubled spot the other side of the world, enjoying what one member of the international reporting set has summed up as 'a front seat on history'.

That is probably a perfect example of the greener grass syndrome, for there are certainly some reporters who would dearly love to exchange their front seats for what they regard as the calmer back rows in the newsroom, where the real power lies in pulling the strings. Even experienced television reporters privately admit that, after a while, the apparent glamour and excitement of their lives begin to pall. Some learn sooner than others to detest rushing to catch planes or deadlines, living out of suitcases, eating hurried meals in unhygienic places abroad, witnessing at first hand unspeakable horrors of which the audience may ultimately see very little.

All this is in addition to the real personal dangers involved in covering the stuff of modern television news: war, natural disaster, civil unrest. That professional newsmen doing their job are just as much at risk as the combatants has been proved time and again by events in South East Asia, the Middle East and Central America. In 1984 alone 23 journalists were killed and 81 wounded according to the International Press Institute, which has produced a survival manual for newspeople operating in dangerous situations[1].

Many reporters are married with family responsibilities, and live with

[1]*Journalists on Dangerous Assignments: a guide for staying alive*, Louis Falls Montgomery, ed. (International Press Institute, 1986).

the uneasy feeling that any birthday party, wedding anniversary or other normal domestic occasion may be interrupted by a sudden telephone call commanding them to be on the next flight to somewhere or other. The wife of one former television news general reporter used to say that the one thing which unnerved her above all was the sight of the small suitcase containing spare shirts, underwear and shaving kit, which stood permanently in the hall as a daily reminder of the emergency assignment which might come at any time; that, and not knowing whether the news 'event' would last a couple of days, a month, or more. Understandably, not all marriages endure that sort of strain.

Of course no sensible reporter pretends it is all hectic. Most will readily recall hours wasted at airports, in draughty corridors of government or other buildings, waiting for events to take place or people to turn up. Sometimes they did not. At other times, doors slammed, telephones went dead, the answer was 'no comment' or something less polite.

In contrast there are pleasant, well-ordered and interesting assignments, at which the reporter is greeted with enthusiasm, hospitality and a genuine invitation to call again. Do not forget the opportunities for keeping up with professional friends: 'Reporting television news is the only profession in which you can fly 5000 miles, drive 200 miles to a town you've never visited before, walk round the corner and meet 52 people you know.'[1]

The result of a job well done may be two or three minutes of good pictures, a visual by-line and an enhanced reputation, yet the dominating factor of it all is that the reporter cannot work alone if the assignment is to be carried out properly. For while the solo newspaperman and the radio reporter in the field are as close to the office as the nearest telephone, the television news reporter has to work with a camera crew, an outside broadcast unit, or a television studio linked in some way with home base.

Even in these days of compact, mobile equipment, this is bound to put the television news reporter at a distinct disadvantage when it comes to the scrimmages which are frequently inseparable from world news gathering. There is little point in pushing through a crowd of other equally pushy newspeople, only to discover that the cameraman has been left behind struggling with his gear.

Yet to be effective, the television reporter cannot be content to hover aloof on the fringe of a story in the hope of eventually being granted special dispensation by the other participants. Despite the fact that the obtrusiveness of the camera, microphone and lights makes the entire team a target for attention and occasional abuse, any reporter who is not up with the herd and sometimes in front of it does not last very long in the job.

And then there is the irony that perseverance and initiative at times work to the reporter's own detriment.

How often it seems that the fruits of a good television interview, grabbed against all the odds, are picked up by other newsmen in the crowd and, with minimal embellishment, are turned into highly acceptable accounts for their own branches of the news business. At other times during the scrum it is impossible to discover who has asked the questions which are eventually heard on the sound track, but that has not always stopped the

[1]Michael Cole of BBC TV News, quoted in *Executive Travel* (September 1985).

critics from blaming television reporters for any bullishness or poor grammar.

In the end, though, the reporter for television news is only as effective as his last report. There is no glory to be won from the production of a brilliant piece of work which arrives too late to be edited in time for transmission. Time, effort and money are wasted if, at the conclusion of an expensive foreign mission, the material is confiscated, never to be seen.

Reporting as a career

Few television reporters begin their careers as such. Most graduate from newspapers, news agencies or radio, and so lack only the knowledge of television techniques to become successful. Some turn out to be competent enough without ever fully understanding how to construct the well-turned phrase which complements rather than competes with the pictures, and it is not surprising that the best exponents of the reporting art are often those who have served apprenticeships as news-writers.

Leaving aside the matter of journalistic ability, a modicum of which must be assumed, the two basic qualities every reporter must have before being let loose in front of an unsuspecting public would seem to be a reasonably personable appearance and clear diction.

In Britain, ideas have undoubtedly changed about what constitutes diction good enough for broadcasting, for the general increase in news outlets, particularly since the arrival of local radio in 1967, has allowed all manner of accents and speech impediments to become suddenly more acceptable. Whether this is interpreted as a lowering of standards or a welcome move towards more genuine spoken English is a matter for individual opinion. However the cruel truth about television is that some expert journalists simply lack credibility in front of the camera in the studio or on location, and that the most carefully researched, well-written material is totally lost to the nine-tenths of an audience fascinated instead by a nervous tic, bobbing Adam's apple or inability to keep the head straight.

That is not the only difficulty. What some viewers consider to be incorrect pronunciation is guaranteed to induce near apoplexy on the part of the critics, amateur and professional alike. Bernard Levin, writing in the London *Times*, devoted hundreds of words to reprimanding certain broadcasters, television news reporters included, for sometimes pronouncing the word 'thee' instead of 'the'. To the uncaring it may have been so much wasted printers' ink. Yet Mr Levin was undeniably correct in his assessment of the result, that the 'ugly, flat, distorted and meaningless noises made by the chief sinners are so boring that they have the inevitable effect of making the listener's attention wander, though they may be telling us of important things we need to know.'[2]

Still, at least such misdemeanours are capable of being cured, unlike the expressionless monotones and nasal whines which apparently defy the best efforts of the voice-coaches. Little can be done, either, it seems, for those

[2] *The Times* (January 29, 1975).

with voices so light and high-pitched as to make virtually no impact for broadcasting.

Women figure largely among the sufferers, which may account in part for what some interpreted as discrimination against female journalists in television news, although the million-dollar wooing of Barbara Walters from one American network to another, and the astonishing upsurge in the recruitment of women which followed the inclusion of Angela Rippon in the BBC *Nine o'clock News* team of newsreaders may help to give the lie to that notion. Another, more cynical, theory about women television journalists is that male viewers spend all their time nursing lewd thoughts about them during their screen appearances while other females among the audience either hate them on principle or wonder who does their hair. (That may cause cries of 'sexist', but there's no denying human nature.) Either way, all is lost.

For these reasons, chocolate-box good looks and speech which is too precise are considered equally off-putting, whether found in men or women. Among all except those who mourn the demise of the Hollywood glamour factories, the preference is for people who look and sound as though they lead real lives off screen.

All this merely goes to emphasize how easy it is to be critical. Given the curious chemistry at work in everybody's likes and dislikes, it is interesting to speculate on the fruits of a computer programmed to produce a picture of the reporter most likely to win universal appeal. No doubt that has already been done. But without the benefit of the computer, it must all be down to intelligent guesswork and a single, old-fashioned word — style.

Learning the ropes

The novice reporter quickly discovers that there is no short cut on the tortuous route that may eventually lead to general acceptance as a competent television reporter. There is likely to be very little in the way of formal 'coaching', as the average news service cannot afford to have any operational staff missing from its line up, and expects its newcomers to pick up everything except the basics as they go along. This is sometimes euphemistically described as 'on the job training', and comes as a complete surprise to novice reporters who may be expected to be able to master the intricacies of 'filming' from their opening assignment, whether it is an interview with the distraught parents of a missing child or with the beaming winner of an angling contest.

Once some initial progress has been made, usually after a few painful lessons on the way, the new reporter may be taken aside by a more senior colleague and told gently about some of the most obvious flaws. Some of these might be avoided in the first place by attention to three factors which add to or detract from any on-screen performance: speech, mannerisms and dress.

Speech
Everyone who appears regularly in front of the camera develops a natural, personal style of delivery and emphasis, and although this individuality is to be encouraged, the aim in every case must be clarity, with delivery at an

even pace. It must be neither slow enough to be irritating, nor fast enough for the words to run into each other; no audience is able to take in much of what is told by an excited reporter speaking at full gallop.

As part of a general tendency to group words and phrases in a manner which sounds odd as well as ungrammatical, one of the most frequent is the addition of non-existent full stops in the middle of sentences.

The cure could not be simpler; sentences which are too long should be broken up into shorter ones.

Fluffed lines and hesitations inevitably mar otherwise fluent performances and perhaps lead to loss of confidence. The answer is for the reporter to become familiar with the contents of the script by rehearsing as thoroughly as possible (mumbling to yourself in a corner, though a poor substitute, is better than nothing).

When serious mistakes do occur there is no shame in asking for a second 'take', for even the most experienced performers expect to trip over their words from time to time. Where any faults persist there is no harm in seeking the advice of speech therapists, who are able to devise little training routines for the tongue which can only increase the performer's confidence.

Mannerisms
In reporters with easy going, relaxed personalities, tiny mannerisms may become endearing to the viewer. An occasional frown, raising of the eyebrows or head movement to emphasize a point, probably comes across as genuine involvement in the story at hand. For the rest, stiff, awkward movements, facial contortions and continual passing of tongue between dry lips are among the many tell-tale signs of stage-fright. Usually this disappears once confidence comes, although not always. I know of one former reporter who, while completely at ease before the microphone in the radio studio, betrayed his nerves during appearances on television by prefacing almost every sentence with the word 'well', even though he knew it did not appear once in the script he had written.

Nervousness is not shared equally between recorded and live performances. In many ways the studio camera seems to magnify mannerisms which, to the consternation of studio staff, reveal themselves only under the strain of live transmission. Some reporters slouch back in their chairs, others tilt like the Leaning Tower or hunch their bodies so that one shoulder is thrust forward aggressively across the desk. Possibly worst of all is the fear which has the reporter sitting literally on the seat edge. The result is a close resemblance to a jockey on horseback, except that to the viewer the rider here seems poised to leap out of the set and land in the front room. At least twitching hands are usually hidden by the camera angle.

To all those who suffer from it, this stage-fright (no respecter of persons), can become increasingly confidence-sapping. Practice will make the biggest contribution towards overcoming it, especially if backed up by the close scrutiny of recordings of personal performances. The advice of production staff, given and accepted in the right spirit, will also help the novice to isolate and then dispose of the main problems which, if left to develop, might lead to permanent bad habits.

Dress

The medium itself imposes some restrictions on dress; the sensitive mechanism inside electronic colour cameras seems unable to digest certain striped or checked patterns which set off disturbing visual hiccups known as strobing, and some colours (notably shades of blue) create 'holes' through which studio backgrounds appear. Aside from that, some news-type programmes have recognized how dress contributes as much as set design to the identity they wish to create.

Breakfast programmes in particular seem to like the casual look, and some ask anyone who appears, visitors included, to dress accordingly. This fits in with the general requirement for reporters to wear what is in keeping with the programmes they are working for and the stories they are covering. For example, an open-necked bush shirt and denims would be entirely appropriate for reporting a desert war, while a pin-striped business suit and Homburg would not, while a formal studio interview calls for jacket, collar and tie so long as these remain convention. The important thing for any reporter of either sex is to avoid clothes and colours which the majority of viewers would consider eccentric or inappropriate. For women there are enough smart, business-like styles available to preserve femininity without resorting to anything fussy, although almost anything they wear on television seems to be regarded as fair game for criticism and comment from fashion writers and others. As for grooming, it would be unfair to expect the viewing audience to accept uncombed hair or a two-day beard where the reporters' families would not, except in those situations where such appearances are relevant to the story.

Beads, jangling bracelets or long earrings are best avoided, as their movements are inclined to create distraction at the wrong moment, especially if they fall off. Lapel badges, in particular those which just defy identification, are fraught with danger. So is the whole range of 'club' ties. The possibility here is that the viewer might miss all that is being said while concentrating hard to see whether the coloured blob three inches below the knot is of real significance or just a gravy stain.

The reporter's role

While local television stations may expect their reporters to find and collect many of their own stories, then supervise the detailed editing of them, in most centrally run news services the reporter's duties are more limited, with daily on-location assignments carried out on the instruction of programme editors or the semi-independent assignments staffs who control news-gathering activities.

A certain amount of briefing is usually given, even if it is limited to the approximate outline any contribution is expected to follow to enable it to take its place within the rest of the programme. Where an assignment is foreseen as representing only one segment of wider coverage of a single topic, briefing is much more detailed. Good preparation is vital at any time. Given reasonable warning of the nature of an assignment, a diligent reporter will make a virtual fetish of reading up any available background material. On foreign assignments, this may run to dossiers built up from previous visits and include a diversity of facts ranging in importance from currency exchange rates down to the names and localities of reliable laundries.

Travel arrangements vary. To ensure speed off the mark, those news services able to afford it provide individual reporters with office cars, complete with two-way radio telephone links, or at least contribute fuel costs towards the reporter's private transport. For those unwilling or unable to tie up large amounts of capital in fleets of cars, reporters are expected to travel with the camera crews or simply jump in taxis, either paying as they go and recouping the money later, or as part of official arrangements with taxi companies, signing the driver's log at the end of each journey.

Some news services operate a pool transport system to ferry all operational staff to and from assignments, but this has its drawbacks. There are apocryphal tales of news teams stranded miles out of town at headquarters officially unable to move until an office car became available, while some government building went up in flames at the hands of rioters.

Once on location, technical matters are clearly the business of the camera crew, but except on those occasions where the unit is accompanied by a field producer, it is the reporter who has to shoulder the 'managerial' mantle, with overall responsibility for the shape and content of coverage.

In between lies a fascinating, ill-defined area of ground which in non-news location work would be covered by a director. For reasons chiefly of cost and mobility, it is generally accepted that television news does not need to have separate directors, the role being shared by reporter and cameraman on the spot. So it is probably here that the greatest scope exists for disagreement between members of the crew. The ideal working compromise consists of a reporter with journalistic skills and an eye for pictures sketching an outline to be filled in by a sympathetic, experienced camera crew. Detailed discussion about the best way of achieving the desired end product is advisable before a single shot is recorded. But, in the final analysis, it must be the cameraman who decides what is technically possible, depending on numerous factors including the available light and distance from the subject.

Once a general storyline has been agreed, the reporter then has to trust the crew to supply what they say they are supplying. Long arguments about the closeness of a close-up or the speed of a pan from left to right only hinder the completion of an assignment, and no professional news cameraman would tolerate a reporter's demand to look through the camera viewfinder before every shot.

Relationships are therefore important, particularly on some dangerous foreign assignments, where the degree of mutual trust between members of the team could make all the difference, literally, between life and death. Sometimes a reporter and crew will build up personal friendships and respect over a series of difficult, successfully completed assignments. Between others, the chemistry will be all wrong, and no amount of attempted peace-making will put it right. To team a lazy reporter with a go-getting crew or vice-versa and still expect the screen to reflect only successful results is wishful thinking. Far better to ensure that, where possible, incompatible factions are kept well apart.

Even when prospects for co-operation are good, there is no sure recipe for success. The reporter must always remember to be considerate and tactful in the treatment of his professional colleagues, resisting any attempts by misguided outsiders to create separate categories of 'officer' (reporter) and 'other ranks' (crew). The reporter who allows himself to be swept off to the executive dining room while the crew makes do in the factory canteen deserves the inevitable opprobrium.

Equally the camera crew must be patient with a nervous or out-of-sorts reporter. After a long, tiring day with very little to eat or drink, it is often tempting for the cameraman to give the thumbs-up to a reporter's performance he knows deep down to be flawed, just as the timid reporter, suspicious that something may be wrong, is prepared to accept a personal second best rather than risk offending the crew by encroaching on meal times.

Getting the story right must come first. As one experienced cameraman has put it: 'If the reporter fails, we all fail'.

In addition to the constant awareness of deadlines, there also has to be recognition of the need to be economical in the use of tape or film, not so much for the sake of cost as for the reason that the greater the volume of material, the longer the time necessary for viewing and editing.

With the assignment completed and the pictures received at base, the reporter's role becomes blurred, for one of the main planks of the intake-output system is that it is the editorial staff back at the office who assume the final responsibility for shaping material for inclusion in the programme. Although the reporter's guidance may be sought, the theory is that those most closely involved in the creation of items are not necessarily the best placed to make objective judgements about their value. This is apart from the possibility that all manner of developments may have taken place which downgrade the original importance of the assignment. Yet many reporters, as specialists in their subjects, quite understandably resent being told which are the 'best' bits of their interviews. Modern video 'packages' especially are so dependent on the reporter's ability to mesh the various pieces together, no producer or news-writer coming cold to a project would probably be able to understand much of it anyway.

It is at this stage that the strict dichotomy of intake and output must seem an expensive luxury for the smaller, less wealthy news services. For them, the solution lies not in sealing their editorial talent into watertight compartments, but in seeking to create genuine all-rounders.

Each would be an amalgam of news editor, researcher, director, scriptwriter and reporter, well-versed in the skills of overseeing picture editing and writing studio introductions for themselves to read on transmission.

6

Reporting techniques

Although electronic news gathering has almost entirely superseded 16mm film as the main means of originating news material, most of the reporting techniques being used to present items in a fluent way for the television screen are just as applicable as they were 20 or more years ago, when they were first introduced. Then, as now, no reporter was considered to be competent until he or she had achieved at least partial mastery over a small range of basic skills which go beyond any proven journalistic ability.

These techniques, whether for use on videotape of any format, live on location or in the studio, are used to some extent separately or collectively in every contribution a reporter makes to a programme. Each demands its own careful study and development to a point where it can be applied smoothly and instinctively to add the same veneer of professional gloss to the news report that the experienced actor brings to the play.

Pieces to camera

Of all the skills needed for television news reporting, the piece to camera is among the most frequently used. Although it is sometimes fashionable to consider it dated (some experienced reporters consider they have failed if they have to resort to it), the piece to camera, which is essentially a vision story told on location in the field, remains a sure means of giving the news lucidly.

It has three advantages. It immediately establishes the reporter's presence on the spot; it is extremely simple to execute, and it is fast enough to be considered a kind of contingency sample, rather like the dust scooped up by the first men on the moon in case they had to return to earth rather hurriedly.

Chiefly because of its speed and the fact that there may be no other pictures to supplement it, the piece to camera can be designed as a complete report by itself, yet it probably has greater worth as one ingredient within a comprehensive news report, being versatile enough to be slotted in at almost any point, not necessarily at the opening or closing stage.

The term *piece to camera* is self-descriptive, being those words which the reporter speaks aloud while looking directly into the camera lens and, through it, to the viewer. The fact that the majority of them are spoken from straightforward standing positions gives rise to the alternative name of *stand-upper*.

The technique depends on an ability to write spoken language and to remember it word for word when delivering it to the camera. But in some respects what matters more is the choice of location for the operation. For example there seems little to be gained in travelling thousands of miles and then pointing the camera at the reporter standing in front of some anonymous brick wall. Unless the brick wall is germane, or there are legal problems such as exist in filming within court precincts, the aim should always be to show that the reporter is actually where he says he is. To say proudly that our reporter is there is one thing. To prove it to the viewer is something else.

That does not mean going to extraordinary lengths to find a background which is visually exciting but irrelevant to the story. It should be enough to place the reporter in a spot which is appropriate, interesting, but not too distracting. Even if the welcome which greets the news team is not overwhelming, the piece to camera is capable of being completed within a very few minutes, provided that the camera and sound equipment have been tested and are known to be working properly, and the reporter is ready with the words.

Most pieces to camera are recorded as the reporter stands full-face to the lens. But the effect of putting the reporter to one side of the frame rather than in the centre is that any action in the background is not completely blotted out and the figure becomes a part of the picture rather than a superimposition on it.

Sensible variations are to be welcomed as long as they do not seem to be too contrived. On occasions these may be forced upon the reporter by the situation: sitting in aircraft, cars or trains, crouching under fire or walking along a road. So much depends on the styles programmes establish for their reporters to follow.

PIECES TO CAMERA

Fig. 6.1. Putting the reporter in the centre of the frame has the effect of masking some of the picture.

Putting him to one side improves composition, making him seem part of the action not just a superimposition on it.

Fig. 6.2. A way out for those unable to remember their words. The cameraman frames the reporter in medium shot for a first chunk of script of about 45 words.

Cameraman changes to close up for second chunk. Picture editor cuts the two together to produce one continuous take. Unsightly, but effective. Note that the reporter in both shots is framed more centrally than in Fig. 6.1 to avoid exaggerating the jump between edits.

Knowing the words

Much of the apprehension felt by novices about their first pieces to camera is caused by doubts that they will be able to remember their words. Admittedly this can pose a real problem, for it is a knack achieved more easily by some than others.

Newcomers to television news reporting are haunted by the possibility that even a short, apparently simple piece will require several attempts, resulting in a waste of time, temper and a humiliating starring role on the private tape of mistakes that television technicians love to compile for showing at office Christmas parties. They can take comfort from the admission of some experienced reporters that, even under the least difficult circumstances, they are unable to remember more than a few words at a time. Others get them right at the first attempt or never. The majority have occasional off-days but generally survive the ordeal without too much trouble.

Relatively few have memories which allow them to recall prodigious numbers of words without a moment's hesitation.

For everyone else there is no infallible formula, certainly not ad-libbing, which is inclined to come across as uncertainty rather than spontaneity. Perhaps the only answer for the beginner is to keep the length of commentary down to the maximum capable of being remembered without difficulty, and not forcing more. Little is worse than watching someone totter to within the final few sentences of a piece clearly too long to memorize.

While there is no way of avoiding the problem posed by the limits of memory, and assuming no portable electronic prompting device is available, three possible escape routes suggest themselves. Two are relatively ugly to look at and are therefore strictly second-best, but, in a tight corner, are preferable to a halting performance which seems likely to grind to a full stop at any moment.

For *escape no. 1* the reporter needs to ensure that the opening paragraph at least is word-perfect. The rest may then be read from a note-book or clip-board which is clearly in shot so that the viewer is not left wondering how the memory is being refreshed. Subsequent raising of the head from written script towards camera for a sentence or two at a time may add just enough refinement to make the performance tolerable.

Escape no. 2 requires even more than usual co-operation from the camera crew. Here the reporter does not attempt to speak the lines in one continuous take. Instead, the script is learned and recorded in two separate chunks of, say, 15 seconds (45 words). For the sections then to fit neatly together the two shots of the reporter must be framed in a sufficiently different way to avoid an awkward jump cut in the middle (Fig. 6.2). The use of this technique should give the reporter some confidence early on. Later, attempts should be made to train the memory to accept longer and longer pieces so that eventually there is no need for the split.

Escape no. 3 has been devised by the reporters themselves. It involves pre-recording the words on to an audio cassette machine small enough to conceal in a pocket and listening to the replayed tape through a tiny ear-piece while repeating the commentary to camera at the same time. It is an ingenious technique which seems to many to require more effort than that merely needed to learn the words, but practitioners say the recorders give them a confidence they would not otherwise feel, and if it improves their performance for the camera, then it is thoroughly worthwhile.

The method is not without its hazards, though, for there is enough evidence on film and tape to prove that the all-important ear-piece has a habit of popping out into sight at the wrong moment, and the cassette recorders have been known to malfunction and leave the reporter speechless.

Finally, there is no point in any piece to camera script which fails to refer, even obliquely, to what is going on in the rest of the picture behind the reporter. Where the background is general rather than specific, it is essential that script and location, however fragile the real connection between the two, are tied together as firmly as possible, preferably by the opening words.

Studio spots

If the piece to camera is a vision story recorded on location, the studio spot is one description given to a vision story read in the studio by someone other than the programme's main presenter or reader. Usually it is a specialist correspondent or a reporter who is called on to draw together the elements of a news story and tell it to the electronic camera in the studio, sometimes with the aid of tape or other illustration.

For many reporters, these appearances exacerbate the underlying nervousness already discussed, largely because of an awareness that such performances are invariably live ones made in the context of a programme as it is being broadcast, and that the smallest mistakes are therefore incapable of being corrected. That said, there are considerable advantages for those making studio appearances. First, the script can be prepared up to the time of transmission, making it possible to include the latest information about a running news story. Second, the performance is made in reasonable comfort at a desk in the studio. Third, and probably most important, the reporter may not need to rely on memory, for as well as the written script available out of shot, there will be a device displaying the words so that the speaker appears to be looking directly at the viewer while reading.

These devices, used by news presenters in particular, are often referred to by the general term of *prompter*. The *Autocue* system, as widely used in television news studios, comes in two parts: a tiny television camera which scans the script that has been re-typed on to a standard 102mm (4 in) roll or as separate sheets of A4 or foolscap, and a mirror unit which is mounted on the front of the studio camera.

The words are superimposed electronically on the lens photographing the performer, who looks straight ahead and reads at the same time. The scrolling movement of the script is regulated by an operator, who keeps pace as the words are spoken by the reader.

In recent years the use of prompter devices has been seized on and adapted for use by politicians who need to appear as fluent and at ease as are television performers in the studio.

Fig. 6.3. Autocue, one of the electronic prompting devices which allow studio performers to read scripts while looking directly into the camera. The typed words are fed under a camera-like device at a speed controlled by the operator to match that of the speaker. *Computerized* generation of prompter scripts is becoming commonplace. (*BBC Central Stills*)

Some of these machines are free-standing and are positioned slightly below or to one side of the camera. The drawback here is that unless placement is perfect the performer may appear to be looking down or away from the viewer.

Portable prompting machines, some more sophisticated than others, have been developed for use in small studios or in the field. One television news service has invented its own. Here the script is typed by the reader. One copy is kept for reference, the other is fed into a simple projection system which throws the words on to a light cardboard screen set up on a tripod at a suitable point below the camera lens. An extra refinement allows the reporter to set the machine's speed to match his own personal reading pace, something which can easily be assessed after a short trial run. A field version, operated by battery, has also been devised, the intention being to make a prompting device as much as part of the reporter's hand-baggage as a notebook and pencil.

Other developments include computerized systems using the same superimposition principle to create scripts electronically. These units can be supplied independently or can be linked with the newsroom computer systems which also come with their own built-in auto-prompt facilities.

The main benefit of this is that very late changes made on the master script on a terminal in the newsroom are carried out simultaneously on the 'prompter'. Where computer systems are in use, 'hard copy' scripts are also likely to be printed out for readers who do not wish to rely entirely on electronic viewing aids.

All these machines, if used with care, are capable of producing fluently

Fig. 6.4. Sharp, clear lettering gives readers complete mastery over the most detailed scripts. Some news services make do without any kind of prompting device, giving their audiences a constant view of the top of studio performers' heads as they refer to script pages on the desk in front of them. (*BBC Central Stills*)

professionally performances from almost anyone able to read with some expression. It is true that some reporters and programme presenters consider themselves above using any mechanical aids. But for most, the use of a prompter is infinitely preferable to the alternative: the sight of the top of the head during a performance because constant reference has to be made to the script on the desk.

Prompting devices are as capable of being misused as any other tool, and many nervous television performers tend to depend on them as lifelines from which they dare not be parted. The frequent result is a near-hypnotic gaze which seems to bore into the viewer. The really skilful and experienced user of the machine treats it as a valuable friend and ally, yet is sensible enough not to depend on it entirely. Occasional references to the written script, particularly for figures or statistics, reassure the viewer that details are not just being conjured up out of thin air, although by now most members of the public must be aware that no reader could possibly have learnt it all. Prompting devices in general have proved a real boon to news performers, and have helped programme presentation to the extent where it is difficult to know how any modern television news service can afford to be without them.

Interviewing

Probably more indignation is aroused by interviews than almost any other aspect of factual television, even though the objections may arise less frequently over news interviews than over those which come under the loose heading of 'current affairs'.

Complaints tend to fall into three categories. There is, first of all, the matter of intrusion, where instead of respecting the privacy of, say, the newly bereaved, interviewers are seen and heard callously asking questions apparently without a qualm. Any questioning in these circumstances would seem to be extremely difficult to justify in a civilized society, yet a surprising number of people are willing, anxious even, to talk about their tragic experiences, either as a form of mental release, or as a genuine attempt to avoid similar misfortunes occurring to others.

Certainly some reporters are guilty of overstepping the mark by asking penetrating questions of those still too dazed to realize quite what they are saying. But such interviews have long been considered legitimate journalistic practice, and will no doubt remain so. The most that can be asked of television reporters is that they respect the privacy of those who wish it, put their questions with tact and sympathy, and do not demand answers as of right.

The second category of complaint concerns the attitude taken towards the subject being interviewed. There is no doubt that there is a substantial body of opinion which takes exception to any form of questioning that seeks to probe beyond the simple elicitation of facts. This objection is usually framed as a right to know 'How *dare* they ask . . .' this or that, or what qualifies the interviewee to appear to doubt what he is being told (especially when the interviewee is a respected figure)?

Rather more serious are the criticisms levelled against those whose techniques do smack of bullying, the '. . . very skilful (not to say ruthless) questioning by young men highly trained in "loading and leading"'[1]

At its worst, this technique has been termed 'trial by television', and has been most graphically illustrated by programmes, probably not quite so prevalent any more, in which interviewees have been browbeaten into making sometimes damaging personal admissions by relentless questioning bordering on interrogation. A secondary complaint about this kind of television is that the interviewers seem as much concerned with projecting their own egos as in producing serious answers to serious issues.

Perhaps it was only to be expected that the pendulum would swing so far the other way after the bland, deferential questioning general in the early fifties, when interviewers seemed entirely content with any platitudes uttered by public figures, and shrank from querying the answers, however unenlightening they might have been.

The precise moment at which a recognizable change of attitude took place is impossible to identify, although many television professionals consider the interview between Robin Day and President Nasser of Egypt in Cairo for ITN in 1957 to be a watershed. Here was a head of state answering with apparent frankness and sincerity questions which diplomats would probably have hesitated to ask. It was done politely yet firmly, creating a real impact on the viewing audience and, unknown to the participants, setting a pattern for future generations of reporters.

Since then attempts have been made to strike a reasonable balance between a persistent, unshakeable seeking after truth and the asking of legitimate questions in a non-truculent manner, although it is interesting to note that even in some Western democracies hard-edged political interviewing scarcely exists, and it is not unknown for Government ministers to decide not only the questions but who the interviewer will be.

At the same time, many present-day interviewees have become as conversant as the interviewers with the rules of the game. Some are even better at it, because the questions they are being asked are connected with subjects on which they are experts, and a reporter who is unsure of his ground for lack of briefing or any other reason can be made to look very foolish. Really experienced interviewees have the knack of being able to answer any awkward question in a way which suits them, and they can use their knowledge of studio routines and the programmes they are appearing on to make sure there is no time for dangerous supplementaries. It can be an uncomfortable education to watch an experienced journalist being given the run around by a wily interviewee who has been through it all before.

The British coal miners' strike of 1984–5 threw up one of the most difficult-to-pin-down personalities for years. The mineworkers' leader, Arthur Scargill, became a pathfinder for others, laying down the conditions under which he was prepared to give interviews and then, no matter the question, sticking doggedly to his prepared line. It was probably the first time since modern television interviewing techniques began that an interviewee exercised such domination over his questioners.

Others in public life go for coaching at television schools created by enterprising businessmen, often ex-television professionals themselves.

[1]Bishop George Clarkson, letter to *The Times* (April 7, 1975).

Would-be spokespersons of all types pay handsomely for the privilege of submitting themselves to grillings intended to simulate as closely as possible the battleground of the television studio. Others have begun to equip themselves with audio recorders, which they place in prominent positions during interviews of all types for use as an insurance against being quoted out of context.

Some interviewers have raised objections to these methods on the grounds that they are designed only to provide the interviewee with enough skill to evade the difficult questions. But the schools are here to stay, and it seems churlish for the professional to quibble because the odds (which are nearly always stacked heavily against the inexperienced interviewee) should have become slightly more even. And since the whole object of the exercise is supposed to be to give the viewer a wider knowledge of what is going on in the world, anything which helps an interviewee to achieve that end ought to be welcomed.

The able, intelligent, well-briefed interviewer should always be capable of extracting something worthwhile in the course of reasoned argument. Where there is evidence of evasion, the reporter should not hesitate to pursue, although without bullying. That is ill-mannered, unnecessary and always counter-productive, since viewers are much more likely to be sympathetic towards anyone they regard as the underdog. Besides, an evasion or point-blank refusal to answer speaks eloquently enough for itself.

The third main area of controversy surrounds the editing of interviews. Politicians and other public figures who appear frequently are well aware that in countries where editorial freedom exists, not all they have to say is going to find its way on to the screen, however important they consider it to be. Even where live contributions are concerned, they know that there is never likely to be enough time available to go through all the arguments, and are therefore content to try to restrict themselves to making those few main points they consider essential to their platform, in the belief that even minimal exposure to the public is far better than none.

It is usually from the interviewee inexperienced in the ways of television that the loudest cries of 'misrepresentation' are heard, and there can be only sympathy for those whose parenthetical comments are construed as the real substance and are extracted for use from a recorded interview. In all cases, reporters should make it clear that they are under no obligation to use the whole of an interview, or indeed any of it, and give the subject an opportunity to make out a case in a cogent fashion or withdraw altogether.

Neither should any doubts be left about intended usage. An interviewee has the right to be told of the context in which the contribution is being made, and whether contrary opinions are being sought from others on the same subject. For although it would be intolerable for journalists to lose the freedom to edit as they think fit, they should be equally jealous in guarding the rights of their interviewees to fair and honest treatment.

Four main forms of news interview

Interviews probably represent the highest proportion of contributions made by television reporters to news programmes, even though they may be of miniscule duration and the credits given collectively ('We asked the general secretary . . .') rather than individually ('Tom Harrison asked the general secretary . . .').

Of all the different types seen on the screen, possibly the one presently in most frequent use is the *set-piece*, conducted on the interviewee's own territory, in some other appropriate setting, or in the news studio for recorded or live transmission. The important thing about the set-piece is that it presupposes the interviewee's willingness to participate, and that arrangements are usually made far enough in advance for the reporter to do some proper homework, including the preparation of questions.

Such luxuries are not normally afforded reporters assigned to *eye-witness* or *spot interviews*, where the most important journalistic quality in demand is the speedy rooting out of those who are willing and able to talk about their experiences of events which may just have occurred. The questions here are more likely to concern facts rather than opinions.

Much the same can be said of the *doorstepper*, probably the form of questioning most loathed by reporter and subject alike. The reporter waits, perhaps literally on the doorstep of a building (hence the name), in order to snatch a few words, any words, with the main participant in some newsworthy event.

These hit-or-miss affairs are scarcely worthy of the name 'interview', yet they have become familiar sights on many a nation's television screen. In the general melee all too often associated with these matters, the television reporter may get no farther than thrusting the microphone forward to ask such elementary questions as 'What's been happening?' or 'What's next?' in the hope that what may start out as non-committal, even grudging answers, may, with patience, become proper interviews in which some real information is forthcoming. Even the refusal to say anything other than 'No comment' is often considered worthwhile screening if only to show the manner of rebuff.

This method of interviewing is one stage removed from the *vox pop* (vox populi), an entertaining but often inconsequental sounding out of opinion among people, usually ordinary members of the public, stopped in the street. The aim is to achieve a cross-section of views or reactions to a specific topic, with each contribution usually boiled down to one or two pithy comments lasting a few seconds. The technique demands that the same questions be put in the same way each time so that the answers may be edited together without the interviewer popping up in between to spoil the flow.

All interviews may be said to be variations on these four broad themes, including the *news conferences* so beloved of politicians and others. These occasions are meant to avoid the need for separate interviews, and so are usually held somewhere large enough to accommodate all the television, radio and press people who wish to attend. The numbers are likely to run into hundreds, presenting enormous difficulties for the television news reporter, who may not get the opportunity to put a single question.

At other times, paths may be smoothed by the organizers' imposition of an advance order of questioning, and this can be taken to extremes, as those who still remember the superbly stage-managed 'news conferences' conducted by President de Gaulle of France will testify.

Settings for news conferences, as for many other newsworthy happenings, take the choice of location for questioning entirely out of the hands of the reporter and camera crew. Then it is a matter of making do with whatever site is available, relying on good picture composition and sound quality to make the result as satisfactory as possible.

Far more desirable from the reporter's point of view is the selection of a background appropriate to the story being told. It makes far more sense to interview the scientist in the laboratory rather than in front of a plain office wall, to talk to the newspaper editor against a background of bustling newsroom activity, to the shop floor worker on the shop floor, and so on. Relevance should always be the aim where possible.

Here is one word of caution. There is a very fine line between a background of interest and one so absorbing it distracts the viewer from what is being said. Being too clever can also create unexpected problems with editing. I once chose to locate an interview with the managing director of a motor company on the brow of a hill overlooking the firm's test track. It was certainly relevant, the cars making a very pleasant sight as they whizzed across from one side of the picture to the other behind the interviewee's back. Unfortunately, it dawned on us only in the cutting room afterwards that one particularly crucial editing point coincided with the moment when a car was in motion halfway across the screen, and that a straight edit into a later section of the interview had the effect of making it vanish into thin air.

Although the composition of the picture is the responsibility of the cameraman, it is a poor reporter who allows the subject to be so badly framed that trees or other obstacles appear to be growing out of the interviewee's head. On one occasion a serious interview was reduced to near farce when it was discovered, too late, that what was apparently an ideal background of ornamental swords hung horizontally on the wall behind the interviewee had wholly unexpected results when seen on the two-dimensional television screen. A long, heavy blade appeared to protrude from the side of the subject's neck, and what made it all the more fascinating was that he did not seem to notice.

Putting the questions

Most journalists have had considerable experience as interviewers before they come to television, but there is a vast difference between the casual questioning which takes place in the quiet corner of a pub or over the telephone, and the paraphernalia of lighting, camera equipment and technicians.

The newspaper journalist is able to phrase the questions in a conversational, informal manner, interjecting now and again to clarify a point, jotting down answers with pen and notebook. Questions and answers need not be grammatical or follow a logical pattern. The same ground may be gone over again and again. If either participant has a cleft palate, stutter or some other impediment, no matter. The printed page on which the interview appears does not communicate that fact to the reader without the writer deliberately choosing to do so. In television, journalistic judgement and writing ability alone are not enough.

Sir Geoffrey Cox, one time editor of ITN, saw the significant difference between the two forms of interview very early on in the history of British television news:

'The best newspaperman will often take plenty of time stalking around his subject, taking up minor points before he comes to his main question, noting a fact here, or an emphasis there, and then sifting out his material later when he sits down at the typewriter. But the television journalist is forced to get to the point at once, as bluntly and curtly as is practicable. His questions must also be designed to produce compact answers, for although film can be cut, it cannot be compressed.'[2]

Michael Parkinson, an experienced practitioner in both newspaper and television interviewing, put it more forcefully, describing the newspaper interview as 'child's play' compared with that for television.

'A three-hour chat over lunch, a carefully written, honed and edited piece and the journalist has created something beyond the reach of any interviewer on television who tries to do his job without the luxury of being able to shape his material after the event. One is instant journalism, the other retrospective. It is the difference between riding bareback and sitting astride a rocking horse.'[3]

Not every television interviewer would put it as baldly as that, but it is undoubtedly true that the screen interview of any type makes considerably more demands on the person conducting it. The essential requirements include an ability to think quickly to follow up topics outside any originally planned structure of the interview, and a capacity to marshal the thoughts in a way which builds up logical, step-by-step answers. Each interview, however brief, is capable of taking on a recognizable shape. Questions which are sprayed in all directions, as topics are chosen at random, make the live interview difficult to follow and the recorded one doubly hard to edit intelligently. In any case the 'office' would much prefer to select a chunk of two or three questions and answers which follow a logical pattern.

Apart from that there is the waste of time involved in asking questions which have no real relevance to the occasion. The same goes for any attempt to produce a relaxed atmosphere by lobbing one or two innocuous 'warm up' questions at the beginning.

The phrasing of questions also needs to be considered. Too many inexperienced reporters, rather fond of the sound of their own voices early on in their careers, tend to make long, rambling statements barely recognizable as questions at all.

At the other extreme are the brusque, two or three word interjections which, apart from anything else, do not register on the screen long enough if faithfully repeated as cutaways.

Next come to the cliché questions. My favourite remains

'How/what do you feel (about) . . .?'

[2] *The Daily Telegraph* (July 7, 1958).
[3] *The Sunday Times* (December 15, 1974).

a question which almost cries out for a rude answer.

Others which crop up all too often include

'Just what/how serious . . .?'
'What of the future . . .?'

Then there is the tendency to preface virtually every question with some deferential phrase or other which is presumably meant to soften up the interviewee:

'May I ask . . .?'
'Do you mind my asking . . .?'
'What would you say if I asked . . .?'
'Could you tell me . . .?'
'Might I put it like this . . .?'

each of which invites curt rejection. Shooting straight from the hip has its drawbacks, of course. Without proper care, questions which are too direct are quite likely to produce a simple 'yes' or 'no' without further elaboration:

'Is it true you've resigned because of a personal disagreement with the Prime Minister?'
'Is there any chance that you might return to the Government?'
'Have you decided what you're going to do now?'

If the television news interview is to be of any value at all, the questions must be constructed more skilfully, in ways designed to draw out positive replies:

'What do you say about reports that you've resigned because of a personal disagreement with the Prime Minister?'
'How would things have to change before you'd consider returning to the Government?'
'What are you planning to do now?'

As for general demeanour when asking the questions, no interviewer should allow himself to be overawed in the presence of the important or powerful, or overbearing when the subject of the interview is unused to television. As Robin Day once put it in a ten-point code for interviewers he suggested as far back as 1961:

'. . . a television interviewer is not employed as a debater, prosecutor, inquisitor, psychiatrist or third-degree expert, but as a journalist seeking information on behalf of the viewer.'

Sometimes, in seeking that information from an agreeable and fluent interviewee, it is tempting to try out the questions in a 'dry run' without the camera. That is a mistake.

No journalist worth his salt ever compromises himself by submitting questions in advance. Secondly, an interview based on known questions is almost certain to lack any feeling of spontaneity. Thirdly, even the most apparently loquacious people are inclined to 'talk themselves out' during a formal try-out, becoming tongue-tied when the real thing begins. So while a brief discussion about the general scope of an interview is a sensible preliminary, any full-scale rehearsal should be eschewed.

Coping with the answers

It is all very well for the reporter to ask the questions the average member of the public would dearly love the opportunity to put. Actually coping with the answers poses a problem by itself.

The experienced politician is quite capable of turning aside the most difficult question with a disarming smile and a reference to the interviewer by Christian name. The others who are adept at ignoring questions and going on with their prepared answers can be 'chased' with repetitions until they are caught. But the reporter's real troubles begin when he does not listen to the answers. This is by no means as uncommon as it may seem. The pressure on a questioner conducting an interview can be almost as great as on the interviewee, and it is all too easy to concentrate on mentally ticking off a list of prepared questions instead of listening, poised to follow up with an occasional supplementary. If the reporter lets his concentration waver, any number of obvious loose ends may remain untied. Ideally it should be possible to forget the camera and the rest of it, relying on sound journalistic instinct to take over.

Jumping in too soon with a new question before the interviewee has finished speaking produces an ugly overlap of two voices and may also be uneditable. If an interruption is necessary, it is better to wait until the subject pauses for breath. If the question is genuinely misunderstood, the reply halting, gobbledygook or off course in some other way, the reporter is well advised to call out 'cut' to stop the camera, so that the problem can be discussed before restarting the interview. This is far more sensible than stumbling through until the bitter end and hoping there will be enough time left to try all over again.

Set-piece interview, step by step

As an example of the way a typical set-piece interview might be conducted, consider the sequence of actions taken in this fictionalized question and answer session in the third-floor office of a government economics adviser. Assume both participants have been adequately briefed. Time is important as the reporter has an early-evening programme deadline to meet, and the adviser has to leave for another meeting within half an hour.

Step One; setting up.   The office is of medium size, the furniture consisting of a large desk with a swivel chair behind it, one easy chair and a coat stand. The only natural light comes from a single window overlooking a main road and heavy traffic. The ENG team consists of three: senior cameraman, recordist and lighting assistant. Their equipment, having been manhandled from the lift a few yards away, now litters the floor. The recordist unstraps the legs of the tripod which the cameraman sets up opposite but slightly to the left and in front of the interviewee's chair and about 12 feet away. The camera is mounted firmly onto the tripod, the cameraman consulting the built-in spirit level to ensure the picture will be absolutely square in the frame, as well as steady. A straight-backed chair for the reporter is brought in from an outer office and placed about three feet to the left and in front of the camera. The lighting assistant, having found the office power socket outlet, is asked by the cameraman to put up three 800 watt lights. All are extended to their full height so that the lamps can be angled towards the swivel chair without blinding the person who is to sit in it. One becomes the 'key' light behind the reporter's chair, the second is placed to the right of the camera to fill in the shadows, and the third is positioned behind the subject, out of shot, to provide backlight.

This, then, is the classic interview set-up. The camera is in position as the observer of a discussion between two people (Fig. 6.5). But as it will concentrate entirely on the interviewee, compensation has to be made for any impression that no one else is in the room. For this reason as the lens looks over the reporter's shoulder, it frames the subject in three-quarter full face, slightly off-centre, making him look across the empty side of the screen towards the question (Fig. 6.5). Moving the camera more to the left would have the interviewee looking directly into the lens suggesting a party political broadcast or some form of appeal. More to the right would produce a full profile, making him look right out of the picture — television's equivalent of allowing the subject of an end-column newspaper photograph to face out of the page. The height of the camera is set so that the cameraman's view is two or three inches above the subject's line of sight (eyeline). Going below the eyeline and looking up has a distorting effect.

Step Two; final preparations.   The two main characters emerge from an outer office where they have been having a brief talk about the area the interview is intended to cover, although the reporter has been careful not to go into detail about the questions. As they settle into their seats all three lights are switched on. Now, with the recorder cable plugged into its socket on the camera, the recordist asks each participant in the interview for a burst of 'level' to ensure that both voices are heard with equal volume. Traffic noise from the street three floors below is minimal thanks to the window blind, but the sound of the typewriter intrudes through the thin office wall and the recordist asks the secretary next door to stop for a few minutes and also to intercept any telephone calls which would otherwise interrupt. Satisfied, he squats on the camera box a few feet from the camera, making sure not to trip over the connecting cable.

The lighting assistant stands by one of the lights in front of the desk, careful not to throw a shadow or distract the interviewee. The reporter refers again to the questions scribbled on his notepad and switches on the tiny audio cassette recorder he has brought along. The cameraman plugs in the battery to drive the camera motor, gives the focus on the 14:1 zoom lens a final tweak, checks automatic exposure, and takes one last look around the room to ensure that everything is properly in position.

Step Three; interview in progress.   'Quiet please', calls the cameraman. A second or so later he flicks the motor switch into the 'on' position, checking to make sure that inside the U-matic video recorder tape is beginning to roll from the new 20-minute cassette loaded at the end of the previous

SETTING UP THE INTERVIEW

Fig. 6.5. Classic interview position, with the camera looking towards the subject over the interviewer's shoulder.

Camera's eye view of the same shot. The subject is framed in three-quarter full face, looking towards the questioner, not the lens.

Subject should be set slightly to one side, looking across the empty side of the frame.

Too square framing suggests a 'Party Political' or other direct appeal to the audience.

'Profile' shot has the subject looking too far out of the frame.

Camera height should be set to give the cameraman a view two or three inches above the subject's eyeline.

assignment. For the first six or seven seconds he records what is known as an establishing two-shot, taking in the back of the reporter's head, the interviewee and the top of the desk, to show the respective positions of the two people taking part. As long as the interviewee has been warned not to speak at this stage, the two-shot can be dropped in by the picture editor over any of the questions or used as a means of joining chunks of interview neatly. This shot complete, the cameraman now frames the interviewee on his own, calling out 'action', 'running' or simply 'go ahead' as a cue for the reporter to begin asking the questions.

As a typical news interview is rarely longer than six or seven questions, the cameraman goes through his usual sequence of shots, using the zoom lens to give a pleasing visual variation and to aid swift editing later.

He does this without stopping the camera or the interview, but makes sure any movement is made only during the questions, otherwise editing would be made more difficult. He holds the first two questions and answers in a steady medium shot, from the waist up (Fig. 6.6). As the third question is being asked he tightens to a medium close-up, from the chest upwards; during the fifth he focuses nearer, to a close-up of the head and shoulders.

At this point, with the digital time-code display on the camera showing that six and three-quarter minutes of tape have been used, the reporter calls out 'cut'. The cameraman switches off, asking the lighting assistant to turn off the three lights which have made the room rather warm, and inquires whether that is all. 'Yes, thanks', says the reporter. The interviewee is disconnected from the microphone lead, shakes hands all round, excuses himself and departs for his meeting roughly ten minutes earlier than he had expected.

Step Four; cutaway questions.   Now comes the time to complete the cutaways, or reverses. Because the shots during the interview were concentrated on the subject, the reporter now repeats his questions to camera for possible use by the picture editor. It is a way of bridging different portions in a way which looks smooth on the screen, but it is a

INTERVIEW IN PROGRESS

Fig. 6.6. Medium shot (from the waist up)

Medium close-up (from the chest up)

Close-up (head and shoulders)

device which has fallen into disfavour with some news services which prefer to 'jump cut' between sections to show that interviews are edited.

Cutaways are carried out in two ways: the reporter can play back the conversation as recorded on his own audio machine, or if the team is equipped with the appropriate model of video recorder he can ask the recordist to rewind the tape and replay the interview sound and picture through the camera viewfinder.

The aim in either case is to ensure that the questions follow both the phrasing and tone of the original. On this occasion the reporter settles for his audio tape recorder, and jots down the information he needs alongside some of the original notes he made as a guideline before the interview.

The cameraman now has to concentrate on the face of the reporter, which he was unable to do during the course of the interview, and it means moving either the subject or the camera to a new position. The cameraman concludes that in this case it is simpler to ask the reporter to move his chair round and to adjust the lighting accordingly. Now he re-focuses, taking great care to ensure that the reporter's eye-line is correct. If it is not, the edited story would give the impression that interviewer and subject were looking in the same direction instead of at each other. To make sure there is no slip-up the cameraman follows the simple rule he made for himself years earlier: the ear that the camera saw during the interview proper must be the same ear the camera sees in the cutaway questions (Fig. 6.7).

As extra insurance the interviewer is framed throughout in a medium shot, so that wherever the cutaway is inserted the reporter will seem to complement and not dominate the subject. The questions themselves follow the original sequence. Although they are now being asked of no-one, the reporter tries hard to re-create the spontaneity of the interview which took place several minutes earlier, taking the opportunity to tidy up one or two small grammatical errors. After the each of the cutaways he looks down at his pad to refresh his memory, pausing deliberately for two or three seconds before asking the next question. He knows that if he speaks while still looking down at his notes, the picture editor will be unable to use the shot.

To finish, the reporter may do several 'noddies', fairly vigorous nods of the head to simulate reactions as they might have occurred at various

CUTAWAY QUESTIONS

Fig. 6.7. Cameraman's rule: the ear the camera sees during the interview . . .

. . . must be the same one the camera sees in the cut-away, however the interviewer is positioned.

points during the interview. These serve the same purpose as cutaway questions, acting as bridges between edited sections. But reporters generally seem to be unable to carry them out with much conviction, and so the technique has been falling into disuse over the past few years. There is also a feeling among newspeople that in some interviews the inclusion of a 'noddy' might create the impression that the reporter was agreeing with what was being said. As an alternative cameramen sometimes record 'steady listening shots' of an attentive but otherwise immobile reporter and, when time allows, a close-up listening shot of the subject is also added to give the picture editor maximum choice of cutaway material.

Studio interviews

To record or transmit live a typical studio interview between two people, most directors use at least two electronic cameras, each concentrating largely on one participant.

As parts of news programmes rather than as programmes in their own right, live interviews have the merit of being malleable. Those which are not getting anywhere can be savagely shortened. Really good ones can be allowed to continue at the expense of other items dropped during transmission. Then there are some producers who, without much regard to quality, will happily tailor their interviews to fit whatever odd spaces remain in their programmes, and there are still more who have cause to be thankful for the interviews which are able to fill a void created by a sudden breakdown in another technical area.

The satisfaction for those conducting any one of these battles of wit is that the outcome depends on the judgement and ability of the reporter alone, and has to stand without the benefit of editing after the event. The techniques required are generally no different from those used in other types of interview, except that the reporter probably needs to be more mentally alert than ever, and that deeper briefing is needed to ensure that there is no 'drying up'.

The one extra skill that has to be developed is a sense of timing. The interview must not be so hurried there is nothing left to say and still some of the allocated time to spare. Neither must there be such dalliance over the first part that important ground remains to be covered and the interviewee has to be cut off in full flight.

Helping to achieve that fine degree of timing is the floor manager, an important member of the production team, who is positioned out of camera range yet within clear signalling sight of the interviewer.

Various timings are given as the interview proceeds, the most crucial time being the final minute. A circular 'winding up' motion of the hand usually indicates the last 30 seconds, time enough for the interview to be brought to a proper conclusion. The final ten seconds are counted down separately, usually with much exaggeration, by finger signal. Over-running will produce frantic cut-throat signs to show that the proceedings must be brought to a halt immediately. The most experienced interviewers have become really adept at this timing exercise, able to wring the very last ounce of value from their interviews right up to the dying seconds.

A newer hazard is the popular technique which has the interviewer in one studio and the subject in another. These 'down the line' interviews are usually necessary when they cannot be conducted in any other way. The main difficulty this presents for the interviewer is that more often than not he is carrying it out without being able to see the subject, although the interviewee's image may appear on the screen behind him. This is done electronically, and means the interviewer has to turn round to face where the subject *appears* to be. It can be an awkward technique for the inexperienced to master, especially without any rehearsal. There are occasions when extra monitors can be placed on the desk to enable real visual contact to be established, but this calls for the setting up of additional shots on the studio cameras and at some stage during the programme the equipment may have to be removed.

7

Packaging the news

On numerous occasions, a brief interview or a simple piece to camera is all that a reporter is required to contribute to a news programme. That each calls for its own special expertise should not now be in doubt. Yet a far greater test of a reporter's television technique comes when those separate skills have to be fused together in the form of a news *package*, an all-picture report which appears on the screen complete in itself apart from the introduction read by the presenter in the studio.

It is often by his ability to package an item about any subject that a reporter may be judged, for its success calls for more than the performing talents so apparent in the piece to camera, or the stubborn persistence needed in some interviews. It demands conscious organization, the ability to fit different pieces together to produce an effective continuous narrative, and a news-writer-like mastery over words and pictures. And when all that is accomplished, enough information must be communicated to ensure that the report is capable of being assembled quickly and accurately by other people, no matter how far away they are.

Packages do not have to be complicated just become they are invariably of substantial duration. Experienced reporters and camera crews, working closely towards a common goal, are well aware of the dangers of wild over-shooting, while at the same time making sure that they do not skimp their coverage in any way.

Broken down into its separate components, a typical package might appear to the viewer in the following order:
1. A picture sequence accompanied by the reporter's out-of-vision commentary.
2. An interview.
3. More pictures and commentary linking into —
4. A final piece to camera.
The chances are, however, that the sequence in which they were completed was very different.

Some news services like to stamp their own individual styles on package formats, although these preferences may be only as straightforward as insisting that they always begin with the reporter's piece to camera (to establish presence and authority at once), or never ending with an interview, expecting the reporter to complete the report with a visual pay-off.

But these are really minor considerations. From the reporter's point of view, the versatility of the package technique ranks high among its most satisfying aspects, with the separate ingredients capable of being mixed together in any number of ways, according to story demands. The one proviso is that during shooting reporter and camera crew keep the eventual shape of their item firmly in mind, otherwise there is a strong possibility that there will be too much or too little material to cover a particular section. The latter fault may make it impossible for the picture editor to assemble the report without blatant disregard for visual grammar, or else become involved in the difficult, time-consuming, reporter reputation-wrecking operation known disparagingly as a 'salvage job'.

'Picture' packages

For an example of the way a typical picture report might be constructed, take this routine, fictional piece about the increasing economic pressures on small dairy farmers. Assume the item has been commissioned by the programme editor for the lunch-time news to accompany an announcement of a rise in milk prices expected later the same day. Arrangements will have been made well in advance to secure the co-operation of the farm owner.

Although an unrepentant 'townee', the reporter has briefed himself well enough on the subject of farming to be aware of the general ground the assignment is meant to cover. A short talk with the farmer immediately on arrival fills in the other necessary detail. The camera crew, meanwhile, take the opportunity to spy out the land without the encumbrance of their equipment, and the cameraman is already taken with the potential for vivid pictures.

Friendly, helpful and articulate, the farmer has a number of important duties to perform about the place and is anxious to complete his own part in the proceedings as quickly as possible. The first ingredient, therefore, must be the interview which the reporter and cameraman originally envisaged taking place later on, set up against a background of the prize herd being milked. But the farmer's declared intentions have now forced a change of plan so, too early for the milking, they settle for an exterior view of the shed, with half a dozen milk churns clearly visible.

Six questions and answers follow smoothly, rounded off with the obligatory two-shot and cutaway questions, all completed with under four minutes of tape on the digital counter. The reporter and crew, now left to themselves following the farmer's departure, decide after a brief discussion to concentrate on other buildings, activity, people and animals around the farm, working from the perimeter in towards the farmhouse. It is an attractive building and the cameraman takes several shots of the exterior from various angles.

Next they move inside to the kitchen, where they find the lighting assistant has already prepared the way for shots of the farmer's wife making her account books up-to-date. All that takes another two and quarter minutes of tape.

Over a break for coffee, the reporter — now able to imagine how the rest of the item will go — writes and memorizes the script for a piece to camera, a little over 30 seconds summing up the dilemma for farmers of this type. Once outside again, he asks to be framed in a fairly loose medium shot against the background of a haystack to emphasize a point about increased feeding costs. He is virtually at the end of the piece when an unseen tractor starts up noisily, drowning his voice. A second take is necessary. This is completed satisfactorily, and so far less than eight minutes of tape have been used.

The crew are just preparing to pack up and move on to a new location, when milking time suddenly arrives. In fact, the herd can be seen in the distance, already beginning to make their way up from the lower grazing field. The cameraman and the recordist grab the Ikegami camera, tripod and Sony BVU50 recorder and make off at a brisk trot in the direction of the advancing herd, the reporter in pursuit. They are only just in time to get the shots the cameraman has been thinking about. Within a few minutes he has recorded on tape close and medium shots of cows and cowmen on the move. The crew then sprint to a conveniently elevated vantage point to capture the long shot of the procession filing past on the way to the milking shed.

As the crew follow the cows they see the farmer emerge from an outhouse and engage one of the farmhands in animated conversation. On this scene they record another 30 seconds of pictures on tape before the farmer makes off in another direction, and the cameraman stands watching through the camera viewfinder as the figure recedes into the distance.

Inside the shed milking is in progress. The lighting assistant, who has de-rigged from the sequence with the farmer's wife in her kitchen while the crew were outside, has already pre-lit the scene. The crew set up the camera on the tripod close to where the action is taking place. The clatter of the machinery and the lowing of the cows make effective sounds to accompany the pictures. After he has recorded about a minute of pictures, the cameraman is satisfied.

At this point the soundman asks if they can return to the field outside the milking shed so that he can record a minute of 'wild' sound of country ambience to cover the long shot of the cattle coming in, as he now realizes the original track was marred by voices and traffic noise carried by the wind from the main road not far away. Only one more shot, of the farm entrance, remains to be recorded, and that will be done on departure.

The reporter, meanwhile, has found a quiet spot away from all the activity and has begun to replay his own audio cassette recording of the interview with the farmer. After hearing it once all the way through, he decides that the second and third answers are easily the most relevant, summing up the issues most succinctly. Timed on his wrist stop-watch they account for a total of 1 min 25 sec. This is too long, he considers, for a package he was told would be allocated no more than three minutes on the screen. Listening even more carefully to a second replay of the tape, he decides that by coming in later on the first of the chosen answers the interview can be pared down still further without destroying the core of the farmer's argument, although one particularly colourful reference to government policy is lost. It is now down to 50 seconds, which is much better. Going back over the rest of the interview yet again he makes notes about some of the other points raised, adding them to the references made during his original research. These are for possible use in the commentary he must now write to cover the rest of the pictures.

The reporter made sure to accompany the cameraman through the entire process of picture-taking, and now he consults the detailed list he made as they went along. With the full knowledge of the content and duration of each shot, he can visualize how the edited pictures will eventually look on the screen when accompanied by the commentary. Without that essential information it would have been guesswork, and would have shown as such.

The rough outline of the package is beginning to take shape as the reporter starts to weave the commentary around the pictures. Conscious of the need to identify the location as quickly as possible, he opens by setting the scene, trying to imagine the shots of the farm entrance which have yet to be taken:

'As farms go, Topfield is very much in the miniature class, not even one hundred acres.'

Next he wants to sketch in the background as briefly as possible, to convey an idea of the type of work being carried out. There were plenty of good shots of general activity immediately after the farmer's interview, and he rejects the phrase 'pig-rearing' as being too explicit, favouring the all-purpose 'stock-breeding' so that the picture editor will be able to select the most suitable:

'But, thanks to a mixture of stock-breeding and milk production, every one of the past twenty years has produced a profit. Until this year, that is, when despite increased production and higher Common Market subsidies, Topfield — like so many farms of similar size — is facing a loss. It's potentially so crippling that the rise in the basic price of milk may be too late to save . . .'

At this point the commentary begins to approach the central issue of the prize Jerseys and their future. The reporter remembers the series of shots taken by the cameraman as the cows were being moved from the lower grazing field, and he sees the sequence extending naturally to the noisy scenes in the milking shed. Although continuity must be maintained, he deliberately avoids too rigid a construction which would leave the picture editor no scope to put in extra shots without having to make drastic alterations to the sound track:

'. . . the herd of seventy prize Jerseys from being sold off. Since the first of the strain was bought five years ago, the farm's average milk yield has more than doubled. Recent investment in a new, automated milking system seemed certain to increase production still further. Despite modernization, things have gone seriously wrong.'

The next paragraph leads into the interview with the farmer. For this, the reporter expects that the picture editor will want to use the two-shot, taken with the milk churns in full view. The last few words have to pose the question, phrasing it in a way which makes the chosen answer follow naturally:

'Topfield's owner, John Brown, has survived other years of crisis. What's so different about this one?'

Including the 50 seconds allocated to the interview, the reporter estimates that, depending on the way the milking sequence is eventually cut, between 1 min 45 sec and two minutes have so far been accounted for. Although he might actually get away with another 20 seconds or so on top of all that, he prides himself on turning in his items to length, besides which he knows the programme editor on duty today gets extremely annoyed with reporters who go beyond their brief without good reason. So a maximum of 1 min 15 sec is all that is left for the remaining ingredients, including the piece to camera which took 32 seconds. The reporter makes the most of the obvious link between the farmer and the pictures of his wife, and thinks the farmhouse exteriors make a neater transition than by going straight to Mrs Brown from the interview:

'The Browns bought Topfield when they married in the early sixties. At the time it was virtually run down, but Mrs Marjorie Brown, who used to spend weekends here helping out the previous owner, persuaded her husband it had potential.'

If necessary, the reporter reckons, the next line could be omitted to save space, although it would be a pity:

'She comes from a farming family and had her own ideas about how to put matters right financially.'

The final two sentences are important, about the future. Here the reporter is in two minds whether they are better illustrated by shots of the farmhands and general activity, or by the conversation between farmer and helper recorded just before the milking sequence.

He decides to let the office choose:

'Now the Browns are considering that if the herd has to go they might as well sell up completely. If they're hesitating, it's because they're in no doubt about what it would mean for their tiny workforce — redundancy in an area where unemployment is already high.'

The commentary leading on from the interview adds up to 35 seconds. Adding on the piece to camera brings the total length to a maximum of 3 min 7 sec. 'Just right', thinks the reporter. If the office is desperate to save space, six seconds can be trimmed back by taking out the additional reference to the farmer's wife, and a few more by keeping a tight hold on the prize herd sequence. The whole scripting exercise has taken no more than 25 minutes. Seeking out the recordist, who has now returned to the camera car, the reporter finds a place on the farm where no single sound is dominant and reads his commentary, interspersed with cutting instructions for the picture editor into a microphone plugged into the videocassette machine, the signals recorded on to the second of the two audio tracks on the three-quarter inch tape. He stumbles once, over the phrase 'here helping out' and after a deliberate pause substitutes 'working here for' for the offending words when he repeats the whole paragraph.

With the commentary now successfully recorded, the camera crew take their leave of the farmer, the cameraman remembering to stop briefly for his final shots before they drive out of the farm gates. The whole operation has taken a little over three hours for a total of well under 20 minutes of tape — less than a single full cassette.

The team now face the propspect of getting their story back in time for their lunchtime news deadline, in just over an hour's time. As Topfield Farm is located approximately 50 miles from base, there is no prospect of driving the tape back and having it edited in time for the programme.

Fortunately, sensible plans were laid long before they set out. A Facilities Engineer has already been detailed to rendezvous with them at a local Post Office microwave link point midway between Topfield and the nearest town.

Leaving the lighting assistant to go his own way to a new assignment, the reporter and crew set off for the microwave point, a grid reference on their map, ten miles away. When they reach it the 'Facs-man' has already arrived and entered the tiny hut housing the telecommunications equipment which will relay the signals to the next link in the electronic chain and so on back to base.

The duty engineer shows the Facs-man where to connect his equipment to the video and sound lines, and then checks to ensure the signals are being received at the other end. The Facs-man takes the cassette and plays it from his own replay machine to base, where it is recorded by another Sony U-matic in the main videotape area. The picture editor and the writer from the newsroom are also there, watching anxiously and making notes about content and quality as the rushes are played over.

As the news-writer has a question for the reporter about one aspect of the script, the two have a brief discussion about it over the link. The videotape operator has meanwhile made a swift spot-check to ensure that the recording has 'taken' and then hands the cassette to the picture editor, who rushes off towards his editing suite.

Editing the package

One of the features of ENG is that it offers to the expert a variety of editing options. 16mm film packages were invariably assembled by re-recording the reporter's commentary from high-quality quarter-inch audio tape on to a 16mm separate sound track and then cutting the pictures to match it (in contrast to the usual procedure of cutting the film and letting the news-writer fit the commentary round it). It was this technique, known as overlay, which gave modern television news reporting much of its professional gloss, and it remains the principle method of package making, even though present-day picture editors may not construct it in exactly the same way.

Editing a package is a fairly slow process as a rule, but excellent results are possible so long as the reporter in the field has played his part by taking detailed notes of the pictures and preparing the script with them in mind.

The best reporters are always prepared to adjust their commentaries to take account of interesting picture sequences for which they might not originally have made allowance, and they avoid over-scripting sections for which there are scarcely sufficient shots. Otherwise they would leave the picture editor with no alternative but to cut back on the commentary track to make it fit.

The main drawback of an ENG report-by-link is that conversations conducted at a distance are not always as enlightening as they should be. An item which arrived directly back in the office would usually be accompanied by a minimum of paper work; in some cases, particularly with overseas assignments sent home by air, a detailed script and shot list. This time our 'Topfield' picture editor has to waste precious minutes listening to the commentary to get the proper 'feel' of the report, although he does have as an aid the notes he scribbled during the transmission of the rushes.

After another viewing of the pictures and listening to the interview with farmer Brown, the picture editor decides it is less time-consuming to match the pictures to the commentary, rather than vice-versa, so he goes into 'fast forward' mode on the editing machine until he reaches the beginning of the reporter's recorded sound, which includes the spoken guide to the way the edit should be carried out.

'This is the Derek Ward commentary for the Topfield Farm milk prices story for the lunch time news of January the fourteenth. Beginning in five seconds from now.' (Pause . . .)

'As farms go Topfield is very much in the miniature class — not even a hundred acres. But thanks to a mixture of stock-breeding and milk production, every one of the past twenty years has produced a profit. Until this year, that is, when despite increased production and higher Common Market subsidies, Topfield — like so many farms of a similar size — is facing a loss. It's potentially so crippling that the rise in the basic price of milk may be too late to save the herd of seventy prize Jersey cows from being sold off. Since the first of the strain was bought five years ago, the farm's annual average milk production has more than doubled. Recent investment in a new, automated milking system seemed certain to increase yields still further. Despite this modernization, things have gone seriously wrong. Topfield's owner, John Brown, has survived other years of crisis. What's so different about this one?'

'The interview with farmer Brown should come in at this point. I suggest you use the second answer beginning "This time, we've not been able . . ." which lasts about fifty seconds. The out words are "whatever the government says." Commentary continues:'

'The Browns bought Topfield when they married in the early sixties. At the time it was virtually run down, but Mrs Marjorie Brown, who used to spend weekends here . . . um . . . er helping out.'

'(oops! Going again with that paragraph. In five.)' (Pause):

'The Browns bought Topfield when they were married in the early sixties. At the time it was virtually run down, but Mrs Marjorie Brown, who used to spend weekends here working for the previous owner, persuaded her husband it had potential.

She comes from a farming family and had her own ideas how to put matters right financially. Now the Browns are considering that if the herd has to go they might as well sell up completely. If they're hesitating it's because they're in no doubts what that would mean for their small workforce — redundancy, in an area where unemployment is already high.'

'The piece to camera comes in here. Use the second take. It lasts about thirty seconds. There's one other obvious trim if needed. That's in the paragraph after the reference to Mrs Brown working for the previous owner.'

The picture editor starts his assembly by re-recording Derek Ward's scene-setting paragraphs on to one of the two audio tracks on the tape he has loaded into his recorder. Then he searches the rushes on the player until he finds the matching shots of the farm entrance and general activity. He considers the camera team have done well to capture the air of bustle about the place, and wants to make sure that this is reflected in the final assembly. When the picture editor edits those scenes to the reporter's opening words he also records the natural sound effects on to the tape's remaining audio track at a level which ensures that the commentary will still be heard comfortably above the noise. When the reporter pauses in the narrative the editor increases the volume of the background sound.

Thus the completed story will have the commentary recorded at maximum level on one sound track and the 'actuality' on the other, the level of this one falling and rising. When the item is transmitted the two sound tracks will be played simultaneously, reproducing the 'mix' at levels of volume the picture editor has created at his machine.

If he had opted to edit the pictures first and add the commentary later, the picture editor would not have been able to record the actuality sound with these delicate falls and rises because he would not have been able to judge where the gaps in the commentary were going to occur. The onus would have been on the reporter to shot list the item after editing to make sure the words fitted the pictures, pausing where it was necessary to accommodate the actuality sound. A sound mix would still have been required, and this would have been achieved by putting the edited cassette into the playback machine and recording it on to another tape, mixing the tracks at the same time. The disadvantage here would be that the picture and sound quality of the resulting final story would have been degraded by being one more generation away from the original. The alternative, slower, method, would have been to use a 'dubbing studio', asking a 'dubbing mixer' to re-record the sound tracks on to a separate audio tape, adjust the levels as he went along, and match this new version with the edited pictures.

On the occasion of our fictitious Topfield Farm story, the picture editor's task has been made fairly easy because the reporter and camera crew have done a full, competent job — partly because they have had the time to consider what they were going to do before they did it. The amount of tape they used was also economical.

The main problem is that on viewing the rushes, the picture editor and the news-writer are not impressed with the milking scenes which were slightly out of focus, and they would have preferred to leave them out, cutting the reporter's reference to the 'new, automated milking system' and keeping the next sentence: 'Despite this modernization, things have gone seriously wrong,' which would have stood in its own right. But having already recorded the commentary on to his assembly tape and built up the first 40 seconds or so of the pictures, the picture editor is reluctant to start all over again, as any 'surgery' to remove the offending words would otherwise be impossible.

As the item also looks like being over length, they are therefore left with the option of trimming back the interview with farmer Brown or chopping the piece to camera by a few seconds; the picture editor prefers the second alternative because it is simpler, but the news-writer believes that because the reporter has chosen to construct the item in this way, losing the final words would make the report incomplete. As for the interview, that has already been pared to the limit and would scarcely be comprehensible if cut back still more. It is a dilemma the two have faced many times before, and they solve it now by listening again to the piece to camera and deciding that, at a pinch, they can lose the opening sentence of it without affecting the overall sense. That saves ten seconds, bringing the total duration of the item to 3 min 2 sec, which is just about acceptable.

Writing the intro

Getting the story right in the first place and organizing the coverage so that it can reach the screen with the minimum of delay is not the limit of the reporter's responsibilities. Just as much effort is needed to ensure that even before it reaches the transmission stage the package is not made out of date, either by a commentary which makes no allowance for the delay between the gathering of the material and its screening, or by ignoring any possibility that other events might affect its significance. ENG has helped shrink the time gap, but the reporter still has to be aware of the possibility that events outside his control might yet take place.

For that reason, Derek Ward's Topfield Farm script has deliberately made no more than a passing reference to the expected milk price rise, even though this was the basis on which the report was originally commissioned. His phrase '. . . and the rise in the price of milk may be too late . . .' remains relevant no matter what the size of the increase or the date of its implementation. He has also made the sensible assumption that the full details will be included by the news-writer and read by the programme presenter in the introduction to the report:

> 'Milk is going up in price. The rise, two pence a litre, takes effect from midnight. The government says it's necessary because the cost of fertilizer for cattle feed is making it uneconomical for some dairy farmers to carry on producing milk, despite subsidies. Union leaders and consumer protection groups have already criticized the rise as contributing to inflation. The farmers themselves say two pence isn't nearly enough to save some of them from going out of business. Derek Ward has been finding out how one farmer's livelihood would be affected:'

How the 'hard' facts of a news story are normally shared between studio presenter and reporter is a matter for item-by-item assessment, perhaps more than ever now journalist-news-readers have begun writing more of the programmes they present. Without formal apportioning, which is impractical, the prime objective is to ensure that, at almost any cost, the reporter's script — the opening words especially — does something more positive than repeat word for word what the presenter has only just finished saying.

Although the temptation to take in all the details is at times practically overwhelming, the reporter has an inescapable obligation to the newsroom to leave at least some of them for the introduction. The choices open to those at the output end would otherwise rest between the evils of a bland, uninformative introduction (which no programme editor would willingly tolerate) and surgery, the carving out of some of the facts from the report itself for use as part of the introduction.

Fortunately, the need for such drastic action is usually unnecessary. After a sharp lesson or two, most reporters soon learn an acceptable level of self-discipline. Some achieve it by writing a full introduction of perhaps three sentences, each completely self-contained, and beginning the commentary proper with the *third*. The other two sentences are then sent off with the script details or passed on in some other way to provide cue material for the newsreader.

This admirably simple technique is capable of being used by any reporter in any situation. Yet it still manages to create difficulties for those whose imaginations are not as sharp as they might be. Deprived of the two most obvious opening sentences, some reporters are reduced to beginning the third in a form which, instead of helping the viewer pick up the thread formed by the introduction, has become a cliché —

'It/The explosion/accident . . . happened.'

8

Camera crews at work

Of all the people regularly employed in routine television news work, members of camera crews must be included as among the most resourceful and energetic, rarely allowing themselves to be more than temporarily set back by the occasional failure of equipment or by the petty bureaucracies which beset so many news stories.

Crews frequently work on their own without reporters or other editorial supervision of any kind and, as a result, have built up a reputation for roving independence which others envy. Partnerships between cameramen and their recordists often last for years, the rapport between them occasionally developing to a point where their mutual understanding resembles the virtual telepathic state existing in some good marriages. Hardly surprising, say some, since many crews spend more time with each other than with their wives.

As they work in so many different ways according to local custom and requirement, it is impossible to generalize either about the standard camera crew methods of operation or the equipment they use. But a fairly broad idea of both can be gained by examining a typical two-man team working for BBC TV News in London.

Transport

Early experiments with ENG suggested that transport requirements for the coming electronic era might best be met by emulating American methods and using small vans as self-contained mobile units complete with all the microwave equipment necessary to transmit material directly back to base. The idea was discarded in favour of a system where the camera crews maintained their independence from the engineers, who were given a special role providing the communications links as and when needed, rather like the lighting assistants who do not work permanently with camera crews but join them at locations where their services are required.

In this respect, little has changed since the days of 16 mm film. For all except foreign assignments (where it is usually necessary to hire a suitable vehicle on arrival), the crew drive to every location in the saloon car assigned to them. It is probably one of the larger, more powerful variety of mass-produced models, and is devoid of any special identification which might mark it out for unwelcome attention. Apart from extra security locks for all doors, and a radio-telephone link with base, the car is outwardly little different from any normal production-line model.

The only other special requirement for a camera car is that it must have a roomy boot to accommodate all the equipment. This is stowed carefully away in silver-coloured metal boxes robust enough to withstand all the inevitable ill-treatment it will receive. The trunks are packed and repacked by the crew with almost obsessional care to a definite and unchanging pattern so there is minimum delay before they are ready for action.

Camera equipment

Like so much else in television news, camera equipment has had to undergo radical and continuing change to keep pace with the demands of the users. One result is that crews need to carry marginally less than they did in the days of 16 mm film. This was how a typical BBC news crew was equipped in mid-1985:

Ikegami or Sony ENG camera
Canon or Schneider 14:1 zoom lens
Sony BVU50 video recorder (U-matic system)
Medium weight metal tripod
Six 12 volt batteries for camera and recorder
Fast battery charger
Mains power unit
Two connecting cables (camera to recorder)
Waterproof cover for camera
Radio microphone
Stick microphone
Gun microphone and windshield
Two personal microphones
Three-way audio mixer
Three boxes (30) 20-minute videocassettes
Miscellaneous audio and video cables and connectors for use with different sound and vision sources.

Total value: £35,000 approx.

The batteries give enough power to drive the camera through three full cassettes (an hour of material) depending on conditions, before re-charging is necessary. The mains power unit is used when the crew know they will be able to plug it in to a suitable indoor location where they may have to be on duty for long periods.

Microphones

The choice of microphones, usually up to the sound recordist, is dependent on weather conditions and location. For interviews in particular the most favoured type is the *personal microphone*. (See Fig. 8.1). This is small, light and clips to clothing at about chest height. The trailing lead is easily hidden. As it is placed fairly near the mouth, this type of microphone is particularly useful where background noise is high, but it is also sensitive to wind noise or crackles from the movement of nylon clothing.

MICROPHONE TYPES

Fig. 8.1. (a) Neck microphone. Useful for interviews where background noise is obtrusive, but it may sometimes pick up the crackle of nylon clothing or ties.

(b) All-purpose stick mike, easily made ready for action and used by the reporter. It needs to be held firmly in the fist.

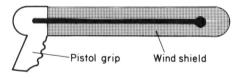

Pistol grip   Wind shield

(c) Gun mike, usually held by the sound recordist. It is versatile but obtrusive, with or without the metal or foam windshield. Could be considered dangerous for the user because of its weapon-like outline.

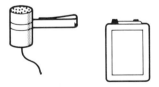

(d) Radio mike. Excellent for the way it frees the user from linking cable. Neck-type mike can be clipped to the clothing and the transmitter slips into a pocket. Effective over several hundred yards.

The *gun* or *directional microphone* is aimed at the speaker by the recordist. It is usually covered in a light metal tube as protection against wind noise. The gun mike picks up sound through a narrow angle over long range, which enhances its versatility. But it is also inclined to restrict the cameraman, as the recordist or the microphone can easily creep into shot by mistake. Its shape is also unfortunate; from some angles it closely resembles a weapon, and in some situations this might draw dangerous attention to the user.

The third and possibly most popular type is the simple *stick microphone*, held by the reporter rather than the recordist. It has no handling noise, can be prepared for use in a very short time, and has the extra benefit of giving the nervous or inexperienced something useful to do with one of his hands when facing the camera. The stick mike should be grasped firmly near the top by the fist, not truncheon-like until the knuckles go white, or so delicately by the finger-tips that it waves about out of control. If used for interviewing it should be 'favoured' gently towards each speaker, preferably at an equal distance from every mouth to help the recordist keep sound levels balanced. It should not be thrust forward so aggressively that the speaker recoils in fear that it is about to be forced up his nose or down his throat. Although the stick mike remains rather ugly to look at, it is probably the best all-round microphone for news use, especially with the addition of a foam shield to keep out wind noise. Nevertheless, like all the other types, it has the built-in disadvantage of allowing the reporter to be only as far away from the camera team as the microphone lead and any extension will allow.

A fourth type in use does get over this inconvenience. This is the *radio microphone*, which comes in two parts: a personal-type microphone clips on to the clothing and a transmitter slips into the reporter's pocket. It is possible to transmit over several hundred yards without the need for the umbilical cord connecting reporter to recorder. Used sparingly, the radio mike is extremely effective, but some types are inclined to be temperamental and need to be treated with care.

Other microphone types are rarely standard equipment, but may be available from a general pool for special assignments. These include those fixed to booms above speakers' heads, and stand mikes, which are well known for producing high quality sound at the expense of obtrusiveness.

Camera crews, being acquisitive by nature, also manage to gather spare parts and various other bits and pieces of equipment over the years in an effort to make their working and personal lives on the road that bit more comfortable. Gum-boots, warm clothing and a small case containing passport, other documents, razor and shirts can usually be found in an odd corner if they are sent unexpectedly on a foreign assignment. Special protective equipment is usually available when their duties take them to likely trouble-spots.

The duties of cameraman and recordist have become more interchangeable with ENG, although it is the cameraman — the senior partner — who places the camera in position, composes the picture and shoots the scene. Sometimes the recordist will take on that responsibility, since it is only in this way that he will gain enough experience to earn promotion to cameraman.

The recordist is mainly responsible for ensuring that sound levels are correct and that the right microphone is chosen for each assignment. His technical expertise has been extended to first line maintenance of highly complex equipment. As number two in a film team, he would also usually double as magazine loader. Today, it is up to him to see that a cassette is always in the recorder ready for use. When necessary he arranges for the despatch of completed tapes.

The recordist is also regarded as the team's main chauffeur and trouble-shooter, the smoother of the ruffled brows of porters, commissionaires or anyone else barring the way towards completion of an assignment. It is sometimes said that a recordist's ability to find the right palm to cross with silver outweighs any shortcomings he might reveal as a technician. However true that might be, it is clearly understood that the best camera team in the world are useless if they are stranded, unable to inveigle themselves and their equipment into the position where they can be of any use to their programme.

Basics of camerawork

As with other television news areas, there are few rigid rules which camera crews must follow. So much depends on the time, place and type of story involved, and on the experience of the team, but there are some basic principles which the most conscientious crews have adopted and apply instinctively under almost all circumstances.

There is no substitute for a sharp, rock-steady picture wherever possible. That means not only having a tripod or strong shoulder/chest harness but *using* it. Sudden jerking or shaking of the picture is entirely compatible with the coverage of riots or in other situations where the camera might have to be hand-held. But such movements are out of place in set-piece interviews conducted at relative leisure. Although fashions have changed with programme concepts, it is still acknowledged that news work should be kept direct and straightforward, without 'arty' camerawork for its own sake. That means keeping unnecesary pans, zooms and other extravagant movements to a minimum, making sure that if they are used the ends of such shots are held long enough for the picture editor to 'get the (electronic) scissors in' if he so desires. 'Hosepiping' (the rapid spraying of the camera in all directions) belongs to the world of the bad amateur home movie maker. But the professional cameraman does try to avoid the boringly static scene which could just as easily be captured by a still camera.

At all times the best cameramen shoot their pictures with the editing suite in mind, trying to imagine how the picture editor will set about assembling the material, especially on those occasions when they know time is short. They avoid single, isolated shots and aim to produce sequences of long, medium and close shots, with plenty of variation in angles. Overdone, though, this can lead to complications. Senior picture editors and news-writers have been known to come almost to blows with camera crews who, they maintain, have swamped them with pictures they have simply been unable to view in the time available, and have therefore omitted key shots they were not aware existed.

Few camera crews doubt the advance that ENG represents. Bill Nicol, an experienced BBC professional who worked his way up from being a sound recordist in the days of 16 mm film and has since won awards for his efforts with the camera, sums up the difference this way:

'For me ENG is a wonderful medium When I look through the viewfinder I can really see what the pictures will look like. Gone are the old worries about exposure and working against the light. Tape is much cheaper and the equipment allows such tremendous flexibility in being able either to record on the spot for later transmission or to connect up to a link system and transmit live pictures straight into bulletins.'

'Topfield' live

That flexibility is perhaps demonstrated by taking the Topfield Farm milk story one stage further on from the lunch-time news to an early-evening bulletin.

Let's suppose the Government department responsible for the milk price rise decides to hold a news conference presided over by the minister one hour before the *Five o'clock Report*. The camera crew and reporter involved in covering the original item are assigned to return to Government buildings to up-date the story. They set up their equipment in the news conference room and, bearing in mind that they will probably be shooting the scene continuously, use the mains adapter to power camera and recorder. But already there is a snag; an aide announces that the minister has been delayed by important other business, so the start of the news conference is postponed. For the *Five o'clock Report* team it means their pictures will be fed back so late the news-writer will have little time in which to select an extract for the programme.

Other technical arrangements are continuing, nevertheless. The assignments desk has supplied a microwave link mounted on top of a van, which parks close to the building where the news conference is due to take place. Contact between van and base is quickly established, the signal bounced off a nearby high building so that it reaches one of the permanent receiving aerials on the other side of town. Now the engineers turn their attention to what should be easier, getting pictures from the nearby news conference when it starts. As the only suitable site they can find is across the road from the Ministry building, a cable is out of the question. So now they bring into use another special piece of equipment, a short-range microwave relay system known as a 'window link'. This takes the pictures and sound from the camera output, combines them into one signal, and transmits it the short distance to a receiver in the van, where it is re-transmitted onwards towards the studio.

The news conference finally gets under way 15 minutes before the *Five o'clock Report* is due to begin. The Topfield Farm story has now become part of what will be quite a substantial sequence, and to round it off with the latest information, the editor has decided he wants a piece to camera from the reporter on the spot. He calculates he will come to it live, 12 minutes and a few seconds into his programme.

By now the news conference is well under way. The minister's main argument has been made. Six miles away the news-writer watching the scenes has managed to select a pithy 40 seconds from almost a quarter of an hour's continuous speech. But, having completed his prepared statement, the minister is now having to fend off questions from other newsmen, and the signs are that he will be doing it for some time yet. At this point, because it would be impossible to conduct their broadcast with the news conference still going on around them, the reporter and crew decide to abandon their original plan, and go for their prepared fall-back scheme.

Quietly they disengage themselves from the news conference and make their way quickly to the van across the road, setting up the camera on the tripod so that the ministry building is clearly visible over the reporter's shoulder. The engineers have prepared cable ends for the crew to plug into, and a monitor showing the output of the studio is wheeled into position within the reporter's eyeline. He will use that to cue himself into the programme, which has already been going for almost ten minutes. Two minutes before they are expected on air, the crew are ready. The reporter has been catching up on the latest from the news conference and has finished preparing his piece. It consists of only five sentences lasting 30 seconds, so he has been able to learn it, but he has the script written out legibly on his clip-board, just in case.

Because of the way the whole sequence has now been arranged, the reporter's finale is immediately preceded by the extract from the ministerial news conference. Everyone is now in position, a friendly policeman from the ministry building keeping back the handful of inquisitive passers-by. The production team in the studio can see the reporter in shot, stick mike in hand, ready to begin. On the monitor screen, the minister's animated face appears. The reporter continues to watch closely until the shot changes and he sees a picture of himself. He pauses, looks into camera, and starts to speak: 'Here at the ministry the news conference is still going on. But the minister's opponents . . .'

9

International assignments

For world television news services with internationally minded audiences, the task of covering important events in far-off places can be daunting, fraught with uncertainty and at times almost crippling in expense. This means that while the less well-off are forced to rely on agency or pooled material picked up at relatively bargain-basement rates, the larger organizations which demand exclusivity and speed to enhance their international reputations have no choice but to join the rat-race, praying that the budget will stand it and casting anxious glances over their shoulders to see how the competition is faring.

As a matter of course, any staff or freelance journalist who contributes regularly to a television news programme from a foreign base is expected to make sure he establishes good local working arrangements and secure lines of communication. Different criteria are applied to what are known as *fire brigade* operations — those occasions when news teams are sent direct from home or the nearest suitable location to cover particular stories for as long as they last.

Television news crews operate abroad under frequently untried conditions which vary according to country and circumstance. Local attitudes range from enthusiasm, with an offer of every facility, through tolerance, to downright hostility leading to restriction of movement, harassment or arrest. 'They say no foreign correspondent's training is complete until he has been arrested, and you get extra marks for being actually imprisoned or expelled . . .'[1]

Even where there is a genuine readiness to co-operate, language and culture barriers, unfamiliarity of terrain and a whole catalogue of major and minor differences provide their own natural obstacles in the path of efficient news-gathering. This does not include making any allowances for the solution to the other, perhaps more important half of the equation — how to get the material on the air at home within scheduled programme times.

[1] *Today and Yesterday*, John Timpson (George Allen & Unwin, 1976).

128

Getting it home

Three options suggest themselves. The first and most obvious is for the crew to collect the material they have gathered and take it home at the end of the assignment. This may appear to be simple and foolproof, but 'hard' news has a notoriously short shelf-life, and the method is practicable only for the news-feature type of material, where the time factor is not of over-riding importance.

The second option, almost equally simple and obvious, is to send home, by air, each separate stage of the assignment as it is completed. Part of every camera crew's routine at any foreign destination is a thorough check of all airline flight times for the quickest and most direct routes home. Consequently, what appears on television screens around the world is unwittingly influenced to a surprising degree by those responsible for the construction of flight timetables. This 'shipping' of news film or tape has become much simpler since airline staff employed in cargo departments began to handle large numbers of those precious 'onion' bags. Arrangements can be made for the entire cost of shipment except local taxes to be met at the receiving end. All it requires at most friendly airports is enough time (sometimes no more than half-an-hour before the flight) in which to conclude the formalities of a customs declaration and to obtain a form of receipt called an *air waybill*. To speed clearance and collection at destination the waybill number is telephoned or telexed to those at home.

Scheduled passenger flights are not the only answer. Freighters and charters play their parts as well, and there are rare occasions when the material is considered important enough for the news services to hire their own aircraft to fly the story out.

An alternative to shipping material is *hand-carrying* it as the personal baggage of a member of the unit, air crew or cabin staff. On occasion it is entrusted to a willing passenger, sometimes referred to as a 'pigeon', who is met personally on arrival and gratefully relieved of his burden. Although this method is used frequently and with success, it has always seemed to me to carry enormous risks. Having spent a large sum of money sending a camera crew and equipment halfway across the world, it would appear to be the height of folly to hand over a valuable piece of merchandise to a total stranger who, at the last moment, may have second thoughts about completing the errand. In these days of international terrorism, two or three hours aboard a crowded jet is rather too long a time to spend worrying — improved security or not — whether the package thrust at you by an anxious-looking young man is as innocuous as he made you believe before he disappeared among the hundreds at the airport.

Even supposing this latest fact of modern life did not exist to deter all but the most accommodating traveller, there are enough stories about missed rendezvous to make the whole business of using a pigeon a fairly chancey one at the best of times.

So to the third option, open neither to the vagaries of the airline flight timetable nor the whim of some fare-paying passenger. It is the fastest, dearest and most nerve-wracking method of all, sending the pictures home direct via land links or communications satellites.

Despite the cost, this is the option being exercised more and more by the big news outfits with sophisticated audiences who have come to expect same-day coverage of major events virtually anywhere in the world.

It was the use of this option which began to change the face of television news in the late sixties and, as many would have it, helped turn American public opinion against the war in Vietnam. Such a powerful phenomenon deserves close examination.

Telling it to the birds

Sitting apparently motionless 22 300 miles above earth, a couple of handfuls of man-made space stations are the agencies through which viewers of television news programmes the world over are able to witness the momentous events of their time — political changes, state occasions, natural disasters, sport, civil unrest, not to forget wars, of which Vietnam has gone down in history as television's very first. It was the drip, drip of nightly newsfilm showing fighting in the jungle and the paddy-fields, which many believe finally sickened the American people into demanding an end to the carnage. Without the communications satellite to speed the coverage on its way between battlefront and living room, it is arguable whether the impact would have been as great, as soon. Vivid, full-colour pictures of this morning's fresh casualties have a gruesome reality that somehow yesterday's do not.

Throwing television pictures across continents is not, however, all that new. Even in its formative days, BBC TV News managed to receive film direct from the United States using a BBC system known as *cablefilm*. This employed conventional transatlantic sound circuits, but it was a slow process, requiring about an hour and a half for every minute of 16 mm film. An extra hazard was that the sound had to be sent separately, making synchronization another technical hurdle to be overcome before the whole could be transmitted.

The impetus for something faster and more reliable came, not surprisingly, from the United States, where there was already a commitment to the exploration of space. The principle was to bounce the picture and sound signals off orbiting satellites from one earth station to another.

The first satellite was launched from Florida in July 1962. This was a tiny piece of electronic wizardry called *Telstar*, a name soon to inspire a popular tune. Every two and a half hours it completed an earth orbit, each one bringing it within range of ground stations built in America, Britain and France. The immediate effect was sensational; the only trouble was that the satellite could be used for only a few minutes each orbit, at those times when it was visible to both sides of the Atlantic.

Within a very short time *Telstar* had proved to be only the forerunner of a world-wide satellite system for public use. This was the International Telecommunications Satellite Organisation, more generally known as *Intelsat*, which was established in August 1964 with a founder membership of 19 countries.

The first satellite launched under the auspices of Intelsat was *Early Bird*, in 1965. Although it was capable of providing only one television channel for use between Europe and North America, this 39 kg satellite has won a permanent place in the vocabulary of television news journalists. To this day, satellites are known as 'birds', and 'birding' has become the accepted term for the entire process of satellite transmission of news.

Early Bird, otherwise known as *Intelsat 1*, was followed over the next five years by bigger and more powerful satellites. *Intelsat II*, placed over the Atlantic and Pacific in 1966–7, extended coverage to two-thirds of the world; the *Intelsat III* series completed the global link by the end of the decade. The seventies brought improvements with the *Intelsat IV* and *IV–a* series, and the early eighties saw the launching of *Intelsat V* and *V–a/b*. By the beginning of 1985, the burden was being shared by a total of 15 satellites, three over the Indian Ocean region, two over the Pacific and ten over the busy Atlantic, although these included several for international and domestic leasing. Each satellite is either fully operational or standing by to cover breakdowns, and appears to be stationary in its appointed position above the equator (Fig. 9.1), not only picking up and re-transmitting the signals, but amplifying them as well. (The idea for a geosynchronous orbit was suggested as far back as 1945 by the science fiction writer Arthur C. Clarke in a now-famous article in the magazine *Wireless World*.)

Work on yet another new generation of satellites intended to last ten years is already under way. This is the *Intelsat VI* series (Fig. 9.2), at $964 million designed to be the most sophisticated yet, with each satellite having a communications capacity equal to 30 000 simultaneous telephone conversations (double that of the *Intelsat V–a/b*) and three television channels. The Hughes Aerospace Company is building five, and there are options for up to another 11. The first was scheduled for launch in 1986,

GEOSYNCHRONOUS ORBIT

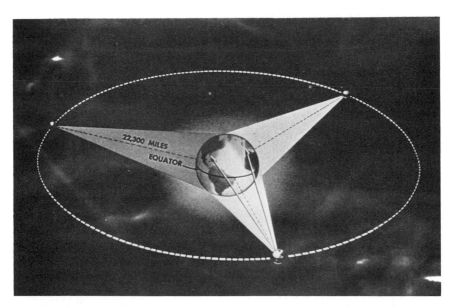

Fig. 9.1. Satellites over Atlantic, Pacific and Indian ocean regions provide global television coverage. (*COMSAT*)

INTELSAT VI

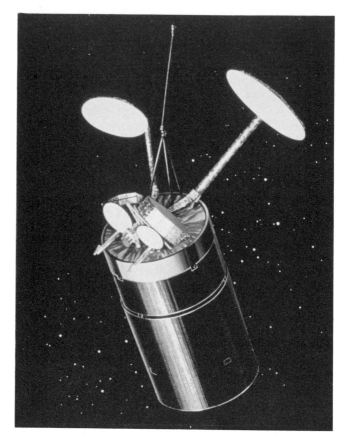

Fig. 9.2. The newest generation of communications satellites for the transmission of telephone, teletypewriter, data and facsimile communications being brought into use from 1989. Each has a capacity of more than 30 000 circuits and three television channels. (*COMSAT*)

but the whole American space programme was thrown into disarray by the disaster which destroyed the shuttle *Challenger*, in January of that year.

Until March 1984, all but two of the *Intelsat* satellites were launched from Florida, on the south coast of the United States, by NASA, the National Aeronautics and Space Administration, which was also responsible for the *Apollo* moon-landing and associated space programmes. The European Space Agency's *Ariane* rocket system carried the others, and is now scheduled to launch the first *Intelsat VI* in 1989. *Ariane* has suffered its own setbacks, and the history of *Intelsat* has included some technical failures, with satellites lost when the launch vehicles went wrong and others not reaching their correct orbits, but nothing on the scale of the *Challenger* tragedy, which killed the entire crew.

Along with satellite development, the construction of earth stations to send and receive the signals has also been continuing at a fast pace. By the end of 1986 there were over 650 of them in the international system, compared with only five at the time of *Early Bird*.

The Intelsat organization itself now has 112 member countries, most of which are represented by their national telecommunications enterprises. Each pays towards operating costs, research and development in proportion to the use it makes of the system. The United States is represented by *Comsat*, the Washington-based Communications Satellite Corporation, and is the biggest investor in Intelsat, with a holding of 24.7 per cent. Other main shareholders as of 1986 were the United Kingdom (13.4 per cent) and France (4.7 per cent). As well as television and telephony, *Intelsat* handles telex traffic, electronic data transfers, the transmission of document copies and tele-conferencing for business meetings. It also provides a 'hotline' between the White House and the Kremlin.

Not surprisingly, the vast sums involved in developing and establishing the system led at first to high tariffs for the users, but the flow of traffic in recent years has been such that costs have actually come down. In 1986, for example, a European service renting the television circuits of an *Intelsat* satellite for the minimum booking time of ten minutes paid the equivalent of approximately £700 from New York or Washington at peak time, plus about £20 for each subsequent minute. A 'cheap rate' (about half price) transmission from America was also available between early morning and lunch time GMT.

These costs, which do not include the use of any facilities provided by local television stations can, however, be shared between any number of organizations. A two-way split is known as a *bilateral*; when three or more organizations agree to share the same material the transmission is known as a *multilateral* feed. Other forms of cost-reducing include the *sequential unilateral* (exclusive use of circuits already established for another organization in the same geographical area). Where unilateral (i.e. exclusive) use is demanded, the hirer bears the whole amount. Since cancellation charges are also high, even the most affluent television organizations tend to look hard at their news judgements before committing themselves to booking unilateral satellite time, even more so when it is necessary to 'double hop', i.e. use two satellites to transmit material across more than one *Intelsat* ocean region.

Despite all this the establishment of circuits between continents for satellite transmission purposes is now a daily occurrence. The administrative and technical procedure can be completed in a very short time, probably well within the hour when necessary, which means that big, late-breaking news stories can usually be accommodated. A new development which makes these links even faster to set up has been the leasing of *Intelsat* capacity on a semi-permanent basis, especially between the United States and Europe.

In 1983, *Visnews*, the London-based television news agency, joined forces with *Western Union* in *BrightStar*, a 24-hour direct video service using dedicated earth stations and microwave links in the United Kingdom and wholly owned earth stations in the USA, to link the transatlantic path with the American domestic satellite system. In February 1985, Comsat signed a seven-year agreement to provide space on an *Intelsat–V* Atlantic region satellite for the live transmission of Cable News Network to Europe. It started on an experimental basis six months later, providing members of the European Broadcasting Union with news 24-hours a day from CNN headquarters in Atlanta, Georgia.

But it is the United States Information Agency which claims to have begun the first permanent global television network by satellite. *Worldnet* was inaugurated in 1983, as a means of getting across US foreign policy through live press conferences between American government officials and journalists in Europe and elsewhere. Two years later, a two-hour transmission service of news, current affairs, science and education features and sport was introduced, coming every day, Monday to Friday, from USIA studios in Washington.

The whole idea of a global satellite system serviced by a single organization now seems to be changing, however. The introduction of DBS (Direct Broadcasting by Satellite), which is intended to bring programme services directly into the home through tiny dish-aerial receivers, promises to bring with it strong competition to Intelsat, particularly over the highly important and lucrative trans-Atlantic region.

Meeting the deadline

Weighty matters such as these are usually far from the mind of the television news reporter who is involved in a brief 'fire-brigade' foreign assignment and is much more concerned with meeting the deadline for his satellite transmission into a news programme thousands of miles and several time zones away. Fine calculations on the spot are required every time to ensure not only that the news material itself is safely gathered in (surprisingly, often the least difficult part of the exercise), but that the pictures are returned from location in sufficient time to complete all the other processes before that ten-minute 'window' opens and closes for good.

Where really big running stories are concerned, the world's most important television news services fly their ENG editing equipment to the nearest possible location and set it up in a hotel or similar centre. It means they are able to be independent of the local broadcasting organizations, which might wish to be helpful but find themselves overwhelmed by foreign demands for facilities they themselves are scarcely able to use. In some places where a big news story breaks, hotels come to resemble broadcasting centres, with rooms converted into miniature studios, cables run under floors, and satellite dishes placed on roofs so that edited tapes can be fed direct. All this costs a great deal of money because, although ENG editing equipment is portable, it is not as portable as all that, and excess baggage charges have the effect of limiting foreign forays for all but the richest organizations.

Nevertheless, once the commitment is made and the bits and pieces have arrived, an experienced picture editor is able to turn almost any small room into a basic edit suite in less than an hour. Certain compromises are sometimes necessary; since the surrounding ambient noise might be loud or unpredictable, the reporter might use a lip microphone (similar to those used by sports commentators) for recording commentaries direct on to the sound track. For the same reason, the picture editor might choose to use headphones instead of loudspeakers, though careful rearrangement of curtains and furniture in a hotel room can go a long way towards creating a passable imitation of studio conditions.

These circumstances invariably help to generate a feeling of cameraderie and closer co-operation between cameraman, recordist, reporter and picture editor than is usually possible at home because they are all working on the same story for a considerable time. The picture editor may be able to see the material being gathered and suggest how it might be shot to help him at the editing stage later, a definite advance over most other stories, to which he comes cold. The cameraman and recordist may be able to spend some time watching the edit and explaining how a particular shot or sequence was constructed; and the reporter may be able to work at the same time as the picture editor, recording his commentary as he goes along during the assembly stage, changing it perhaps minutely to extract the best possible combination of pictures and sound.

When the moment comes to transmit that precious edited package, the team will do so either by feeding it back to base by way of their own satellite dish or, more likely for most, by taking it off to the local television station for feeding. All that, of course, is on the assumption that the necessary arrangements have been made in advance. There is no point in booking satellite time for a five-minute unilateral unless some sort of prior arrangement has been made with those expected to provide the necessary facilities. There is no point in turning up in great haste at a heavily guarded television station without some form of acceptable documentation or at least the correct name of the present local co-ordinator. Trying to explain to a soldier with an itchy trigger finger on a sub-machine gun that it has all been arranged 'by the office', and would he please stand aside to let you, your two colleagues, a large hire-car and a pile of electronic equipment inside at once, is not the most enviable task to be faced with in a strange country. The arrangements may indeed have been made by 'the office', but the office is a good 3000 miles away, and what may have seemed like a firm promise made to them at a high level over the telex yesterday turns out to be a commitment to provide every facility *tomorrow*. Today is a national holiday, and only a skeleton staff is on duty.

Most important there is no point at all in arriving with edited stories or a mountain of cassettes of the most exciting news pictures recorded on a technically incompatible standard which cannot be transmitted or converted. So if disappointment or outright failure is to be avoided, it is essential for someone to do all the necessary homework before the team ever sets out. It might result in a decision to set up a separate facility known as a *Feedpack* — a mobile standards converter through which it is possible to transmit material back to base. But that means another body, another hotel room and more excess baggage to add to the bill.

A better way out, where possible, might be to work on the local standard, be it PAL, SECAM or NTSC, and at the same time take advantage of a phenomenon of the electronic world circus — the degree of co-operation between television news services which are ostensibly rivals. Informal contacts between people on the spot often lead to an interchange of material for mutual benefit. No tv crew can expect to be in more than one place at a time. Suppose several are waiting outside some building for the same VIP to arrive; it makes sense for, say, NBC of New York to watch one entrance, the BBC of London another and NOS of Amsterdam a third so they can *all* succeed. BBC cameraman Bill Nicol talks enthusiastically about this close international co-operation and his part in it:

'To be on location in Beirut as I have when great historical events are taking place, and to take a key shot which can be replayed as soon as you return to the local edit suite, and then to have other networks use that shot all over the world within hours can be a very satisfying experience. 'Gone are the days when we worked in isolation with only a film crew and reporter and if we were lucky a picture editor if there was processing available locally. Now we are part of the travelling circus which moves in a great baggage train from one major event to another like great medieval camp followers. No longer do we shoot exclusively for ourselves on the bigger stories. Coverage is carefully co-ordinated with our satellite partners so that a wide range of events and locations can be covered in short time by a minimum number of crews.'

But he does seem to have a wistful hankering after the old times:

'Gone are the days when one could start early in the morning, do the story by lunch-time, put the film on the afternoon plane and then have a few hours to yourself. Now one still starts early and tries to complete the story in the morning so that the on-site picture editor will have plenty of time to assemble his package for satellite transmission into the first programme at home. Then it's back on the streets or up into the mountains to find the pictures to update the package for the *next* programme.'

The 'Fixer'

An increasingly important figure in that international baggage train is a somewhat indeterminate figure known as a Fixer. Crude though this title may be, it does accurately convey the essence of the task, as a member of the visiting news team to tie up the many loose ends at the scene of a major event, so that transmission into bulletins at home can proceed with the minimum of delay. The fixer's duties are predicated on the fact that the reporter and his camera crew covering any news story are capable of being in only one place at a time, either in the thick of the action on location or back at the local television station or hotel editing suite, taking up valuable time to negotiate such tiny but crucial matters as the allocation of space to keep the equipment safely and the arrangements to supply food and other necessities. Because the fixer is there, the rest of the team can throw themselves into their assignment, secure in the knowledge that at their temporary headquarters, one of their own is protecting their interests, keeping an eye on what the competition is doing, watching for any unexpected developments which might affect the story or their own circumstances, and soothing the anxieties of programme editors and others back home by providing frequent progress reports by telephone or telex.

The fixer therefore needs to be trusted for his judgement, and known to be the possessor of a sound enough technical knowledge to be able to cut corners in a crisis. The work is sometimes extremely boring — sitting about for hours in a foreign television station far from where important things are happening; frequently testing — trying to persuade a disinterested local technician to attend to your needs before those of your national rivals'; but almost always worthwhile. Assignments, usually given on a temporary, story-by-story basis, are much sought after, particularly when they involve foreign travel, and the glamour scarcely seems to pall even though the most important task of one whole mission might be no more creative than jumping into a taxi to find a spare part for a camera that neither the normally resourceful crew nor the local tv station is able to produce.

In some of the earlier, pioneering times of foreign television news reporting, those news services which were unable to delegate 'fixing' tasks to field producers as part of their normal duties, decided to entrust the role to editorial people, sometimes fairly senior ones from the newsroom. But the trend soon moved away from them to picture editors, who invariably had the time to combine their own exclusive role with the special requirements needed for fixing. It also saved money because it was considered that as long as an experienced picture editor was part of a team which included a reporter, there was no need for the additional editorial presence. And as the idea has developed, picture editors have become familiar figures at the scene of world news events, not merely because they seem to be seated all day at their editing machines, but also because they are taking their part in the decision-making which never seems to end for crews on location.

Those who have travelled the world as picture editor/fixers will readily recognize the occasions when editing equipment has broken down and they have either had to repair it themselves or summon expert help (who turns out to be able to speak only an obscure dialect of an already difficult local language); when in the absence of everyone else a snap decision has had to be made about the cancellation of satellite booking time, or the agreement to cover events which go beyond the original brief; when outside attempts to influence the editing politically have had to be resisted; and when it has been necessary to break the legal speed limit in an unfamiliar make of car on the 'wrong' side of the road, in order to get to the feed point in time. Add to that the fatigue which comes with never really being off duty away from base, and it is easy to see that despite all the superficial attractions, fixing abroad is a task requiring real stamina and dedication.

Even on those occasions when all does go according to plan, reporter and fixer find the time towards transmission appearing to melt away at a disconcerting rate. Distances between different departments seem to grow, each stage in the process proceeding at little more than a crawl, accompanied by lengthy and seemingly irrelevant discussions in that language no one else can understand, until the realization comes that now only a few minutes remain and the last edits have yet to be made. For the reporter and crew, on whom the news team at home are depending so much, the tension becomes almost unbearable. Will that effort be wasted, after all, in the dreadful anti-climax of a missed deadline? Fortunately, persistence and a refusal to panic have a tendency to pay off.

Working through Eurovision

A remarkable spirit of professional co-operation exists between television news-people in many countries, not for purely altruistic reasons alone, but for sound, practical ones. The hosts today may find themselves the guests tomorrow, the day after, or the day after that, in maybe identical circumstances.

In Europe, the provision of facilities by members of the European Broadcasting Union is only half the story. The rest is made up by the *Eurovision News Exchange*, the model on which many other similar organizations have been established elsewhere.

The Eurovision News Exchange has been called a clearing house for television news, an electronic market place through which this much sought-after commodity can pass unhindered across the national frontiers of member countries, which include some in the Middle East and North Africa.

Three times a day, news items of European interest are fed into the network of land lines and microwave links for use by the news services, any of whom, in theory, are thus able to receive a complete portfolio of foreign coverage without the expense of originating any of their own. Costs, mainly for the vision circuits, are shared between participating services according to the number of items available to each (there are rules to prevent material contributed by one organization being used by their competitors in the same country) and are based on a concept which allows programme representatives to view and record all the items offered each day before deciding which to use.

The original and still valid idea behind the creation of the Eurovision News Exchange was the common interest which exists between television news audiences of different nationalities. For the journalists there were several attractions. First, there was no reason why those already committed to covering an event for their domestic programmes would be unwilling to make the same material available to others, as long as it did not jeopardize their own operations. Second, there was an accepted principle of reciprocity. Third, coverage by people on the spot was bound to be available relatively quickly. Fourth, the need to send staff crews abroad to cover 'borderline stories' would become unnecessary.

It was mainly at the instigation of Dutch Television, often short of its only foreign film because the London or New York flights they relied on were delayed, that after successful trials in the late fifties the Eurovision News Exchange was born in May 1961. Transmission was every afternoon at five o'clock, Central European Time. Six years later, the first daily exchange took on the title of *EVN–1* when it was augmented by a second, *EVN–2*, transmitted at 6.55. A third exchange, *EVN–0*, with transmission at mid-day, was added in March, 1974, to serve the increasing number of lunch-time programmes. A regular daily satellite feed from North America is recorded in Brussels every day an hour and a half before EVN–0, and extra unexpected items of importance are sometimes offered outside the regular transmissions as 'flashes' or extracts from other news programmes as they are being transmitted.

Depending on the events of the day, EVN–1 is invariably the longest, coinciding as it does with most of the early-evening news bulletins in Europe, and EVN–2 is the shortest.

The items to be exchanged are sent in turn from the originating country, each routed through a technical centre in Brussels. There is a separate administrative set-up in Geneva, and an office in New York, opened in 1970 to co-ordinate satellite transmissions between North America and Europe.

The content of each daily exchange is decided by a *News Co-ordinator* alone or at editorial conferences conducted in the official languages of English and French over the network sound link. Co-ordinators are senior journalists drawn in rotation from member countries, for duty spells of ten 12 hour days, the operation being conducted from a conference circuit in their own office. At times of crisis, EVN co-ordinators are sent to select and edit material on the spot on behalf of member countries.

EVN also has an important working relationship with the international television news agencies, WTN and Visnews, which, together with CBS, have been contributing material since the early days, and there are links with the news exchanges established by Asian and Latin-American countries. Regular contacts between *Eurovision* and *Intervision*, a body within the Prague-based International Radio and Television Organization (OIRT) were begun in January 1960.

The Intervision News Exchange was set up in May 1964, consisting at first of a weekly transmission on Friday afternoons. The main daily exchange, *IVN–1*, now takes place daily between 2.15 and 3.00 p.m., GMT, preceded by a half-hour programme conference during which details of each item are passed on. There is also an *IVN–2* at 5.15 for late items, *IVN–0* at one o'clock every Wednesday for special news items, and *IVN–Sport* on Mondays.

The ten member countries include Bulgaria, Czechoslovakia, Cuba, East Germany, Poland and the Soviet Union. Finland belongs to both IVN and EVN, with Japan, Algeria, Afghanistan and Vietnam among other participants.

The phenomenal growth of the exchange, from about 500 items in 1964 to more than 5000 by 1981, has led to the use of *Intersputnik* satellites for the distribution of material.

10

Constructing a news programme

Fashions change in television news just as much as they do in any other walk of life. The BBC's idea in July 1954, when it decided to replace a highly popular, cinema-style nightly newsreel, was that of a disembodied voice reading solemnly over a series of agency photographs and simple maps, followed at a respectable distance by a succession of film clips strung together.

Although the exercise was greeted with minimal enthusiasm by the critics, viewers in those innocent days were a good deal less demanding. To them, every programme was still practically an adventure, and the fact that some more-or-less up-to-date film appeared on the news was often regarded as being of greater significance than its actual relevance to the day's events. Neither had television in that state begun to offer much competition to the newspapers as the principal medium of information. The audience of the eighties is far more discerning, with the same high standards of presentation and production demanded of the news as of any programme which might have taken months rather than hours to prepare. So because television news cannot appear to be lagging behind in professional gloss or technical excellence, the journalists have been drawn (perhaps a little reluctantly at first) by the need to produce not only news *on* television but news *for* television.

The list of unrelated events has gone, to be replaced by *programmes*, thoughtfully constructed and prettily packaged. Designers are brought in to sweat over the shape, size and colour of studio sets, famous contemporary composers are commissioned to write a few bars of stirring title music. When the time comes to give the programme a new look (usually when a new man takes over at the top), the whole thing is revamped. Old faces disappear from the front of the screen, new ones take over amid much publicity and speculation about their salaries. However much the old hands may deplore it, the public has come to expect an element of 'show biz' about the nightly news, even if it is merely confined to the window dressing at the end, when the presenters visibly relax, allow fleeting smiles to cross their previously grave faces, finger their scripts and exchange pleasantries behind the closing music. (One of the questions most frequently asked of presenters is what they say to their screen partners during the final few seconds they are on the air together.)

The importance of these trimmings should not be underestimated. Just as a newspaper properly seeks to attract its readers with the layout of its pages and its typographical styles as much as with the quality of its content, so the television news programme has to find a way of capturing audience interest and holding it right through to the end 25 or 30 minutes later. Now, even more than before, audiences are being asked to grasp abstract and complex issues that have a direct bearing on their lives. They have no chance of comprehending even a percentage of them unless the subjects are presented clearly and unambiguously. There is, however, one over-riding factor: duration. Television news comes in all shapes and sizes ranging from all-vision summaries lasting a minute or two to marathon feasts of an hour or more; and, like it or not, duration is the fundamental influence on style. The shorter the programme the shorter the items within it, the less room for frills, with only the bare bones of the day's news capable of being squeezed in. The longer the programme the greater the opportunity to spend more time on explaining the issues, to cast the net more widely and to employ the full panoply of television techniques.

But how long is a long programme? Some have said that even the half-hour news, so much the pattern in many parts of the world since it was pioneered in the United States in 1963, is insufficient to communicate anything except the essentials. The argument in Britain in the mid seventies was over what was called a 'bias against understanding', a phrase which summed up the view that although most events formed part of a continuing process and could not be dealt with in isolation, television news,

> 'devoting two minutes on successive nights to the latest unemployment figures, or the state of the stock market, with no time to put the story in context, gives the viewer no sense of how many of these problems relate to each other. It is more likely to leave him confused and uneasy'.[1]

Coincidentally or not, the emphasis does seem to have changed in the past ten years. In-depth reporting, analysis, background — call it what you will — has begun to find its way on to the screen in a form which in the past would more normally have been reserved for the longer, current-affairs type programmes. Nowadays it is not unusual for news reporters to devote several days to the assembly of a single item intended to help explain or interpret news as well as simply report the facts of it. The old idea of the 'bulletin of record' with every item of importance given an airing, however brief, has gone for good. Instead, editors are encouraged to be more selective, to recognize that because their time is so precious, it is better to tell fewer stories, in greater detail.

In that mission, some have also been given more space. In 1982, *Channel Four News* became Britain's first regular hour-long television news programme, making serious attempts to pioneer a new style. (After an uncertain start it was cut back to 50 minutes and has been thriving ever since.) Other news programmes are given the flexibility to over-run their 'normal' durations and, rarely, to interrupt schedules when very important events demand it.

---

[1] John Birt, Head of Current Affairs, London Weekend Television, in *The Times* (February 28, 1975).

All this assumes everybody actually wants more news on television, let alone channels carrying *only* news. There are members of the public who would say there is already too much. Inside, occasional rumours circulate that certain news programmes are to be reduced in duration/moved/axed because they are too expensive or are placed so awkwardly in the schedules that the really popular, audience-pulling shows are losing out. The journalists don't believe it. But while every serious-minded news practitioner is always eager to put forward sound reasons for more and longer programmes, together with enough extra money and resources to support them, the honest ones are equally prepared to admit that, in the crowded world of *conventional* television programming, news is only one tenant. Drama, entertainment, education and the rest have to live in it too, and it would be entirely wrong of journalists to lose sight of the fact that, however much it hurts, they have to fit in with the schedules and not the other way round.

The consolation lies in the knowledge that television news does not operate in a vacuum. If the journalist genuinely believes in the importance of communicating current events to the widest possible audience he will rejoice that others are sharing the burden. Although it may well have been proved beyond doubt that more people obtain their information from television than from any other source, it is equally true that television is not and cannot be the sole provider. Radio, newspapers and magazines all have their own special contributions to make towards the sum total of knowledge, and it would be foolish as well as arrogant for television newspeople to suggest otherwise.

The onus on all those engaged in news programme-making is therefore to make certain that they use every second of their available air time to present the news attractively as well as intelligently. And that demands, more than anything else, recognition that the interests of the audience should be considered paramount. That may be stating the obvious, but perhaps it is a principle which needs to be restated, for in the technological revolution which has all but overwhelmed the journalists during the past few years, the basics are in danger of being overlooked.

Putting it at the simplest, it is all too easy for the professionals to assume that because *they* understand what they are transmitting, the viewing public will do the same, taking it for granted that everybody has equal ability to concentrate on the news for as long as it lasts and that it is always viewed under ideal conditions. Even if this were the case (and it is possible to think of a hundred reasons why it usually is not), it is inevitable that levels of comprehension differ from person to person. Experiments to test the ability of viewers to recall in detail programmes witnessed only a short time earlier indicate that concentration spans fluctuate and attention wanders during the course of a single bulletin.

A survey carried out in Finland in 1981, at a time when important policy reforms were taking place in Finnish broadcasting policy, suggested that one part of the audience seemed unable to realize their own inability to comprehend the news. The lack of understanding by others was put down to the fact that they might be taking television news as a ritual.

'These ritualistic news viewers do not want any information and the only essence of the whole ritual is that nothing has happened that concerns the viewer personally. The active part of the news audience wants the news as a source of new information and so there are several conflicting interests.'[2]

So it seems inevitable that if, for whatever reason, some viewers do not take in what is being aimed at them, a proportion of those expensively gathered satellite pictures or the golden words of highly paid presenters is going to be wasted. The best the practitioners of news can hope to do if they are to succeed is to reduce the comprehension 'fall-out' by keeping their programmes and the items within them direct and uncomplicated. Stories which are well-chosen in the first place, then carefully written and edited to present the most important facts with clarity and simplicity, are perfectly capable of conveying the message, even in a short time. Not so the irrelevancies and repetitions which masquerade under the name of depth but add only length. Swiftly moving picture sequences, miniscule sound extracts woven in and out of complicated packages, jazzy, all-action headlines and beautifully crafted graphics packed with information are all very well in their way. However much they may impress the boss or television journalistic colleagues, if there is any likelihood that they will be lost on the viewer, what's the point?

No one pretends it is easy. The frenetic excitement generated by a busy news day can militate against cool judgement, and the temptation to use all the marvellous new electronic toys now at the disposal of television journalism is sometimes irresistible.

When satellited ENG rushes are flooding in, that most precious commodity, thinking time, can be in short supply or non-existent. The 40 minutes or so it took for film to pass through the processing lab used to give programme editors a breathing space in which to make a considered assessment of whether they would actually want to transmit the stuff when it was ready. Nowadays the instant wonder of ENG can dazzle an editor for choice, and it takes a strong mind and a refined news judgement to decide to reject late material which others have put in considerable effort to supply.

Putting it together

In the past, television news was so short, editors preferred not to waste even a few seconds in reciting the contents. These followed soon enough anyway, items crowding one upon another, unannounced, at breakneck speed, more or less in order of importance. If bulletins looked like over-running, cuts could be made from the bottom up without seeming to disturb such overall shape as there was.

Since air-time has become more generous, this philosophy has been made to seem out-of-date. In its place has been evolved the concept of television news as a programme, dependent for its success on the ability of those in charge to take a series of disparate events and fashion them into something which takes on a recognizable outline of its own.

[2]*OIRT Review*, Vol. XXXV (3/1985).

The criticism is made that in reaching out for that goal, editors sometimes allow themselves to be over-influenced by the availability of pictures. Such a generalization is impossible to prove one way or the other. Yet, if it is true, there seems little shame in admitting it. By what other criterion should a medium which deals in pictures base its judgements? Given a reasonable alternative, no editor would choose to open a peak-time television news programme with an indigestible wad of vision stories and studio reports, leaving the first pictures until ten minutes have passed. It has never meant ignoring the important non-visual story in favour of the trivial pictorial one. What it does mean is encouraging editors to apply to television news the values of television, as opposed to those of newspapers. Ninety-nine times out of a hundred they will be the same. When they are not, editors should beg to differ and go all out to exploit the advantage they have over the printed word.

In many ways the argument is not so much about what constitutes a 'good story' as about emphasis. On a front page of a newspaper, clever lay-out is used to direct the reader's eye quickly to the most important item, or to any one of a number given equal prominence. In television news, the implication is that importance is synonymous with the order in which events are transmitted.

In reality, whether or not they always succeed, some television news editors would prefer to concentrate on making programmes which viewers find easy to follow. Instead of being sprinkled haphazardly throughout the news like confetti, stories are sorted into small groups. An item about domestic industrial output, for example, might lead logically to one about exports, which puts the audience into a receptive frame of mind for a report from abroad. Brick-by-brick the programme edifice is built up in this way: little sequences of events linked together by association of subject, geography or both.

Individual durations and treatments have to be considered in parallel, so that successive items will not look the same. This may lead to some stories being detached from one group to join another, or made to stand in isolation. There is no virtue in constructing a tortuous link for its own sake, or in 'promoting' a story far beyond its importance just because it seems to fit. Without making a fetish of it, the target is to produce a programme which looks as though some thought and care has been given to its construction.

An essential part of the formula has been added with an innovation known as the *menu* or *headline sequence*. This summarizes each outstanding item in the programme, often in no more than a single sentence, so that impatient viewers are not forced to wait until events unfold before them. Over the years, the headlines have developed from being straightforward reads on or off camera into proper sequences in their own right, with combinations of stills, graphics and videotape extracts to whet the appetite.

As well as imparting urgency at the top of the programme, the headline technique has added a previously unknown degree of flexibility. Once the bald details have been given, there is no rule to say that the full reports themselves must follow each other in a block or, indeed, in the same order. Instead, editors have begun to enjoy a freedom to distribute their 'goodies' at points which help news programmes achieve pace, variety and balance.

At the same time, other options have presented themselves for editors and producers eager for some format that will enable their programmes to stand out. Ideas are tried and discarded, varied and tried again. New questions arise: whether there should be one presenter per programme or two or more, and in what combination of male-female; whether studio introductions to moving pictures should be read by one person, off-camera commentaries by another; what kind and colour of background should be used — a plain, pastel studio wall, some illustration to suit each story, or just a static programme symbol; whether correspondents or reporters appearing in the studio should be given the same backgrounds as the main presenters; whether opening and closing title sequences should be accompanied by music or sound effects; whether there should even *be* set titles instead of something which changes daily according to programme content; whether each participant should be introduced by name orally or by means of a superimposition on the screen (and, if so, where on the screen); whether the presenter should preface the first story with a 'Good morning' or 'Good evening' or plunge straight into the day's news; whether studio performers should be framed dead-centre or offset to one side of the screen, and in medium shot or close up.

All this and more has to be decided with as much care and consideration as the way the news itself is reported, for without being offered an attractive programme wrapping, the audience may decide not to wait to examine the contents.

It is debatable, though, whether it is necessary to go as far as some local television stations in the United States, once it dawned on managements that news programmes could attract the lucrative advertising that accompanied healthy ratings. Specialist consultants — news *doctors* — were commissioned to find the magic formula which would first conjure up high viewing figures and then keep them. The result was that, in many cases, accepted editorial standards were jettisoned in favour of sensational-ism, emotional stories of human interest and greater personal involvement by reporters. The one greying, dependable looking newsreader was likely to be replaced by a team of personable presenters recruited to re-create family-style relationships on the screen in a way designed to make the viewers feel more comfortable.

Programme running order

An 'act of faith' is how a senior BBC colleague once described the production process of every television news programme: faith in the certainty that each separate member of the news team is carrying out his or her allotted task while everyone else is doing the same. It is a faith understood on the road at home or abroad, in the newsroom, in the editing suites and in the studio. And the basis of it is good communication without which, in the constantly shifting sands of news, the whole thing would probably sink without trace.

To the uninitiated, the daily home and foreign news diaries, the 'prospects' setting out details of coverage, the wall-charts on which the progress of assignments is ticked off, probably seem confusing and unnecessary. To those engaged on the serious business of constructing something tangible out of hopes, promises and expectations, they represent a comforting reminder of the amount of effort being expended for the sake of a common goal.

While one part of the editorial output team writes scripts and assembles news items, the more senior members of it decide programme shape and content. Central to that is the *running order* or *rundown*, a list composed of the sequence of stories to be transmitted and a guide to the separate elements to be used within each. Without this information readily to hand in some consistently acceptable form, the production staff would be at a complete loss, and the result would be obvious to the viewer in a short time. Presenters would be addressing the 'wrong' camera, introductions would not match their intended reports, graphics would be out of sequence or fail to appear on the screen at all. In short the whole broadcast would disappear in confusion.

Yet, crucial though it is to the smooth transmission of a programme, there is nothing especially complicated about a running order. In some small news operations, it need be no more than a half sheet of paper on which the studio director notes the details as dictated by the programme editor, and then passes them on to the main technical staff. In other cases it is a lengthy, detailed document which emerges only after earnest discussion.

In either case, while practical necessity demands that it may have to be drawn up and distributed at least an hour before transmission (and it follows that longer programmes need longer running orders, which therefore take proportionately longer to compose), the chances are that it will be subjected to considerable change as programme deadline nears. That is inevitable, because even without the need to accommodate newly breaking stories, so much of what is committed firmly to paper is no better than educated guesswork, based as it is on frequently sketchy information about such unpredictable matters as the estimated times of touchdown of aircraft carrying videocassettes, the arrival of satellite pictures from some remote spot on the other side of the world, the duration and substance of a political speech (followed by the ability of the office motor-cyclist to weave his way successfully through rush-hour traffic), added to the notional time needed for editing and scripting a dozen complicated packages.

For all this, the running order is the foundation on which any programme begins to assume a definite shape, and even experienced editors feel uneasy until it has been prepared. Many news-writers, meanwhile, like to know how their work is meant to fit into the overall scheme of things, if only because it enables them to decide whether they will need to construct phrases linking one item to the next.

The running order is invariably put together at a conference presided over by the programme editor who, with or without canvassing colleagues for their opinions, outlines the framework and gives an idea of the approximate time he or she proposes to devote to each separate item. In some longer newscasts, departmental heads — sport, entertainment, etc. — contribute their own regular blocks, having a fixed allotment of air-time without needing to bargain for space with the programme editor.

Some programmes leave their production staffs with the responsibility for constructing and amending running orders, but as so much depends on editorial as well as technical judgements, there remains a general reluctance on the part of the majority of journalists to relinquish this control. It is an understandable point of view, but the traditional methods of producing these important documents have invariably been slowish, and altering them, particularly close to transmission to accommodate late stories, is a chore which probably occupies a senior editorial figure for too long at a time when he should be concentrating solely on journalistic matters.

Fortunately, as with so much else in television news, new technology is coming to the rescue. One of the most important benefits of the computerized newsroom systems now being introduced is their capacity to cope easily with the creation of running orders, and to handle any possible combination of changes (up to and including transmission) within microseconds.

We will come to that later. For the moment let us concentrate on an example of a fairly typical running order produced in one traditional way. Each item is given a page number and title by which it is identified throughout its brief life to avoid any possible confusion in the often chaotic last few minutes before transmission. Where stories are particularly complex, or have several strands to them, they are allocated successive page numbers and titles. This is so that the writers responsible can produce scripts page by page to speed distribution.

Running orders also commonly contain several numbers against which there are no titles. This is a built-in allowance for any new stories to be slotted in without disturbing everything else. Where really drastic changes cannot be accommodated, whole sheets may have to be scrapped and re-written and items re-numbered. Any changes, no matter how minor, have to be communicated to the production staff, so that by the time the broadcast begins no one involved is left in doubt about the part he is expected to play.

The running order lay-out itself is important (fig. 10.1), although it does not have to be complicated. The chief consideration is for it to be easily understood. Essential ingredients are numbers, titles and sources.

Behind what may seem to be a straightforward enough exercise, a great depth of journalistic experience and understanding has to be shown by the editor in the hours between the daily round of formal and informal conferences and the drawing up of the running order.

In this example of *The Five o'clock Report*, it is quite possible to imagine that several 'diary' stories have not come up to expectation and have had to be discarded. Suggestions for coverage of a handful of new, borderline stories have been weighed then rejected. A special report from one of the staff foreign correspondents has failed to arrive in time for the programme because of technical problems at the airport of departure and it had already been decided not to send the item by satellite. The extra news agency stories put forward by the copytaster for possible use all turn out to offer no advance on what is already in hand.

Much of what is listed for inclusion is therefore as predicted, and the one remaining doubt in the editor's mind, two hours before transmission, is whether to begin his programme with something which *was* unexpected: an early morning explosion and fire at a factory just over 100 miles from the

PROGRAMME RUNNING ORDER

THE FIVE O'CLOCK REPORT: Running order, Monday January 14
Studio Two.   Rehearsal: 4.25 p.m.
Director: Bert Brown   Presenter: Phil Jones

TITLES & SIGNATURE TUNE (15")

```
 1.  MENU                          PHIL/CAPS
 2.
 3.
 4.
 5.  PRIME MINISTER                PHIL
 6.  PM/INTERVIEW                  ENG
 7.  PM/REACTION                   PHIL/CAPS
 8.  PM/POLITICAL                  INJECT (EX PARLY)
 9.
10.  STRIKE                        PHIL
11.  STRIKE/LIBRARY                VT/SUPER
12.  STRIKE/MICHAEL                SS (CSO FACTORY)
13.  STRIKE/PAY OFF                PHIL
14.
15.  FIRE                          PHIL/CAP
16.  FIRE/MIDLANDS                 VT/SUPERS
17.
18.  COLLISION                     PHIL/CAP
19.  COLLISION/CHANNEL             ENG
20.
21.  PARIS DEMO                    PHIL
22.  PARIS/EVN                     VT
23.  GORBACHEV                     VT
24.  U.S.                          CAP
25.
26.
27.  MILK                          PHIL/CAPS
28.  MILK/TOPFIELD                 ENG/SUPERS
29.  MILK/MINISTER                 VT/SUPER
30.  MILK/UPDATE                   LIVE/SUPER
31.
32.
33.  AIR FARES                     PHIL/CAPS
34.  NEW PLANE                     PHIL
35.  PLANE/REPORT                  ENG/SUPERS
36.  PLANE/ADD                     PHIL
37.
38.
39.  LA SALVA COUP                 PHIL/CAPS
40.  LA SALVA/HARRIS               TAPE/COMPOSITE
41.  LA SALVA/BRITON               PHIL
42.  LA SALVA/2-WAY                PHIL/LIVE/SUPER
43.
44.
45.  MISSING PAINTINGS             PHIL/CAPS
46.
47.  BABY                          PHIL
48.  BABY/HOSPITAL                 ENG (2ND VOICE?)
49.  BABY/STEWARDESS               ENG/SUPER
50.  BABY/ADD                      PHIL
51.
52.  ENGLAND TEAM                  PHIL/CAPS
53.  MARATHON                      PHIL
54.  MARATHON/MAN                  VT/SUPER
55.
56.  WEIGH-IN                      PHIL
57.  WEIGH-IN/TODAY                ENG
58.
59.
60.  CLOSE                         PHIL/CAP/SIG.TUNE
```

Fig. 10.1. RUNNING ORDER FOR THE FIVE O'CLOCK REPORT.

capital. Two people are known to have died, by international standards no great loss of life, but factory safety has been a matter of great interest everywhere since the Bhopal gas disaster in 1984, and staff from the local station, quick off the mark, are at work putting together what seems to be an excellent account of the accident, with pictures and interviews. Added to that, a collision between two foreign ships a few miles off the coast, with a possibility that up to eight seamen have been killed, makes the temptation to lead with the double disaster a considerable one.

But with a certain amount of reluctance, the editor decides to give pride of place to the Prime Minister's forecast that the economic situation is showing signs of considerable improvement. A statement along these lines has been expected for some days, but it has now come out in a rather less cautious form than the political correspondent has been led to believe. Moreover, the Prime Minister's willingness to be interviewed on the subject is an additional factor. So economics find their way to the top of the news running order, the sequence completed by reaction from opposing politicians and a live report from Parliament by the political correspondent to put everything into perspective.

The economic theme is continued by placing second a report about the strike at a factory which makes components for the motor industry. It is significant because it could lead to lay-offs, affecting in turn exports and the Prime Minister's hoped-for economic revival. The industrial correspondent is expected to return in time from a meeting between the management and the union, from which it is hoped some news of a settlement may emerge. It means a second correspondent appearing high up the programme, but since both stories do really need authoritative explanation, the editor decides there is no alternative.

Fig. 10.2. Television newsroom. The author discusses programme running order with BBC newsreader Moira Stuart. (*BBC Central Stills*)

With the economy out of the way, the reports of the two accidents come next. On sheer numbers alone, the ship collision ought to merit the higher place in the running order. But there are other factors to be considered. First, the factory explosion is a domestic story and has potentially serious ramifications, while the collision seems to have been the result of a simple navigational error in fog. Second, there is full coverage of the factory disaster, but the visual material available on the other story is expected to consist of no more than a minute of pictures, taken from the air, of one of the damaged vessels under tow. Third, and decisively, the incident at sea makes a far neater transition from a sequence of 'home' stories to a sequence of 'foreign' ones. These concern a workers' demonstration in Paris and a military parade in Moscow (both offered on the Eurovision News Exchange) and comments made by the United States President about East-West arms talks.

The editor did wonder whether to extend the foreign sequence by reporting a military take-over in a small but important South American republic, especially as some impressive stills have come over the wire and there is a telephoned dispatch from the local correspondent. Eventually, he decides to save the item for the latter half of the programme, which is looking distinctly thin without the substantial foreign report that will not now arrive until tomorrow.

Casting around for something with which to 'come home', after the foreign sequence, the editor briefly contemplated putting in a vision story about a tourist thought to have been bitten by a rabid dog during a continental camping holiday, but discarded it as too trivial. He opts instead for a clear change of emphasis with the milk price rise and Topfield Farm sequence. At one early stage in the afternoon this was considered as a strong candidate for second story, but it had soon become obvious that not all the ingredients would be completed in time. So now it comes just over 12 minutes in, about halfway through the programme. A proposed new structure for domestic air fares seems to follow naturally, and that coincides with the pictures of the maiden flight of a revolutionary new passenger aircraft.

From there the programme takes off on another new direction with the South American coup report, rounded off with an interview with a businessman who got out of the country on the last flight before the take-over. A vision and still story about some stolen paintings acts as a useful buffer in front of an unusual 'human interest' tale about a baby girl born prematurely in mid-flight over the Atlantic. There are pictures of the child in an oxygen tent in hospital, and an interview with the stewardess who helped deliver her. The editor spotted the possible link between this and the report of the new plane, but decides to ignore it.

Towards the end, after the ritual announcement of an England cricket touring party, come two more lightweight sports items. The editor hopes that the rest of the programme will come to sufficient length to enable him to discard at least one of them, but for the time being, uncertainty about the duration and availability of the factory explosion report has forced him to include both.

To close the programme there is the usual recap of the main points of the news, and the closing titles.

An alternative to the formal running order is to leave the final permutation until shortly before transmission. Although this method is known to work perfectly well in some circumstances, it does seem to introduce another, unnecessary element of uncertainty into a process which is already fraught with difficulty. It is something I would hesitate to recommend for any except the least intricate programmes.

Setting out the script

Hand-in-hand with the numbered running order goes a need for the careful lay-out of every page of script. The discipline is perhaps not as necessary where very small editorial and production teams are concerned, but big services, especially those operating on shift-working lines, need to conform to a house style readily understood by anyone.

Just as the running order dictates what elements the programme contains, the written script influences how and when they are introduced. The studio director, glancing at a fresh page arriving in the control room two minutes before air-time, must be able to feel confident that following its instructions without hesitation will not lead him to disaster. Poor typing or idiosyncratic lay-out could easily lead to misunderstandings among the production staff, with predictably chaotic results.

The scripts are produced in the newsroom according to the convention which says each page must be typed in nothing less than double spacing, technical and production instructions being given on the left-hand side, text on the right. Computerized systems allow this split-page format to be generated by no more than one or two key-strokes. Numbers and titles must correspond with those given on the running order, and the duration of separate components added to help those constructing the programme keep in step with the projected overall length.

The number of script copies required for each newscast must depend on the number of people concerned with production. In some cases half-a-dozen may be sufficient, turned out on typewriters with jumbo-sized lettering for feeding straight into teleprompting devices. In other establishments, 40 or more complete sets have to go round. My own view is that it is far better to have too many script copies than too few.

Some services responsible for several newscasts a day give each its own paper colour code. In that way there is no chance of a spare script page left over from, say, the afternoon news, creeping into the late evening programme by mistake.

Figure 10.3 gives an idea of how the opening few pages of *The Five o'clock Report* might be set out.

As can be seen from the examples, the production instructions are bald, to say the least.

PHIL IN VISION

does not go on to say how the shot of the presenter should be framed. The instruction when to introduce the

CAPTION

does not go beyond identifying the subject. The rest is left to the discretion

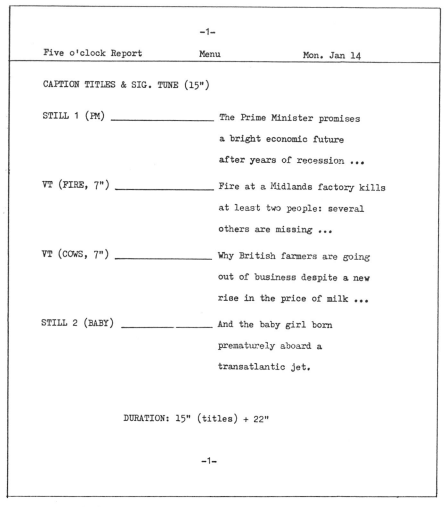

Figure 10.3. Script for the five o'clock report.

of the studio director and production team, although sensible suggestions of where electronic wipes, mixes or other techniques might add variety to the presentation will probably be followed if the writer has taken the trouble to include them.

Directors in some news services prefer their scripts to contain much more detailed technical information. There seems to be no accepted standard, either, for the terminology employed. For instance some stations are content to use *videotape* as a generic term and do not bother to differentiate between three-quarter, one inch or other formats, and it is possible to find a variety of expressions for the same production instruction:

TAKE VT

or

```
                                    -5-

        Five o'clock Report      Prime Minister        Mon.Jan 14
```

PHIL IN VISION _____ The Prime Minister has forecast
                               an end to the economic recession
                               and high unemployment. She told
                               MPs this afternoon that the
                               situation has improved so much
                               over the past six months that a
                               dramatic drop in the number of
                               unemployed now looks likely, and
                               she's optimistic that figures out
                               next week will prove the point. But
                               she's also warned against complacency.
                               There is, she says, still a
                               difficult time ahead. John Jennings
                               asked if that wasn't too rosy a
                               picture of the future:

ENG FOLLOWS

              DURATION: 29"

                                    -5-

TAKE ENG

or

TAKE TAPE

or

TAKE SOT

(sound on tape)

    Some day, somewhere, some bright spark will no doubt embark on a project to devise a detailed set of television news production instructions for worldwhile acceptance. Until then, however desirable uniformity may well be, as long as the staff concerned understand and react correctly to the local terminology, it hardly seems important.

-6-

Five o'clock Report   PM/Interview   Mon.Jan 14

ENG (1'47")

SPEECH BEGINS: "No, this time I am ..."

SPEECH ENDS: "... wouldn't like anybody to
                      believe that."

                 DURATION: 1'47"

                      -6-

-7-

| Five o'clock Report | PM/Reaction | Mon.Jan 14 |

PHIL IN VISION _____ The immediate reaction from
                                the Opposition parties was one
                                of disbelief.

STILL 1 (JONES) _____ Mr Albert Jones said the Prime
                                Minister was deluding herself
                                and the country if she really
                                thought the worse was over.
                                And

STILL 2 (SMITH) _____ Mrs Aga Smith, for the National
                                Noncomformists, said any
                                improvement was probably more
                                to do with the recovery of
                                world trade than successful
                                Government policies.

          DURATION: 20"

-7-

11

Production and presentation

Having collected and selected the news items, and put them into an acceptable order, we now consider the production and presentation of that programme. The key to this is the studio control room.

The control room

Like the bridge of a modern supertanker or the cockpit of a long-range jet aircraft, the control room of a television studio is a world of its own, dominated by electronic gadgetry of seemingly overwhelming complexity. It is cramped, dim and claustrophobic. The main source of light comes from a bank of television monitors which reflect the seeing eyes of the cameras in the brightly lit studio next door. Other small squares of light shine from the illuminated buttons on control panels, at which sit shadowy figures, heads bent over scripts. Tension and excitement lie close beneath the surface air of calm efficiency.

This, then, is the nerve centre of a television news broadcast, the one and only place where the editorial function, supreme until now, has to take second place. For this is the moment when the production and technical team hold sway as they set about the intricacies of translating paper plans into a living television programme. No matter what the number of sources — live, recorded, visual, oral, static, moving — they have to knit the whole structure together, each dovetailing neatly into the next to produce a continuous, seamless whole, based on split-second timing.

That is not over-stating the case. Split seconds make all the difference between a programme which flows from item to item without a hiccup and one which is ragged, with awkward delays between presenter introduction and videotape, clipped sound, momentarily blank screens and missed cues. Yet there is a very fine margin indeed between success and failure. The most ambitious programmes, especially, court disaster night after night, pushing men, women and machinery to the limits by the deliberate policy of trying to squeeze in the very latest information. New stories are added, some are dropped and others are altered right up to and including the time the programme is on the air. The only deadline most editors are prepared to accept is the closing signature tune.

As a result, the professionalism and expertise of the control room staff is continuously on trial. One slip, and all the time, effort and money spent by others might be wasted. Fortunately, real disasters are rare, despite the knowledge that one minor misfortune has a habit of begetting another, and the prickly feeling that, one day, an entire programme is going to collapse on air like a house made of cards.

Responsibility during transmission lies with the *Studio Director*. In the days when news came in short bursts of 10–12 minutes, it was reasonable to expect directors to be responsible for several broadcasts during a single duty period. Since programmes have become not only much longer but technically more complicated, proper preparation is essential, and a director is now more likely to be associated with the same programme every day. The aim is to provide continuing production advice to the journalistic team on the ways items might be prepared for the screen and to help maintain the overall continuity in presentation which gives the programme its identity.

The director attends the daily editorial conferences, organizes and supervises recordings of graphics sequences or studio interviews, and perhaps helps select headline sequences and stills. If there is time he might go into the field to supervise the shooting of stories. But his over-riding concern is to keep a close watch on the running order, ready to sound the warning bells over any potential difficulty, and to keep abreast of changes as they are made. In short the director should be the focal point for everything to do with the ultimate transmission of the programme.

One of the main tasks, in conjunction with the technical staff on duty, is to help in the deployment of the production resources necessary to

THE CONTROL ROOM

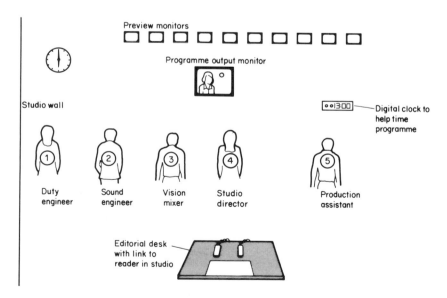

Fig. 11.1.

Fig. 11.2. In the control room, nerve centre of a television newscast. The studio director is in charge, selecting video sources from banks of preview monitors in front of him. To his right is the production assistant. The director here is taking advantage of the final few minutes before the BBC's *Six o'clock News*, to rehearse the opening sequence. (*BBC Central Stills*)

transmit each item, preferably in a way that ensures the greatest editorial flexibility. Videotape stories, for example, are not always played in by the same machine (unless there *is* only one or moves have been made to feed stories from carousels of transmission-only machines stacked in central areas). Spreading the load reduces the likelihood of the programme coming to a complete standstill in the event of a mechanical failure, as tapes can be switched physically between machines. It also gives the programme editor freedom to 'drop' stories for any reason, even while on air, because a tape set up on one machine can easily be discarded while another item on a separate recorder is being broadcast. For similar reasons, wherever it is possible, the widest range of equipment for the transmission of graphics and stills is also brought into use.

Control room lay-outs vary, especially as some are incorporated within the newsrooms from which programmes are transmitted. CNN at Atlanta accommodates its production team in a newsroom area known as 'the pit', but a more typical lay-out would have the director seated more or less at the centre of a desk which runs virtually the whole width of a completely separate room. Immediately to one side sits the *Production Assistant*, armed with stop-watches to see that the whole programme runs exactly to time, and that an accurate count-down is given into and out of the separate videotape and other inserts as the newscast proceeds. On the other side of the director is the *Vision Mixer*, hovering over an organ-like keyboard on the desk top. Banks of levers and glowing buttons represent the selection of cameras and other sources he will put on the screen under direction.

Next to the vision mixer may be either the *Sound Engineer* busy at a panel of faders which control volume levels in the studio and those from other sources, or a *Duty Engineer*, whose prime responsibility is to ensure that technical standards are maintained throughout the broadcast. This, then, would be the basic studio control room production and technical team, although there might be a second sound mixer, and operators for the sophisticated, remotely controlled cameras favoured by some news organizations (see later). Some services make do without the sound engineer's presence, locating him and his equipment in another nearby area. Others expect the director to double as vision mixer by punching his own buttons.

Places are usually found for the programme editor and a senior colleague or two, together with representatives from other departments which have made special contributions — perhaps someone from graphics, stills and videotape. With all those experts on the spot, answers to any problem which may crop up during transmission can be supplied very quickly.

The studio

Unless it is autonomous or carries considerable prestige, the news is likely to be only one of a number of programme types queuing up to take turns in using whatever studio facilities its parent organization has to offer. It is still possible to find places where the news cannot be transmitted until sets from the previous programme have been dismantled and taken away from the only studio. Big television productions need plenty of space and technical support; studios exclusively for news tend to be small and unelaborate, and it remains fashionable in some quarters to put the cameras in the newsroom as a way of conveying an air of bustle and excitement to the audience.

A close look at almost any half-hour news programme will show how little of it is spent *in* the studio compared with the time devoted to routing videotape and other sources *through* it. Even so, as it is largely on studio-based items that programme identity is maintained, considerable thought has to go into their technical presentation. To do that there might be four or five electronic television cameras. One concentrates on a head and shoulders shot of the presenter, one on a wide shot of the whole studio, two on maps, stills and electronic switching (see below), and a fifth is reserved for additional performers (reporters and correspondents) and the occasional interviewee. Movements are so few and unfussy that the BBC, for example, has found it just as effective to use colour cameras remotely controlled by operators sitting not in the studio but at joysticks and banks of switches behind a glass wall in the control room several feet away. Each camera is equipped with an electronic memory capable of storing pre-selected shots for use on transmission, thus removing much of the mental strain from the camera-work needed for a fast-moving programme.

IN THE STUDIO

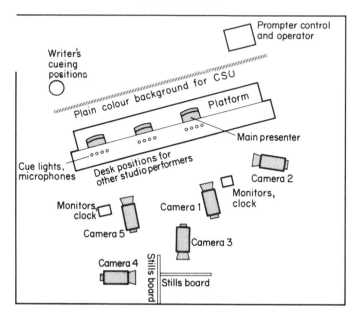

Fig. 11.3. Possible five-camera lay-out for a news studio. If necessary camera five could be dispensed with and camera four moved to cover any other contributors.

Sound and sets

Studio sound is fed independently from microphones sited in pairs (in case one fails) at each of the reading positions. Overhead, individually adjustable banks of lights hang down from hoists close to the ceiling, throwing their beams over studio sets designed to enhance the special qualities of the programme. Some sets are elaborate and expensive. Much in favour are desks on raised platforms surrounded by simulated bookshelves or 'windows' which allow the viewer to look out on familiar views, photographically or electronically reproduced, which are changed according to season. Other sets are of stark simplicity, consisting of plain backgrounds against which the presenter sits at an ordinary desk equipped with only the bare essentials of telephone (to talk to the director in emergencies) microphones and cue lights.

For some years now it has been the vogue to present the reader against a background which changes to give a visual representation of the story being read. This might be a still picture, a graphic, or a frozen frame of video. The most sophisticated way of achieving this is with what is known as *chromakey* or *colour separation overlay* (CSO). This enables a plain background to be reproduced electronically by another visual ingredient without affecting the subject in the foreground of the picture. The key to the system lies in the colour chosen for the studio backcloth. It is often blue, of which there is very little in human flesh tones. At the touch of a switch, the electronic camera locks on to that background colour, filling it with a picture coming from a second source, perhaps another studio, a

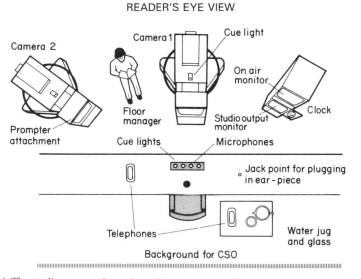

READER'S EYE VIEW

Fig. 11.4. The studio, as seen from the main presenter position.

camera, a stills store or videotape recorder, effectively merging the two images into one. What is created for the viewer is an electronic illusion. Should the presenter in the foreground look over his shoulder he would see nothing except the plain studio backcloth, which can sometimes make two-way interviewing a tricky matter while this device is being used.

At one time when CSO was used, the foreground subject would occasionally take on a curious, blue-tinged outline, particularly around the hair, and zooming in movements by the camera had the effect of making the foreground leap forward by itself. Most of the minor flaws in the system now seem to have been overcome, but performers still need to select clothing colours for the studio with considerable care, as the device is extremely sensitive. It will be triggered by any strong foreground colour which matches the background, punching an electronic 'hole' through anything in the way, human bodies included, and replacing it with the background picture.

Other floor space in the studio is taken up by coils of camera cable, large pin-boards or stands to accommodate non-electronic artwork or still pictures, and portable monitor sets which enable the presenters to keep a discreet check on both the output and themselves. Tucked away in the studio corners are the controls for the electronic prompting devices, together with an operator or two, and possibly a small table at which the writers sit to work the cue lights on the reader's desk during voice-over commentaries.

During transmission, the *Floor Manager* stays in the studio as a go-between for the director in the control room and the presenters at their desks, making sure that any late instruction or alteration is passed on, helping to count the readers in and out of the various sequences, and giving whatever visual cues may be necessary. In recent years, some of the floor manager's tasks have been lightened by the introduction of *deaf-aids*, miniature loudspeakers tailored to fit snugly into the ear of each regular performer. These are linked directly with the director's microphone in the control room, but some readers prefer to switch them off for long periods during transmission in case they are distracted by the breakthrough of babble by production staff. Some programme editors like to be able to give instructions directly to their presenters during transmission and have a telephone link into the ear-piece which is activated when they pick up the receiver.

Countdown to transmission

An hour or so before transmission (the exact timing depends on the duration and complexity of each programme), the production staff gather in the studio control room for the *script conference*. At this stage in the proceedings the director has the running order, at least some of the alterations which have inevitably been made, and a good idea of what other changes may occur before the programme goes out. Now he is able to begin issuing detailed instructions, referring to the items on the running order in sequence, page by page. Everyone with a part to play in the newcast has to be made familiar with the camera shots, the machine-by-machine allocation of videotape inserts, and the order of graphics and stills. Instructions are marked on whatever pages of script have been distributed up to that time. Whatever details are known about pages yet to come are written on a *skeleton*, a sheet which is left completely blank apart from the corresponding page number of the script. When the completed page eventually turns up, the skeleton will be discarded, although in fact the director could work from the blank as a last resort.

New methods are evolving with the introduction of newsroom computers, but the need for communication between all production and technical departments remains, and the dialogue for part of a script conference for *The Five o'clock Report* will be something like the following:

(*Director speaking*:) '. . . so it's page ten next — Strike. That'll be camera one for the presenter, into library pictures — the first on VT–2. OK? They've written in a page twelve for the Industrial Correspondent's studio spot, though it might not happen. If it does we'll seat him in front of camera four with a CSO of the factory, using a freeze frame from the stills store. I suppose they'll want to superimpose his name and title as well — if so it's yours, scanner two. Right, then it's back to Phil and camera one for page thirteen, the pay off. No page fourteen, so fifteen is next, Fire. Camera one for Phil, plus map. Cardboard this time. We'll pin it up in sight of camera four, which will have had plenty of time to line up on it after the studio spot. The writer wants us to zoom in on the street name becuse it's near a primary school. We'll rehearse that later if we can. From there it's VT–3 with Fire, Midlands. That's going to be very late, so there's a strong chance it'll have to go live . . .'

The conference continues briskly in the same vein, with pauses for the director to answer queries from other members of the production staff.

Eventually every page on the running order has been covered, and allowance made for those items about which very little is known so far. Everybody concerned with the production is now fully aware of the part he or she is expected to play, while being quite prepared to accommodate any sudden change of plan. It is a fairly routine day for news, however, and with the favoured editorial shift on duty, the production and technical teams are keeping their fingers crossed for a smooth, good-looking programme.

Rehearsal and transmission

Rehearsals for television news programmes tend to be sketchy affairs because so much of the material to be used on transmission is unavailable until the last few minutes before air time. Scripts are still being written, ENG edited and graphics completed. In fact, the assembly of items goes on so late, programme editors are often heard to grumble that they scarcely have time to see some of them to make editorial judgements, let alone hope to have them rehearsed.

Just the same, any director must take the opportunity to go through whatever he can, and the one responsible for *The Five o'clock Report* is no different. The early availability of one of the videotape machines gives him the chance to check a recorded item which would have been tricky to transmit live, to try out the zoom in to the map on page 15, and to see whether the script for the end item, running order page 57, will match the pictures, by asking the presenter to read through it. As the minutes tick away the flow of completed scripts coming into the control room begins to quicken. The corresponding skeletons are thrown out to accommodate the new pages, everybody remembering to transfer the marks made so carefully at the script conference 40 minutes earlier.

Editors who for no apparent reason make wholesale changes to their programme running orders at the last moment are not popular with even the most experienced of production teams, and acquire reputations for being indecisive. Inevitably, though, the duration of some items will turn out to be longer than planned and others will have to be adjusted or omitted to fit them in, so minor alterations at least are unavoidable:

Director: 'Page thirty nine, everyone. There's an extra still for the frame store. All right?'

Sometimes there are deletions, ordered by the editor speaking on the intercom from the newsroom:

Director: 'Page forty five. Missing Paintings — out. That means we shan't want your Goya portrait, frame store, thank you.'

In between, the Industrial Correspondent wanders into the studio, and is motioned into a seat facing camera four. The floor manager's voice booms into the control room from his microphone next door:

Floor manager: 'Can you try the voice level for Michael now, please? He's got to go back in the newsroom to check on his story.'
Director: 'Yes, right away. Sound?' (He presses a button on his desk, so

the correspondent in the studio can hear him.) 'Just a few words then, Michael.' (After no more than a sentence the sound engineer in the control room has adjusted the fader and given the thumbs up). 'OK, Thanks.' (To Production Assistant:) 'Better get the make up girl in here. He'll need a touch of powder before he goes on.'

With not much more than 15 minutes to go, the editor in the newsroom is suddenly confronted with the sort of dilemma he has nightmares about. The reporter in charge of the factory fire story has telephoned the home assignments desk to say that a search of the gutted building has revealed another five bodies, bringing the known death toll to seven. What is more, police have told him that at least a dozen more workers are unaccounted for, although it is not yet apparent whether they had reported for duty that day, and the checking procedure is a slow one. He speaks enthusiastically of the pictures, which are still being edited.

The editor curses the timidity which led him to regard the economics story as the most important one, inconclusive though it was. The fire now has all the makings of a major disaster. There is still time to switch the lead, but it would mean wholesale changes to the running order and destroying much of the carefully planned structure of the programme. Another thought occurs: the assignments desk ought now to be chasing a senior executive from the parent company which owns the factory, so that he can be interviewed live from the nearest studio available.

He also wonders whether there is time to throw together a brief background item which would recall similar disasters. One more question remains to be answered:

Editor: 'What's happening about the strike talks? Does it look as though they're going to settle?
Writer: 'Michael's on the phone now — it doesn't look as though the meeting has finished yet.'

The editor makes up his mind.

Editor (to his no. 2): 'I'm going to switch the lead. We'll move the fire up to page two, with vision, map and the Midlands vt. Find a writer and get him to put together a quick backgrounder and we'll see if the home desk can get hold of some bigwig from the factory. Just warn the control room what's likely to happen. Tell them we'll have to play it by ear. For now we'll move the Collision story up to page three — that means fifteen, sixteen, eighteen and nineteen are out. I'm just going to see about the interview, then I'll go and talk to the director. And don't forget to have the headlines re-written.'

In the semi-darkness of the control room a few yards along the corridor, the director is still in the process of catching up with earlier changes:

Director: 'There's a new story at page thirty seven, Commons Debate. Camera one for the reader and a still of Frank Smith on camera three. And pages fifty six and fifty seven are out. That means we don't need your last piece, Weigh-in Today, on VT–4 thank you.' (To floor manager:) 'Tell Phil we go straight from the Marathon Man vt on page fifty four, to the close. OK? Right, script check in five minutes, everybody.'

By now the messengers are bustling in with the last scripts. Everybody is writing furiously. The floor is littered with discarded skeletons and 'dropped' story scripts. In the studio, the make-up girl is applying a light touch of powder to the Industrial Correspondent's forehead. The presenter is checking the roll of prompter paper against the printed pages of script.

The editor has arrived in the control room, out of breath after confirming that the managing director of the factory has agreed to appear on the programme. The only snag is that he has already promised to be interviewed by the main opposition news programme, which is on the air first. A taxi will whisk him from one studio to the other, and *The Five o'clock Report* presenter, an experienced journalist, will have to do it live down the line to the local studio, 100 miles away. (No one has dared to tell the editor that *that* studio will be occupied by a children's programme until approximately two minutes before the news is due to begin.) A senior writer is already briefing the presenter about the interview. The director listens, unperturbed, to the catalogue of changes being made. He speaks calmly into the microphone linking him to the studio and the other technical areas:

Director: 'Change of lead coming up. I'll tell you in a moment, during the script check.'

The final changes are scribbled in on the running order. The editor, relaxing briefly, looks around the room, and indicates the preview monitor for camera three, which is just lining up on its still picture for the late story:

Editor: 'Is that the Frank Smith still? I thought he'd shaved off his beard.'

The stills assistant hurries off to check with the writer back in the newsroom. Five minutes to go. 'Script check', orders the director. This is the last check before transmission, and everyone is expected to pay full attention. Loss of concentration here could result in disaster later on. Again the director is in command, going through the complete script, page by page, at a rapid pace, in confirmation of all that has gone on before and since the first script conference nearly an hour earlier:

Director: 'Here we go then. We start with the Five o'clock titles and signature tune on VT–1. Then there's a re-write of page one, Menu, on its way. That's Phil's voice over VT–2 of the fire, followed by a frame store of the collision, then camera three for the economy and VT–4 Milk. Don't forget to bring up the natural sound of the cows! And that's it — no baby still then. The new lead is numbered page two, Factory Fire. Phil on camera one, the map we rehearsed on camera three. That's a quick change for you, Two, remember. Then, fingers crossed, back to VT–1 for the Midlands Fire story. It was numbered sixteen. I'll explain when I get there. At page two-a, two-a, we're putting in a new piece called Fire Background — some library pictures from VT–4 with Barbara Andrews' voice over, if it makes it. And there's a page two-b, two-b, which is a two-way interview — Phil and some top cat from the factory. We'll bang him up as a CSO using camera four, with camera one for the single of Phil. Next is page three, Ship Collision. Camera one, map on the frame store, vt on VT–3. Then page five. Prime Minister. Camera one, interview on VT–2, camera one again for the Reaction, plus stills on the frame store and scanner one. Page eight, PM Political is live again. Brian will end by handing back to the studio . . .'

The director rattles through it all, remembering to explain how pages 2, 2a and 2b have replaced 15, 16, 18 and 19. The few queries take only seconds to answer.

'Two minutes to go', calls the production assistant. Red flashing lights outside the studio and control room doors warn that transmission is imminent. The studio begins to settle down. The prompter operator is at the controls of her machine. The presenter glances down at the scribbled notes for the interview, hoping he will be able to decipher them when the time comes. Music filters into the studio, signifying the approaching end of the preceding programme. (Pictures from the Midlands studio appear in the control room on a monitor to the director's left. Several teams of children are engrossed in some elaborate quiz game.)

One minute. A writer races into the studio with the re-written headline page. At the back of the control room a fierce argument is going on about the Frank Smith portrait. Voices rise.

Thirty seconds. The director reluctantly tears his attention from the monitor bank:

Director: 'Quiet please! Stand by everyone. Stand by VT–1 with the titles.' (There is an answering buzz from the machine operator on the floor below.)

Station announcements are coming to an end in the brief break between programmes. A square dot appears in the left hand corner of the screen which is now showing station identification and a clock.

Fifteen seconds. The dot disappears.

Ten seconds, Nine. Eight. Seven . . .

Announcer: '. . . that's at seven thirty. But now, at five o'clock . . .'
Director: 'Run vt! Stand by VT–2.'
Announcer: '. . . it's time for the news.'
Production assistant: '. . . four, three . . .'
Director: 'Run VT! Coming to studio and voice over.'
Production assistant: 'Counting into opening headline . . . two, one.'
(The titles and signature tune come to an end.)
Director: 'Cue him!'
Presenter: 'At least seven people have been killed . . .'
Director: 'Frame store next . . .'
Production assistant: 'Counting out of vt — four, three . . .'
Presenter: '. . . in a factory fire in the Midlands . . .'
Director: 'Cut!'
Presenter: 'Off the Cornish coast . . .'
Director: 'Camera three next! THREE! Cut!'

Presenter: 'The Prime Minister promises . . .'
Editor: 'Any sign of our factory management man? We're on him in a couple of minutes.'
Production assistant: 'Thirty seconds, VT–1.' (Buzz!)
Duty engineer: 'Can't see him.' (he indicates the preview monitor. The children have gone, but the studio is now ominously empty.)

The Director, following his script, waits until the presenter in the studio gets to within 12 words of the end of his introduction to the Factory Fire story. Then:

Director: 'Run vt!'
Production assistant: '. . . three, two . . .'
Presenter: '. . . this report from Tom Dixon.'
Director: 'Cut to vt.' (He relaxes.) 'A little more headroom on your Presenter shot, please camera one. He's looking a bit squashed. Has our interviewee turned up yet?'
Duty engineer: 'Doesn't look like it.'
Director (grumpily): 'What am I to do if he doesn't make it? Show an empty chair or go on to the next story? We've got about two minutes.' (Wearily) 'Will they never learn?'
Editor (reassuringly): 'He'll be there.'
Production assistant: 'Thirty seconds left on this vt.'
Director: 'Stand by VT–4 with your Fire Background. Coming to camera one next.' (To floor manager in the studio:) 'I take it Barbara is with us?' (To the editor:) 'Are you happy about the Frank Smith picture yet?'
Editor: 'We're working on it.'
Production assistant: 'Ten to go.'
Director (seeing movement on the monitor showing the Midlands studio): 'Aha . . . methinks I detect signs of life in the sticks. Coming to camera one . . .'
Editor (sounding smug as he wipes sweat-damp hands on his handkerchief): 'Told you he'd be there, didn't I?'
Production assistant: '. . . three, two, one . . .'
Director: 'Cue him and cut!

Although they are unlikely to admit it in public, hardened newspeople still manage to marvel at the way production staff throw an almost entirely unrehearsed programme on the air without so much as a tiny hitch. The occasions when minor errors do occur — the director running a videotape insert too soon, the vision mixer pressing the wrong button, the sound engineer fading up the microphone a second late, the graphics artist mis-spelling a place name on a map — are usually the subject of lengthly and heated inquests. Audiences probably do not notice until the mistakes are glaring, and then they seem to take huge delight that their favourite news programme is peopled by fallible humans like themselves, and not robots. Perhaps that accounts for the enormous popularity of those television programmes composed entirely of scenes that have gone wrong.

There is a serious side to it. The reputation of television news rests above all on its editorial credibility (witness all that mail and telephone calls from viewers), and if programmes become so riddled with production errors as to make technical 'cleanliness' impossible to maintain, there is a real prospect that the journalism itself will eventually be undermined.

Most of the mistakes that do occur could be avoided, but that would mean setting strict deadlines to ensure full rehearsals. It is not a realistic proposition for most news programmes. Television newspeople are acutely conscious of the 'now or never' nature of their work. That is why editors are prepared to jeopardize an entire production for the sake of a good story breaking halfway through a programme. By dropping one on-camera item, taking the option of an 'early out' on a videotape insert and striking out all but one of the closing headlines, there is suddenly enough room to squeeze in something which may already be too late for most editions of tomorrow morning's newspapers. And that, television journalists will say with satisfaction, is what it is all about.

News magazines

What has gone before has been principally to do with programmes which bring news to *national* audiences. But these programmes, despite their prestige and the serious followings they command, are easily outstripped in numbers and popularity by those concentrating on local matters: news magazines, which have 'hard' news sheltering under the same roof as interviews and longer reports categorized as 'news features' or 'current affairs'.

Local newscasts in the United States underwent a transformation when managements realized how they attracted advertising revenue, and the professional view is that some went so far over the top it became difficult to tell that they were news-based at all. But at their best, these programmes are more accurate mirrors of society than their network counterparts can ever hope to be, and local politicians anxious to keep a finger on the public pulse often consider them essential to see and be seen on.

Content is a broad mixture of the serious and the frivolous, the contentious issues either purely local, or national ones given a local twist. On the 'magazine' side, the daily reporter packages and studio discussions presided over by the main presenter(s) are supplemented with regular feature items which might include consumer matters, comprehensive sport and entertainment news, and press reviews. The weather forecaster becomes a personality, encouraged to develop an individual style. The 'news' section, sometimes read by a separate presenter, comes in the shape of mini-bulletins containing stills, graphics and ENG inserts.

The pace in a typical local newsroom is bound to be more leisurely, and some of the issues less immediate, but for the aspiring television journalist, work on a news magazine may be far more stimulating than on a nationally-based programme. Staff numbers are invariably smaller and harder pressed, opening the way for those with ambition to turn their hands to many different tasks. As a result, a surprising number who start out as local news-writers, reporters or presenters, soon find themselves lured to the bigger city or national programmes.

There is also something immensely satisfying about being so close to the grass roots. Many of the subjects handled by national news-writers and producers cannot be anything but remote from the vast audiences of millions. Local television journalists live with the knowledge that what they report and write about directly touches the lives of their viewers. It helps to make them more careful. Instead of writing rude letters, complaining members of the public are liable to come round to the office and hammer on the door for an answer face-to-face, or accost any programme personality they recognize Saturday shopping.

Some local programmes are superbly resourced, with enough talent, equipment and facilities to put many a national newscast to shame. Elsewhere, money and technical resources may be limited, frustrating programme ambitions. For the editor of an under-financed programme, the biggest headache is usually how to fill his allotted 10, 40 or 60 minutes every afternoon. There may not be enough staff to allow for a continuously high level of planning, so much of each programme may have to be assembled from scratch a matter of hours before the day's transmission.

That leaves little room for manoeuvre, and should the already meagre ration of stories be reduced for some reason, the alternative to the unthinkable — leaving a hole — is to pad out what remains. The result is not attractive. The live studio interview may have to be stretched by an extra minute even though the subject has been exhausted long before. The 'news' slot may be so crammed with on-camera stories it appears to be a convenient dustbin for dumping the oddments unwanted anywhere else, instead of being a brief, crisply written round up of matters of real interest.

The arrival of the lightweight electronic camera has not provided a complete answer. The speed and flexibility it adds to coverage has, in some places, led to more trivialization of the news, with every minor traffic accident, every fire, every petty crime hyped to a level of treatment it may not deserve, simply because pictures are available or easy to obtain quickly. In the editing suite the picture editor may be encouraged to lengthen shots or include those he would prefer to discard.

Before long, if these conditions persist, standards slip, fundamentals including proper shot-listing are ignored, and the whole programme becomes flabby and over-written. The journalist's ancient battle-cry of 'What's it worth?' is replaced by the anxious inquiry 'How long can you make it?' This may be an understandable attitude, but it is one which does disservice to the viewer. Almost every story has its own 'natural' length', in whatever context it may be found. Going beyond it does nothing except debase the coinage.

That admittedly begs the question of how else a programme is to be filled. Frankly, there is no answer beyond the general hope that somehow resources will be found to enable more effort to be put into the news-gathering operation, even at the expense of temporarily weakening output.

Newscaster or Newsreader?

It was President Harry Truman who immortalized the saying: 'The buck stops here.' Conceivably, in his case, it was true. The widespread misconception about 'The Buck' in television news is that it stops at the desk of the person seen to be delivering the message, good or bad, directly to the viewer. In short, the newsreader.

When a new editor took over BBC News, 'some critics complained of the space that newspapers gave to the story, the way they treated Angela Rippon (one of the newsreaders) as though she had won an Oscar. These critics were wrong. The men and women who read the news play a large, persistent and recurring part in people's lives.'[1]

Newsreaders themselves have been known to compare their role with the town criers of old, the main difference being that the word is passed on to the people from a comfortable seat in a television studio, rather than from among jostling crowds in the market square. They also operate on a much more personal level. 'Television breeds a closeness and intimacy unlike that of any other medium,' says Robert Dougall, who read the news on BBC television for more than 15 years. 'Your image is projected straight into people's homes. You become, as it were, a privileged guest at innumerable firesides. What is more, a newsreader is not playing a role, not appearing as another character, or in costume, but as himself. He therefore builds up over the years a kind of rapport with the public.'[2]

The truth of that can be gauged from the opinion polls which consistently placed Walter Cronkite, veteran of CBS News, as being among the most trusted people in the United States.

The responsibility all this implies is fairly awesome. There is still more. A cough, hesitation or mispronunciation might easily make nonsense of the most serious or important piece of news. An erratic speed of delivery, particularly during the crucial few seconds of countdown into videotaped or other inserts, can have a devastingly destructive effect on the most carefully planned programme.

Yet between the far-off days when the pioneers were expected to present the news anonymously off camera (in case an involuntarily raised eyebrow, twitch, or some other facial expression should be construed by the viewer as 'comment') and the beginning of the electronic revolution, the conventional newsreader was rather a contradictory figure. On the one hand he was accepted as the figure-head, the standard-bearer of the programme, admired and respected as the subject of unwavering public interest on and off the screen. On the other he was among the last to be consulted about content, style and format. Complaints that Reader A made certain grammatical errors that were scrupulously avoided by Reader B overlooked the fact that neither had probably very much to do with the way the words were written, only the way they were read.

So, sitting in front of a camera, reading aloud the fruits of other people's labour with the aid of a written script and an electronic prompting device, directed through a hidden ear-piece by a studio director next door, supplied with a card index or other reference system to aid the pronunciation of 'difficult' words or names, scarcely seemed exacting enough to warrant all that acclaim. No job for a man, as one reader himself wryly describes it.

True, there were nightly butterflies to be conquered for those terrified of

[1] Jeremy Bugler, *The Listener* (April 1, 1976).
[2] Robert Dougall, *In and Out of the Box* (Collins/Harvill, 1973).

making a mistake or losing a place on the page in front of millions. And yes, the hot lights might make the half-hour or so of programme transmission a trifle uncomfortable physically — dangerous occasionally when, as has been known, a studio light exloded in a shower of glass — especially if fairly formal dress was expected on set. But even here the 'standard newsreader shot' usually revealed no more than the upper half of the body. The rest might just as well have been covered by crumpled old jeans or a pair of shorts for all the viewer knew. Before Angela Rippon danced on a BBC Christmas comedy show back in the seventies, critics of news programmes had been known to wonder, rather cruelly, whether newsreaders needed legs at all.

As for the qualifications necessary for the work, these would seem to have been limited to an authoritative screen 'presence', a pleasant appearance, clear diction, lack of irritating mannerisms, and an ability to keep cool when things occasionally fell apart at the seams; talents which, it may be said, bore a striking resemblance to those required for 'ordinary' television reporting.

Not every newsreader was a reporter who had come in from the cold, and some reporters regarded with horror the prospect of swapping their passports for a permanent place in the studio. The original readers of the news were not necessarily fully fledged journalists at all, although they could scarcely have been effective unless they had exhibited a reasonable interest in the subject. Some began as actors, announcers for different kinds of programmes, or were chosen simply because they had the looks and voices to suit the fashion.

The outstanding quality the best of them managed to bring to television news was an almost tangible manifestation of the editorial credibility of the programme they were representing, allied to some superb skills in delivery and pronunciation which gave a de-luxe finish to writing sometimes scarcely deserving of it. For the viewer they became as familiar as old friends, welcome, immovable points of reference on a world map of constantly changing contours and values. No wonder one newsreader of those days is able to recall from memory virtually every word from letters written by lonely elderly women who admitted to kissing the screen every night as he ended the late headlines. Others must have their own stories to tell of receiving gifts, invitations, compliments, threats, declarations of undying devotion, and proposals of various sorts, all from complete strangers.

That phenomenon is unlikely to change, even though the signs are that *non-journalist* newsreaders are about to become extinct. Their demise is being hastened by technical advances, the transmission of live pictures through the studio and the introduction of instant reactive interviewing demanding a journalistic expertise thought to be beyond the capabilities of all but a handful of television professionals.

Some would say the movement began long ago, pointing to the introduction of newscasters, allegedly a different breed altogether. The newscaster, goes the theory, was employed to fulfil the same functions as the old-fashioned newsreader, except that from a position of considerable journalistic experience drawn from inside or outside television, he was also expected to make a positive contribution to a programme, by writing some of it, acting as an interviewer within it, or both. As the price for such expertise, programme bosses were prepared to accept less than cut-class accents and features which, in the case of one much-loved veteran performer, I have heard described politely as 'lived in'. On a practical level, though, the complexities of a television news programme, with its last-minute videotaped items or Eurovision or satellite inserts, make it difficult to see how anyone but an outstanding personality could do much more than ask the questions as suggested to them by producers, pen the occasional headline, or tinker with a few of the news scripts in order to suit a personal style.

The modern approach is to hire *Anchors* or *Presenters* to take managerial as well as editorial decisions as part of their job. Nowhere is this more apparent than in the United States, where because news programmes are perceived as being crucial to prestige and therefore come under constant commercial pressures, the stars chosen to anchor some of them have been invested with powers commensurate with their staggering salaries. The considerable influence they exert extends to programme policy, content and structure, as well as personnel.[3]

So has developed the trend towards 'personalized' news, which deliberately sets out to identify one individual reader so closely with a particular programme that his or her name is included as part of the title. It is a movement which has been greeted with dismay by some of the journalists, who have had to accept that the editorial responsibility which for many years rested with the producer or editor after consultation (and much argument) with colleagues has now shifted to the reader.

'Presenter power' has also found its way to Europe, and if not yet to the same degree, it has certainly reached the point where there is a blurring of the formerly clear-cut division between those who produce programmes and those who read them.

Behind it all, the purpose is to encourage the audience to establish much the same kind of special, trusting relationship with the person bringing them their daily dose of news as they have with their doctors, bank managers and similar professional advisers. The expectation seems to be that the personality reader has a greater chance of building up a devoted following sufficient to resist any opposition from other channels than the man or woman who appears in rotation as part of a reading team. It is significant that audiences are sometimes asked for their comments before presenter appointments are finalized, but it is still arguable whether viewers actually prefer one news programme and its presenting team to another or whether their choice is governed more by programmes which precede or follow the news.

At this point, and at the risk of being considered old-fashioned, I must admit to prejudice. From a working journalist's point of view it seems wrong to sacrifice the broad team concept in favour of one or two dominant presenter figures. It might also come to represent the very antithesis of the idea of television news as a dispassionate provider of information, as the programme would become instead a vehicle for one

[3]See Barbara Matusow's excellent history *The Evening Stars* (Ballantine Books, 1984).

person's interpretation of events for the viewer to swallow undiluted or turn off. The other question to be asked is what happens when the 'star' is temporarily absent, leaves or dies? The answer is that a vacuum is left, the programme becomes rudderless until he or she returns, an acceptable substitute is found or the entire format is changed.

In the final analysis it is difficult to argue with those critics who suggest that *who* reads a news programme is of far less importance than *what* is shown and said on it.

Perhaps the last words on the subject are best left to an outsider. Alan Coren, a humorous, often highly accurate observer of the British television scene, in examining ITN's search for a female newscaster, included a comment which still rings true, nearly ten years on:

'. . . news is, quite simply, something that happens while you're not there. You therefore require to be informed of it in as clear, cool, detailed, objective and interesting a way as possible; news is not entertainment. When the priorities in its presentation shift so that the criteria become glamour, personality and mass-audience appeal, news is no longer news but feature journalism.'[4]

Doing it in pairs

A popular alternative to the solo reader supported by the occasional reporter or specialist correspondent presenting individual items within a programme is the newsreading double act, personified by NBC's highly successful pairing of Chet Huntley and David Brinkley which began in the fifties. Since then single-reader news services all over the world have tended to follow suit whenever they have felt the need for a re-vamped format, and two-handed programmes have at times returned to one reader for the same reason.

The introduction of a second person into a formerly single presenter news programme adds technical complications, possibly leading to a complete redesign of the studio set to make room for another camera. More thought has to be given to backings and lighting so that there is continuity when the two presenters are shown separately in successive one-shots. Where other contributors are also expected to appear regularly there is also the danger that the programme may seem to be cluttered with too many faces barring the way between the viewer and the news.

Most of all, it presumes the discovery of not one but two first-class journalists willing to pool their talents for the sake of the common good. Compatibility is essential; the whole enterprise is as good as doomed if (as has been known) the senior or more experienced member of the team is reluctant to share the studio with anyone else, regarding the new partner as an unworthy intruder.

Although the camera may show them together in the same shot for only a few seconds at either end of the programme possibly half an hour apart, the best pairs are able to give the impression that, however much their individual styles differ, they hit it off as a team, each member of it taking a genuine, continuing interest in what the other is doing, and not acting as

[4]*London Evening Standard* (April 4, 1977).

Fig. 11.5. Two-handed newscast in progress. Cameras in this case are remotely controlled from outside the studio, so apart from the floor manager the news presenters are alone under the lights. Note the monitors fitted into the desk-top to enable the readers to keep track of the programme. (*BBC Central Stills*)

one of two people who just happen to find themselves occupying the same set at the same time. These experts somehow manage to 'bounce' off one another, each using perhaps no more than a hint of a head turn away from the partner's direction before taking up a new story. Their manner is crisp, efficient and friendly, without recourse to the cosy ultra-informality which looks and sounds so phoney.

Long discussions go on about how the work should be shared between presenters, in some cases down to the percentage of time on air an agent can contract for his client. What was special about Huntley-Brinkley was that one was in Washington and the other in New York, which resulted in a fairly natural division of responsibility. Other pairs have been known to split home and foreign stories, to take alternate whole items, or what amount to alternate pages of script. Sequences of out of vision commentaries spoken by alternate readers come across with real pace and punch, particularly when the partnership consists of one female and one male.

Working with the presenter

Other members of the news team are likely to regard their presenter colleagues, whether one, two or more, with considerable professional respect as the instruments by which a series of unrelated events becomes a television programme before their eyes. They know that without the reader that transformation would be impossible. Those programmes which have a succession of reporters popping up in the studio to introduce their own items are deluding themselves if they believe they have done something different. All they have done is to share out one role between many, for the function of linking one news event to the next remains the same whoever does it.

A few of the staff, perhaps other journalists among them, may have a tendency to feel resentful about the way that the job of presenting the news generally rates super-star treatment, especially since readers began to write — or, more accurately, rewrite — so much of the programme. And there is no disguising the effects on programme morale as a whole if those who present the news are careless of the feelings of fellow professionals.

But for the most part, the best advice to give writers is to stop worrying and start appreciating how their work benefits from having it well presented. For while a poor reader can certainly ruin a good script, the corollary of that is that a good reader can improve on a poor one.

The 'writer's reader' has many qualities, mostly invisible to anyone except the insider. These include a natural gift for putting the emphasis in the right place, even on late scripts which have to be sight-read for the first time on transmission, the offer of exactly the right word or phrase which might have eluded the writer for hours, razor-sharp reactions to cues from the floor or control room, and the confidence and ability to smooth over the awkward moments which might otherwise lead to disaster.

At the other extreme is the reader who is over-anxious, egotistical and temperamental, unwilling to accept advice, concerned only that the duties he is called upon to perform do not offend his public image, uncaring about the ulcer-making effects he has on production and editorial staff during transmission by speeding up or slowing down delivery as the mood takes him.

Not all programmes employ their presenters full-time, effectively ruling out close collaboration with editorial staff, but where possible readers should always be invited to attend conferences in order to absorb the feel of a day's news before they might have to read it.

As transmission time approaches readers should be warned of running order changes and awkward or unusual words. Where pronunciation dictionaries do not exist, some form of card index system should be compiled as a reference. Any last minute alterations to completed scripts must also be given (if necessary in a suitable lull during transmission) to the prompter operators where they affect on-camera passages. Where necessary, writers should be prepared to alter words or phrases to suit the reader's style so long as the intended sense is not destroyed. Much depends in the first instance on the writer's skill in constructing the short, easy-to-understand, easy-to-read sentences already discussed. Tongue-twisters of the 'Scottish soldier shot in the shoulder' variety are easily avoided if the writer follows the preferred path of reading the words aloud before inflicting them on the poor newsreader.

Some problem words are unavoidable. One world-famous newsreader, otherwise impeccable in his delivery, used to admit to great difficulty in saying 'hostage', a word much in current use, alas, and one for which there are not many obvious alternatives. Pity even more the former newsreader whose time as a public figure came to an end because there was an almost endless list of words he was practically incapable of pronouncing. For a few weeks, his writing colleagues went through amazing verbal contortions to find words he could deliver with any confidence. Eventually, after considerable suffering, one hit on the bright idea of spelling out the 'difficult' words phonetically on the script. 'Why not', replied the exasperated programme editor, 'we've tried everything else except injections'.

12

Fresh fields for the television journalist

Although the technological revolution in the field and in the studio has attracted most of the attention because of its obvious effects on the screen, an equally far-reaching change is taking place behind the scenes in the newsroom. The computer has arrived.

The electronic newsroom

It is, of course, some years since the industrialized nations began making use of computers for manufacturing and for data processing, but it is only since the miniaturization of components through the development of microprocessors that computer-related equipment has become commonplace. A streamlined visual display unit, keyboard and a few associated devices known as 'peripherals' can be seen on the premises of virtually any business organization that prides itself on being modern and up to date, although at one time such equipment was more likely to be looked upon as a status symbol than a useful tool.

For the newspaper industry in many parts of the world, the latest developments have represented yet another step towards a completely automated printing process as a means of cutting costs and defeating the competition from television and radio, as well as from the burgeoning 'free sheets'. That in itself has serious consequences for employment and industrial relations, because it means dispensing with at least one tier of workers between those who collect and write the news and those who set the printing presses rolling.

The technical advances are such that a journalist sitting at a keyboard in the office is able to type his story and release it into a computer memory for printing in what has become known as the single key-stroke or direct inputting operation. Sub-editors can write headlines, set type sizes, create cross-heads and design pages in the same way. Proof-reading and stone subbing become unnecessary, as the need for typesetting in the conventional sense no longer exists. Advertising and other departments of a newspaper will originate and key in their own material as a logical development of the technique. All this means that newspapers need smaller staffs, theoretically enabling them to survive on lower circulations. This it is thought should encourage others to establish new newspapers, thus creating extra job opportunities.

The unions are not necessarily convinced, as they are inclined to believe that managements will find other uses for the money saved on production staffing. There is also the emotional argument which surrounds any potential elimination of crafts that have been around for a long time; this has been responsible for at least some of the resistance. The dilemma for those involved in the battle is that as laboratories to process news film have disappeared, so the 'traditional' equipment for newspaper production is harder to find. Compromises have been reached in the face or possibility of serious industrial disputes; some newspaper managements have settled for a kind of halfway house, in which editorial copy created at the visual display terminal is re-typed into the computer by the former occupants of the composing room. There seems to be a good deal of merit in that, for there are several categories of material which are unsuitable for journalists to type directly into the computer and, believe it or not, there are still some journalists who cannot (or will not) type at all.

For television, the problem is only just beginning to surface. Inspired by some newspaper owners who have established new projects and others who have over-ridden the objections and gone whole-heartedly into the new technology, a number of television stations began to pioneer the use of computer systems with which to run their news operations. The entrepreneur Ted Turner introduced the system in 1980 when he set up his 24-hour *Cable News Network* in Atlanta, Georgia; Independent Television News in London computerized *Channel Four News* from its inception in 1982 and had linked their three other programmes into the system within three years; both BBC and TV-am used computers from the start of their breakfast services in early 1983.

The advantages to all (and, it must be said, they include a growing number of radio stations) seem similar to those which apply to newspaper production. Not only is it an obvious way of conserving paper, with which most newsrooms have traditionally been awash, but word processing and text manipulation help the journalists process their information and write their scripts more swiftly, enabling deadlines to be put back, and the production process to be speeded up. This contributes to the real savings made in cost and efficiency over the whole operation.

It is true that responses by newsroom staffs have varied. In some places, the arrival of a computer system has been greeted as excitedly as if it heralded the Second Coming. In others, the established members of editorial teams have stubbornly refused to have the slightest involvement in new-fangled methods apparently intended to part them from their beloved typewriters. In yet more newsrooms, management proposals to introduce something which would actually be of benefit all round have been met with implacable opposition from those whose instinctive reaction to any planned departure from 'normal' working is to seize it as a welcome opportunity to negotiate more money.

For all of them, the computer can do no more than offer a modern alternative to the news handling processes they have always followed, so journalistic jobs are not at risk. Until the fifth generation of so-called

Fig. 12.1. The computerized newsroom. Basys terminals in use at Cable News Network headquarters in Atlanta, Georgia. The system speeds up news script-writing and production processes, although in this picture some typewriters are in evidence. (*BASYS*)

'intelligent' computers becomes reality, the most sophisticated machines remain stupid instruments, able to do nothing unless properly programmed and operated by humans.

Setting up a system

Such has been the revolutionary impact of the office/personal computer on modern industrialized society, there must be very few people living in the latter part of the twentieth century who are still unfamiliar with its shape, even if they remain ignorant of how it works, and are fearful of its powers. In my own case, it is still painful to recall that, when first confronted with one of these magic boxes in December 1982, my reaction was one of near panic – a state brought on by the knowledge that within the space of six weeks I would be helping to launch a brand new television service which was going to be entirely dependent on technology about which I knew next to nothing. It would not be true to say that during the ensuing month and a half I learnt to love the machine, because there were times when I would have cheerfully thrown it out of the window in frustration, but thanks to patient tutoring, the computer and I were at least able to co-exist until the point was reached where I was prepared to trust it to do what was asked (most of the time) and could pass a typewriter without having itchy fingers.

In the years since then, I have gained enough knowledge to understand and respect the enormous advantages that computers offer to journalists as journalists, in addition to the advances which the remarkable new technology alone has made possible for those engaged in the production processes of television.

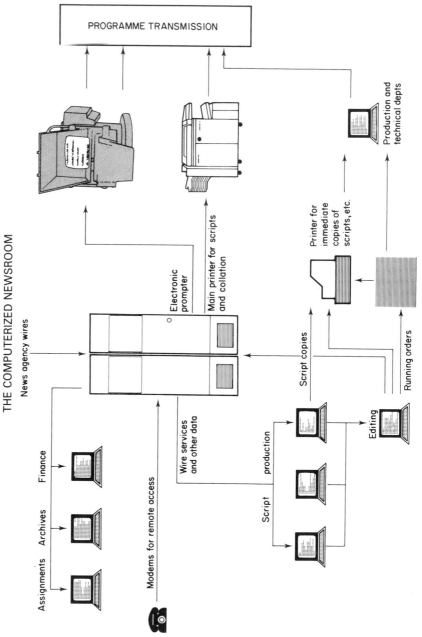

Fig. 12.2.

After those early experiences, though, it is easy to have sympathy for any other poor middle-aged wretches who are computer-illiterate to the extent of feeling completely overwhelmed when facing their first 'hands on' attempts at the keyboard. Trained help is usually always available as part of any package to introduce a computer for serious use, but there are definite advantages to be had in being vaguely aware in advance of what the thing does and how it works.

At the core of the machine is the processor, the 'brain' which sits amid a mass of integrated circuits ('chips'), controlling the tasks it is programmed to carry out. Some of these are already embedded permanently within the computer when it is assembled and so are available for immediate use from the moment the power is switched on. This part of the machine's memory is known as the ROM (Read Only Memory), as opposed to the RAM (Random Access Memory) into which programs are entered as required with the use of magnetic tape or disk and are automatically wiped clean when the computer is switched off. All this circuitry is packed inside a metal box, and a linking typewriter-style keyboard, keypad or similar device allows detailed programming instructions to be entered directly by the operator. The third element is a video screen ('monitor', 'visual display unit' or 'visual display terminal') on which the computer's reactions to those instructions are followed and, if necessary altered as they are put in. Computer, keyboard and screen may remain separate or be combined in different configurations within the same box. This is usually sufficient for the limited requirements of a mini- or micro-computer.

For the larger systems (and those for newsrooms tend to fall into that category), special areas have to be set aside to house one or a series of computers supported by hard disks for electronic storage of the information.

By the beginning of 1987, the total number of fully fledged systems operating in television stations world-wide was probably just over 150, the majority in the United States, though European countries, Australia and parts of Asia including Singapore were also being equipped. Among the best-known makers are *BASYS* (Broadcast Automation Systems), founded in San Francisco in the late seventies, and wholly owned by ITN since 1984, and *Newstar*, part of the Dynatech Broadcast Group of Madison, Wisconsin.

Of these installations, only a few were designed to sustain 100+ terminals linked between main newsrooms and out-stations including bureaux abroad. The rest, excluding those radio and television stations which have bought off-the-shelf or locally designed adaptations of modestly expensive 'personal' computers arranged in networks, averaged between about 12 and 20 terminals, with the flexibility to add more as funds became available.

Money, essential though it is, is surprisingly not always the most important factor in the decision to buy a computer system. From the outset, the management of virtually any news organization contemplating such an investment would understand the financial implications, and would be able to decide very quickly whether it would be beyond their budget. Of a far higher priority is the need to decide exactly what is wanted from any design, and whether it would result in greater efficiency, economy or both.

Small newsrooms with limited output might well conclude that they would be far better advised spending their money on another set of ENG equipment rather than on a computer system likely to be too sophisticated for their needs.

A comprehensive feasibility study should be undertaken, and not rushed. Time must be taken to look at other, completed installations, and to compare the competing merits of a standard package from a big manufacturer with the construction of a complete 'one-off'. Plans to go electronic must also take full account of the need to link all the devices with special cabling, preferably under a raised 'computer floor', the securing of a reliable power system including emergency generators, and provision of proper ventilation to counter the heat from computer, terminals and printers.

There may be unexpected ramifications, too, for the lay-out and design of any existing newsroom and other offices within a news set-up, for example, how the screens and keyboards are going to be positioned on desks originally designed for typewriters. The cost of re-equipping with new furniture, chairs which won't give VDT operators backache, lighting that won't give them eyestrain and the treatment of surfaces to prevent the build-up of static electricity giving them shocks (and affecting the terminals) must also be included in the budget. Proper office design and planning to accommodate the new equipment is needed if the whole move is to be a success environmentally as well as technically. Nothing is calculated to mar the great leap forward more than the belated discovery that the screens are so big they interfere with normal conversation, forcing people to leave their desks in a way they never did before. It can be an expensive mistake in more ways than one, for vibration from the sudden pushing back of chairs has been known to send free-standing pieces of equipment crashing from desk top to floor. Other details to be thought through first include the colour of the text displayed on the screen. Amber or green, for example, may be thought to be more restful on the eye than white.

After that come decisions about the way the computer is to be installed, in all departments at once, or gradually, with different programme areas coming on line after a period of experiment and rehearsal.

It is this sort of attention to detail which will have a beneficial effect on the scheme as a whole, as well as denying ammunition to those who were opposed to the enterprise from the start.

At some stage, preferably sooner rather than later, serious negotiations have to be conducted over the changed manning levels that inevitably accompany the arrival of new technology of any sort. Clerical and secretarial staff clearly face the greatest change of duties in this case, as an essential element of the system is that the television journalists, just like their newspaper counterparts, are expected to key in their own stories. The computer program is designed to turn scripts into accepted television format, so in theory those news services that have traditionally relied on script typists to do the job no longer need perhaps more than one or two to cope with emergencies. Though it does not always happen. Because no agreement was reached over journalistic input at the time their system for electronic script distribution was introduced, several years later the BBC's

External Services newsroom in London still needed to employ clerical staff they had long before affectionately nick-named 'Lolics' (Little Old Ladies in Carpet Slippers).

How many terminals?
Newsroom writers, reporters and programme presenters are almost certainly going to require one each, otherwise the same old hold-ups are going to occur close to transmission time. Presumably the requirements would be marginally fewer in intake/assignments areas, where terminals could quite successfully be shared between two or three. Then there are other departments which could make out a strong case for being linked into the system, among them any regional or remote studios which serve the station regularly. And, finally, no senior executive expects to be left out and will inevitably demand his own terminal.

Logging on
The first thing a journalist does when he starts work at a computer keyboard anywhere in the system is to 'log on' (or 'in'). This he does by typing in his name, followed by a personal password of perhaps eight or ten characters from which the computer identifies him as an authorized user.

As soon as the password has been accepted, the user may be taken automatically into his electronic mail box where messages, office memos or other correspondence await. Otherwise the screen may display the system 'menu', a list of headings representing the functions the computer has to offer. This is rather like a cabinet of office files. It is up to the user to choose the one he wishes to 'open' with a predetermined codeword, keystroke, or positioning of the cursor, the short flashing symbol that tells him where the next character will appear on the screen. Ideally, he should be able to switch forward and back between files or groups of files with as few key strokes as possible.

Every maker of a newsroom computer is bound to claim that not only does his system do everything and more than anyone else's, it is also 'user friendly' — computer jargon for simple to understand and operate. Unfortunately these claims are not always borne out, and the novice user may be faced with equipment that is badly designed or shoddily made and computer programs that either do not meet the exact needs of the operation or execute them so slowly as to make the whole exercise pointless. Speed is important.

Little is more irritating than to sit at a VDT, press the keys which activate the chosen function, and then have to wait and watch the cursor for half a minute or so until the screen display appears. But 'user friendliness' is probably the most crucial of all, because no system will pay its way if every operator has to keep referring to the maker's handbook for instructions before carrying out the most routine procedure.

Getting the best from the electronic newsroom

Possibly the biggest, most obvious advantage any electronic newsroom system has to offer is its capacity to store incoming news agency wire stories and to retrieve them at any time within seconds by a couple of key strokes. It is not unknown for national network news programmes to subscribe to a dozen international, domestic and sports wires. On a fairly average day the big agencies like Reuters, AP and UPI would probably file about 300 000 words between them over a 24-hour period, and not even the best ordered manual system can be expected to cope efficiently with that volume.

Other inconveniences attend conventional tape services. The banks of teleprinters, fairly noisy creatures en masse, have to be found homes at some convenient location where they can spew out all those words each day; people have to be employed to fuss over them and replenish them with new rolls of paper; pages have to be torn off at regular intervals for distribution, either to individual desks or to a central point for the editorial sorting procedure known as copytasting. No matter how diligent those doing it, the tedium of ploughing through that mountain of paper (sometimes double or triple ply) hour after hour leads inevitably to the occasional mislaid item, an end scarcely fitting for the modern technology which sped the words to their destination in the first place.

The trouble with copytasting, copytasters will grumble, is that it is akin to painting the Forth Bridge; as soon as the job is finished, it has to be started all over again. In this case another pile of copy thuds into the tray. So a method of feeding agency output direct into a computer's memory eases the problem considerably. Stories can be scanned quickly, without all that messy handling of newly printed paper (cotton gloves used to be copytasting standard issue at some offices), and as what is discarded is spiked electronically, it is therefore still available to be retrieved if necessary.

Ideally, the computer's storage system should be large enough to hold at least three or more whole days' agency output, and the entry of a name or subject will trigger off an automatic search for every reference over that entire period. The system is so powerful that a great deal of unwanted material will also be produced if keywords are vague or imprecise. Urgent or flash messages sent out by the agencies for really important news interrupt the normal flow, and appear on the screen, accompanied by a sharp beep or pinging tone as a warning. It is this facility, plus the rapid search and story 'call up' from memory to screen, which makes the modern copytaster's role in television news so much less of a chore, allowing him to concentrate more on exercising the editorial judgement for which he is chiefly employed.

Every writer, reporter or specialist handling a story can become his own copytaster. Instead of having to wait for copy to be delivered, he can set his own terminal to sort through the incoming agency material automatically for pre-selected subjects or categories which are routed directly to him, so making the whole process slicker, faster and more economical. The same applies to a wide range of other electronic options, notably script writing, which is undergoing a transformation in technique as a result of the computer. It's not unusual for the introduction of this feature, probably the second most important part of any programme to computerize, to be greeted with the strongest resistance. However progressive journalists like to say they are in their attitudes to society, they can be incredibly suspicious, stubborn and reactionary when it comes to changing their professional working habits. For every newsroom computer buff eager to try out the newest piece of shiny equipment on offer, there is sure to be at least one long-serving veteran who has been hammering out scripts for years on an ancient typewriter and is quite offended at the mere suggestion that something more up to date might be available.

There is, of course, no doubt that some people equate dexterity at a computer keyboard with the ability to solve the most obscure mathematical problems and need to be convinced that non-geniuses can cope. There are a few who never do get to grips with the minimal logic necessary for routine computer operation and quietly go away baffled. But for the most part, after a little persuasion and education (they go hand in hand) the die-hards and the faint-hearts are usually won over once they have been encouraged to find out for themselves how much extra power the electronic method gives them to do the job.

The range of systems on the market has led to such a wide degree of sophistication it is difficult to be specific about either editorial processes or the equipment in use for script creation. But in broad terms it means that instead of using typewriters or dictating to typists, writers at their keyboards select the script creation file from their menu to call up blank 'pages' on which they type their own stories.

Normal word-processing options come as standard. Corrections are made by over-typing, sections of text can be added, deleted or moved around the screen without difficulty. The most sophisticated systems allow the screen display to be split so that journalists are able to write their story on one half of the screen and read the latest news agency message on the other. A built-in dictionary may let writers check doubtful spellings as they go along. They may also be linked with electronic graphics or stills stores, and another keystroke turns words and accompanying production instructions into the proper script format for television, with technical details in the left hand column, text in the right.

As each script is completed, the author signs off with a code word which signals to the producer or whoever may be supervising programme material that it is available to be called up on his or her own screen for checking. Once the story has been called up and cleared, the supervisor keys in his approval for it to be electronically stored by the computer, ready for use on transmission. In that way not only is senior editorial control maintained as usual, step by step progress towards compilation of the whole programme is monitored at the same time. Access to this procedure is sensibly limited so that while all users can 'read' a story simultaneously only one can 'edit' it.

Once the script has been passed at senior editorial level it is held in the computer's memory for use later. Rough paper copies may be obtained for convenience at almost any stage using printers linked with groups of terminals. (Every terminal in the system I first operated had an integral printer able to produce thin paper copies from a roll fixed in the top section of the machine.) In some cases these paper copies are of a high enough quality to be used by the technical team concerned with the transmission of the programme. More often the computer is also interfaced with a separate high speed printer which churns out the completed scripts as hard copies, collating them automatically into the correct order. The day may come when all news production staff and presenters will be prepared to forego paper altogether and to take instructions and read scripts direct from the screen, but there is something reassuring about having printed sheets to hold in the hand, and it is likely to take a long time, as well as the development of fail-proof equipment, to change the habits and superstitions formed over many years.

Some presenters have moved part of the way by reading the lettering generated electronically by the computer's studio prompting device. The preferred display size and colour — white on a black background or vice versa — and the speed at which the lettering is made to move can be altered to suit the reader. Important words can be highlighted. The biggest advantage of computerized prompting is that changes made on master scripts back in the newsroom appear in front of the reader automatically. Most presenters, though, seem to prefer any electronic methods to be backed up by old-fashioned paper scripts, just in case things go wrong.

The computerized running order

It is not only that the use of a computer helps remove the drudgery from compiling long and complicated running orders. Electronics really come into their own when changes have to be made as transmission time approaches. Unless a very efficient chain of command exists, it is often extremely difficult for everyone concerned in the production of a news programme to keep track of important alterations as new stories are added, existing ones grow, contract, are moved up and down the order, or are dropped from the programme altogether.

Every news organization has its own method of constructing its running orders, most probably born out of years of established tradition. They are local, individual and highly idiosyncratic, yet no one minds so long as the routine continues to function efficiently. In some systems, every story keeps the number it is first allocated even if its position in the running order is changed. In others, consecutive numbering is preserved at all costs as it is thought to be essential to the avoidance of any possible confusion on air. This is all very well when there is plenty of time. Changes are just as likely to be made close to transmission and beyond, and those responsible for overseeing them come under extreme pressure. The frequent result is uncertainty, lost tempers and production errors which show up on the screen.

The beauty of the computer system is that changes from the smallest detail to the wholesale re-casting of a programme can be considered, entered and previewed at leisure, then executed in a twinkling. The new running order is then immediately available to everybody who is in sight of a VDT, at once. Story numbers can then be switched or left as they are, according to professional taste. As long as the computer is programmed to tell the master printer the chosen final order, scripts will be printed out in the correct sequence, and will be followed automatically by the electronic prompter.

Programme timing, too, becomes much simpler. The computer not only calculates the time taken by each script in the running order, it adds it to the overall duration, remembering to adjust when new stories are put in and others are dropped.

Terminals in the studio control room remove the guesswork and arithmetical contortions from transmission. As the broadcast progresses, the computer takes account of those items which have gone and those which remain to be transmitted, making minor adjustments to ensure that the programme ends on time a simple matter for the editorial and production staff. In the future, perhaps studio directors will find themselves using the gallery-based terminals to key in production commands on air.

For now, the other big users of the computer are the assignments desks. Details of diary events, and forthcoming coverage are entered by news intake staff and stored for retrieval by producers, reporters and camera crews when they come on duty. In the field, note-book sized word-processors are available for reporters to write scripts and transmit them to base over the telephone. Terminals installed permanently in out-stations including overseas bureaux also link to the main system, and where necessary they are shipped in for the duration of big set piece stories. In all cases, programme editors are able to use their own terminals to follow the progress of stories, helping to reduce some of the tensions which accompany decisions over running orders.

Elsewhere in news, the computer can be used to communicate with other departments, conduct rapid 'global' or selective searches of archives holding large volumes of wire copy, picture and script details, help the administration of staff rosters, payments, and the indexing of names of contacts. The list goes on.

If it goes wrong

Once they have learnt to conquer the early fear of losing everything they have written by carelessly pressing the wrong key, new users of a computer system start to worry about what happens if the whole thing goes wrong, and the computer 'crashes'. Most systems consist of several computers linked together rather than one giant piece of equipment, so if individual units do fail for some reason only localized parts of the system are affected. Installers are usually well aware of the need for an urgent response to equipment failure, and if they do not maintain support staff on duty they will almost certainly have a service agreement under which repair or replacement of faulty parts is guaranteed within a specified time.

The installers are usually also responsible for a computer training programme, at least until they have made sure that there are enough experts on the buyer's staff.

As with other areas of modern technology, newsroom computer systems are advancing all the time, and 'user' organizations have been set up to ensure that those who have bought them are kept up to date and able to upgrade them as new software or hardware becomes available.

A word of caution is necessary. Computers have begun to make an important contribution to the quality and efficiency of television news programmes, and are likely to become commonplace over the next few years. But the keyboard and screen, however much journalists may learn to depend on them, must never be allowed to take the place of normal, human contacts between colleagues. The computer is a tool, like any other. The enthusiasts must make sure that the computer serves them, not the other way round.

Videotex

The history of television broadcasting is landmarked with the exploits of those who have made special contributions towards the creation and refinement of the most influential method of mass communication since the printing press was invented. Between them, in little more than 60 years, they have inspired television to develop from the days when Londoners marvelled at their first sight of Baird's crude, 30-line images, mechnically generated, to an age where colour, videotape recording, outside broadcasting, picture standards conversion, satellite communications, computer graphics and the rest have become accepted as a logical outcome of the unending desire for progress.

Not all this growth could have taken place without the developments which were continuing steadily in electronics and other associated industries at the same time. What has changed the face of television over the past ten years or so has been an unprecedented acceleration of that technological innovation, and few people who have experienced at first hand the extent to which every area of programme making has been affected are likely to believe that the revolution is complete.

Conventional programming has already been touched and the stranglehold of the network schedulers broken for ever because one effect of the revolution has been that other uses have been found for the television screen. Home video owners 'time-shift', i.e. record programmes off air for viewing at times which suit themselves and no-one else, sometimes succumbing, no doubt, to the temptation to 'fast forward' through the commercials. (They don't even have to be around to make the recordings, because the machines can be programmed to do it for them.) Microcomputer users may employ their screens for writing programs or playing games instead of watching the news or *Dallas*.

The other main option is to use the screen to display 'written' text. The first system of this type to be introduced was *Videotex*, the generic name given to the distribution of information as text from central computers to remote screens including television. The broadcast version is known as *Teletext*, the official birth of which was announced in Britain in October 1972. It has since been developed jointly by the BBC and IBA engineers to a world standard which is broadcast in most western European countries, Australia, New Zealand, Singapore, Malaysia and parts of the United States.

The beauty of teletext is its simplicity and economy. A television picture is made up of a number of horizontal lines which appear on the screen in rapid succession. No television system needs every one of those lines for carrying picture signals, and it is in a handful of the unused, blank black spaces that teletext is transmitted simultaneously with the normal programme as a series of coded electronic pulses. These can be seen as bright dots at the top of a badly adjusted television picture. The coded information is translated into text by a decoder built into the receiving set, invariably as an optional extra.

On the screen, teletext is displayed as still pages of writing and graphic diagrams, either in place of, or superimposed on, the normal picture. Coloured headings and text, which can be made to flash for emphasis, add attraction to screen layout. Current practice is to string those pages together in the shape of 'magazines' made up of news, sport, finance, travel and weather information and so on, the viewer (reader?) selecting the required numbered page using a small, remote-controlled keypad.

Each page (and there may be several hundred in a 'magazine') is transmitted in quick succession in a continuous electronic loop. Immediately a selection has been made, the teletext receiver searches the transmitted signals until they match the page ordered by the viewer and then displays it on the screen. A full magazine is broadcast every 12 seconds or so, and the maximum average time it takes for a chosen page to appear is about seven seconds; the more blank lines used, the faster the response or the greater number of pages possible.

Once it is displayed the page remains in place until a new one is selected. Because a single teletext page has limited space (it varies, but is probably no more than 24 rows of 40 characters and spaces), longer features calling for more than one full screen can be linked together in multi-page sequences which are programmed to change automatically after a set interval. In this way the day's main news, for example, can be presented over several pages without the need for any more selection. The sequence is repeated from beginning to end until a new page number is punched into the keypad.

Two full-scale teletext services have been operating in Britain since the mid seventies: *Ceefax* (See-facts) by the BBC and *ORACLE* (Optional Reception of Announcements by Coded Line Electronics) by Independent Television. By 1986, roughly 3 million homes (about 14 per cent of the households in Britain) owned or rented teletext-equipped sets, with the projection that the number would continue to grow by about 700 000 a year.

TELETEXT

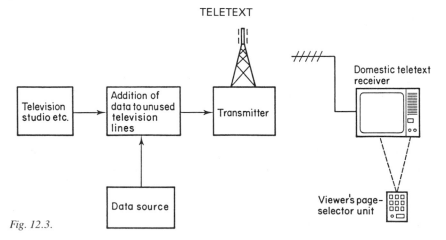

Fig. 12.3.

Teletext news services

A strong news content is an essential ingredient of all teletext services and is usually spread over many pages of a magazine. These tend to be allocated the same numbers every day to encourage regular viewers to go straight to them without the need to consult the general indexes, which are usually very comprehensive. All four British channels offer viewers a choice from news headlines or longer background pieces. There is also a 'newsflash' facility which can be chosen as a separate page and appears in a black background box cut into the conventional programme picture.

The pages are compiled by journalists using all the sources available to other broadcasters and the newspapers. Copy is typed in at computer keyboards for conversion into the teletext signals. The speed of the system allows stories to be transmitted as quickly as they can be created or revised. Oracle says it makes at least a thousand editorial changes a day to its news, sport and business sections alone, and in the 1983 general election updated the results every 20 seconds during the peak period of midnight to 2 a.m. As it is possible to put in material from any number of centres, pages can easily be devoted to purely local or regional news. Writers may also be expected to 'draw' in the simpler graphics.

One of the other main benefits of teletext is its ability to bring information to viewers with impaired sight or hearing. Double standard height teletext characters can be displayed for those with poor sight, and

Fig. 12.4. Teletext — broadcast videotex — makes use of 'spare' lines in the conventional television picture to display text. News is an important part of most services. (*ORACLE*)

either the top or bottom half of a page can be enlarged to cover the whole screen. Sub-titles, ideal for the translation of foreign language films or programmes, can also be added to the picture for those who are deaf or hard of hearing. But this represents a huge commitment by the teletext services. Estimates are that it takes one person a whole week to prepare one hour of sub-titles, so in general they are applied only to pre-recorded programmes. Experiments are continuing apace in several countries with various methods of live sub-titling, which would be a tremendous help to those who are unable to enjoy news programmes with any comfort because of their disability, and the current rate of progress suggests that teletext journalists will work alongside their colleagues in the same television newsrooms, 'translating' the news as it is transmitted.

Other teletext developments include the broadcasting of computer programs — *telesoftware*. The broadcasts are aimed at owners of microcomputers who have bought adaptors able to pick up the programs as they are transmitted. These can then be stored on cassette or disk for later use.

The sophistication of teletext is now at a stage known as Level One. By Level Five the system could be pushing the decoder circuits within the receiver into creating screen images of a much higher quality and better definition than can be achieved with a television camera. The implications for news are obvious.

Another, non-technical, way forward is the provision of specialized information in parallel with present broadcast teletext, restricting access to those who pay for it, perhaps down to individual receivers.

Fig. 12.5. Teletext 'newsflash' facility allows up to date information to be added to the bottom of a conventional programme picture. (*ORACLE*)

Other possibilities exist, because teletext is versatile enough to be carried as a radio signal or by wire as well as during the transmission of television programmes.

A form of non-broadcast videotex which offers a fully personalized service is *Viewdata*. This system, first available to the public in Britain in 1979, enables subscribers to call up information for display on a television or computer screen by using a keypad which links them to computer data banks over a telephone line. Connection with the system takes the user first into a comprehensive index from which the choice of service is made.

Prestel, the British Telecom Viewdata system, makes the information available through independent specialist suppliers known as *Information Providers*. The range and depth of material is growing all the time, but the vast amount of material that can be tapped already runs into hundreds of thousands of pages, with access to information held by international computers available in exactly the same way. It has the extra facility of being a two-way system, so message-exchanging with other users, electronic banking, shopping for goods and services can be carried out. 'Tele-betting', particularly on horse-racing or other sporting events linked to live television transmission, has also proved popular. General and specialized news, including sport and finance, is compiled by journalists working for the information providers as part of the service.

Payment is necessary to view some pages, but apart from standing charges and the cost of the telephone call, much of the service is free.

Cable and satellite

It is already clear that cable and satellite television represent something potentially new and exciting in television journalism, even though they seem to pose an even greater threat to conventional programming.

The future development of the two systems appears to be largely interlinked, because much of what is transmitted and received by satellite is ultimately distributed by cable. *DBS* (Direct Broadcasting by Satellite) which enables programmes to be beamed directly into the home via small dish receivers is, at time of writing, on the verge of being introduced in several countries, but it will probably be well into the nineties before any proper assessment of it can be made.

Cable television, also known as *CATV* (Community Antenna Television), was developed in the late forties for areas which were unable to receive television signals because of geographical difficulties or their distance from transmitters. To overcome these problems, antennas were set up in areas which had good reception, and the broadcast signals were distributed over coaxial cable to subscribers. In 1950, only 14 000 homes in the United States were being served by cable; the Federal Communications Commission calculates that the figure had reached more than 34 million by the beginning of 1984. Belgium, Holland and Switzerland in particular are also heavily cabled, and one projection[1] for western Europe is that by 1995

[1]*CATV Growth Projections, Western Europe* (Communications & Information Technology (CIT) Research Ltd., 1985).

more than 21 million or 16.6 per cent of the 130 million homes will be linked for cable, about 13 million of them on advanced systems offering two-way transmission for viewers to participate in television events from their own homes (voting in talent shows, for example) and giving, like videotex, access to electronic shopping and services.

In Britain, as a result of legislation to allow a much more general expansion of cable, a new Cable Authority has been set up. It has been given power to award franchises, supervise programme services and promote development. Pilot projects have already been introduced, joining some of the original cable operators who have been concentrating up until now on relaying existing broadcast services to improve reception quality. Since 1981, seven cable operators have been providing subscription tv in 13 areas as an experiment.

The development of cable might not have been so important had it been limited to the transmission of only a handful of existing programme channels. But its technical capacity — enhanced by optical (glass) fibres, one of which, though finer than a human hair, can carry two colour television programmes or 2000 simultaneous telephone conversations — means that dozens of channels can be made available, offering not only existing broadcast services but paving the way for the origination of new ones bringing specialist forms of information and entertainment to an extent previously unknown. New cable services have sprung up everywhere, their titles usually giving a clear idea of what they provide, *Disney, Home Box Office, Playboy Channel, The Movie Channel, Screen Sport, Sky, Life Style, The Children's Channel, Premiere* to name only a few. Some have their signals 'scrambled' (encoded) to ensure that their offerings will be seen only by those who pay for them.

By far the most intriguing development for television journalism has been the introduction of two 24-hour all-news channels set up by the American businessman Ted Turner, and based at the headquarters of the Turner Broadcasting System in Atlanta, Georgia. He employs a staff of several hundred, including *Video-Journalists*, who are given their first experience in television.

Cable News Network (CNN) began broadcasting on June 1, 1980 and now reaches more than 32 million American households with its daily mix of news and interviews. Regular coverage includes national and international matters, sport, weather, business, entertainment and technology, usually structured as separate programmes, but the network is also able to devote hours to particular events. In 1984 it carried more than 35 hours' live coverage of a criminal court case in Massachusetts. To complement CNN's news channel, *Headline News* ('Around the World, Around the Clock') was launched in December 1981. Each half hour is split into four segments, the last of which other cable systems are at liberty to replace with their own locally produced headlines.

CNN has reached beyond its national boundaries to more than 20 countries including Japan, where its reports are translated into Japanese, and plans to distribute the service to members of the European Broadcasting Union were announced in 1985.

A possible British-based operation may come in the shape of the *World News Network* being considered by Visnews, the international agency, as a

European news channel, and a truly multi-national newsroom could be the result. To ensure that viewers of different nationalities received equal treatment, the news would have to be voiced over in several languages simultaneously, and there would be no studio presenters, the visual identity of the service being created by computer graphics. The format of a pilot programme suggests that WNN might be similar to CNN's *Headline News*, with an updated rolling half hour of international news, business, sport and so on, segmented so that cable operators would be able to put in their own local news or commercials. Other all-news channels are sure to follow, making use of the communications satellites which have contributed to the expansion of cable.

Before satellites began to be introduced in the sixties, broadcast services in countries with widespread populations had to rely on a combination of land lines and chains of microwave links to reach the bulk of their domestic audiences. Recorded programmes, supplied on film or videotape as air-freight, were inevitably subject to occasional delay or misdirection. As the global satellite communications system began to develop, improving technology helped bring down the cost of building earth stations to receive the signals, changing the situation completely. All types of programmes including news were transmitted by networks booking time on established international 'birds' or on the domestic satellites which were beginning to be placed in orbit, while cable operators found it commercially worthwhile to distribute their product in the same way.

CNN, for example, now transmits its services 22 300 miles into space from dish-shaped antennas in the grounds of its Atlanta headquarters to a satellite which sends the signals back to domestic and international customers on earth. Incoming feeds from overseas bureaux are received similarly.

Years earlier, the upsurge in satellite use was responsible for an unexpected by-product. In 1976 a handful of television addicts, do-it-yourself experts, dabblers in electronics or those who were combinations of all three, started to build small systems good enough to track the satellites and intercept the programmes for viewing in their own homes. Part of the enjoyment lay in being able to watch live, unedited, advertising-free broadcasts made to sister stations for recording and later use, and to eavesdrop on rehearsals which were frequently more entertaining than the programmes.

Soon the 'Backyard Earth-Station' movement grew from a hobby into a cult. Within the next couple of years, home TVRO (Television Receive Only) had spawned satellite equipment shops, specialist publications and the other trimmings associated with a fast-growing industry, especially in the United States, where it is reckoned that up to 1½ million people own dishes able to tune in to an almost unlimited range of transmissions being beamed to consumers all over the world. The legality of individuals to own and use earth stations was confirmed in America in 1984.

The proliferation of home earth stations also had much to do with the small size and falling cost of the receiving dishes. In this, they had something in common with an international movement towards the construction of new services which came under the umbrella of Direct Broadcasting by Satellite (DBS). The idea, which has been around for

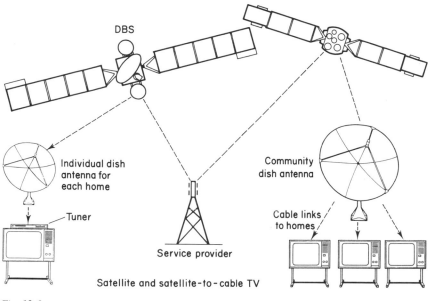

DBS

Individual dish
antenna for
each home

Tuner

Community
dish antenna

Cable links
to homes

Service provider

Satellite and satellite-to-cable TV

Fig. 12.6.

about 20 years, is to meet a world of changing public demand by supplementing existing channels with services received directly by individual households on dishes probably less than a metre in diameter, the signal being transmitted first to new, high powered satellites (see Fig. 12.6), on the principle that the more powerful the satellite signal the smaller the dish, so environmental objections would be reduced. Like cable, DBS offers the promise of infinite variety. It is capable of bringing specialist or minority-interest programmes, educational and other material within the reach of otherwise uneconomical small audiences. It can also carry radio services, data and the 1000-plus line high-definition television pictures which will offer better sound and vision on a wider screen.

In 1977, a formal plan to introduce such a system was drawn up at a World Administrative Radio Conference in Switzerland.

Countries were allocated frequencies and locations in space to establish national television system satellites whose *footprints* (areas covered by the transmission) would interfere as little as possible with their neighbours. Despite initial enthusiasm, progress towards this goal has been beset by many problems, mainly political and financial, and it seems likely that exactly ten years will have elapsed between 'WARC', and the inauguration of the first European DBS services by West Germany and France.

The European Space Agency's own first-generation DBS satellite is not due to be launched until 1987–88, so when the European Broadcasting Union began a fledgling pan-European channel in the autumn of 1985 it used a Dutch transponder on an existing European Communications Satellite, *ECS-1*. The intention was to switch the service directly to homes as soon as the new satellite became available. *Europa Television* was established by a five-nation consortium to complement existing broadcasting systems in Europe. Plans included a nightly, multi-lingual *Europa*

Television News (ETN) bulletin, but the whole project ran into financial difficulties and stopped transmission after a year, though attempts were made to revive it.

An uncertain fate also seemed to be awaiting British DBS when early proposals for a service run by the BBC, the 15 ITV companies and five non-broadcasting organizations came to nothing, chiefly because of the cost of the UNISAT satellites preferred by the Government. Then the Independent Broadcasting Authority offered a 15-year franchise for a privately-financed system, awarding it in December 1986 to the British Satellite Broadcasting (BSB) consortium. Their plans, due to come to fruition in 1990, include a big editorial contribution from ITN towards *NOW*, a 24-hour service of news and events making up one of four channels.

ITN had already committed itself to a weekday news half-hour on the *Super Channel* (largely a mix of ITV and BBC programmes), which was set to begin operating a service to European cable systems via the ECS-1 satellite from early 1987.

As the eighties began to draw to a close the possibility that an international television news programme could be delivered regularly to a world audience – either independently or as services contracted to operators of DBS or satellite-to-cable systems — was under serious consideration in several countries, including the United States and Canada. In Britain the BBC drew up a plan to combine the expertise of their television news department with that of their much-respected External Services, operators of an existing radio news service which attracted 120 million listeners world-wide. A journalistic team was set up to produce pilot programmes, and it awaited only a favourable decision on funding for the project to become reality.

However the problems these advances bring with them are finally resolved, the years to the end of the century promise to give the young profession of television journalism its severest test. The editorial flexibility which has been able to meet every past technical innovation (whether or not the impetus for change has come from the journalists) may have to be stretched to new limits if future audiences are so bombarded with choice the bed-rock of scheduled programming is eventually undermined. In an age of cable and satellite channels transmitting 24-hour services of general and specialized news, the concept of the fixed-slot, half-hour network news programme as all things to all viewers will become as out-dated as radio announcers in dinner jackets.

13

Conclusion

The whole emphasis of this book has deliberately been on method, not motive. Although it might have been tempting to suggest *how* individual news services should perceive their role in society, and in particular how they should approach the hyper-sensitive areas of news selection and process, it would be wrong to have done so and naive to believe that it would make any difference in any case. Why a programme chooses to operate the way it does is a matter between those editorially responsible for it and their viewing public. Each news organization is guided by its own set of principles, most of which have their origins in the political and social ethos of the country in which it is broadcasting. Editorial values are therefore inevitably going to differ, and because increasingly large number of broadcasting organizations are owned by governments, it follows that what passes for news in one country will not necessarily match the concept of what passes for news in another. For every journalist struggling towards the goal of 'balanced objectivity', there are others for whom such niceties are of no concern. To put it another way, one man's objective report revealing government incompetence is another's betrayal of the society which succours him.

One experienced western journalist, seconded as news adviser to the television station of a Middle East kingdom, remembers the frustration of being quite unable to persuade those in charge that their news judgement was at fault because they insisted on beginning every main bulletin with the filmed official activities of the king, following by the filmed official activities of the queen, then the crown prince, and so on right the way through the royal household, the coverage being of a duration which diminished in accordance with position. All this was followed by speeches by the prime minister and the activities of other government ministers.

Domestic news came next, most of it of stunning triviality. Then came foreign news, led by equally trivial events about countries considered friendly to the regime. Only after that, with about two-thirds of the programme gone, was space given to what the adviser recognized as 'real' news, regardless of its importance. The fact that while he was there, Neil Armstrong was taking man's first steps on the moon, made no difference to the rigid pattern.

Later during the adviser's stay, a revolution took place. The monarchy was overthrown and exiled, a republic proclaimed. The editors of the news responded at once. From then on, every bulletin began with the filmed official activities of the president of the revolutionary council, then the filmed official activities of each council member in turn. Domestic news came next, in much the same way as before, followed by foreign news about countries which were considered friendly towards the new leadership. Former allies, together with the royal family, were completely ignored. The journalists made no protest. They merely carried on doing what they saw was their duty, serving the interests of the state. The fact that the circumstances had changed so drastically made no difference to their attitude.

My own experience, some years later, was of a political assassination which aroused immense interest and concern elsewhere in the world, but which rated no more than a brief mention by the television news service I had been asked to advise. Later discussion about the treatment of the story got nowhere; the editors were unconvinced that their decision was wrong in any way, because they preferred to devote air time to reporting matters which they considered more relevant to *their* audience. Who is to say they were mistaken?

It is no business of anyone else if television news in the socialist countries continues to be 'politically involved information services'.

The foremost aim is the 'reliable presentation of news items dealing with topical events and exerting a definite influence upon public opinion. Therefore they do not seek sensation; crimes, disasters, accidents and scandals do not predominate. Such events cannot push aside news items of interest to the majority of viewers. The presentation of acts of violence is very limited.'

On the other hand, television news broadcasts 'do try to portray social processes and the development of the socialist society. The processes of socialist integration constitute a major subject of reporting, too. Moreover events reflecting the fight and struggle for freedom, peace and social progress all over the world are themes occurring very often.'

Editors are well aware that their output is a public commentary. 'They know that it is impossible to present news broadcasts without influencing the audience . . . often the mere inclusion of a particular item in the news service, or its omission, already constitutes a commentary.'[1]

There is nothing to suggest that the change of style apparent with the arrival of a PR-conscious leader in Mr Gorbachev heralds a move towards more westernized news values on the part of *Vremya*, Moscow's equivalent of the *Nine o'clock News*, especially as 150 million Soviet citizens are said to take from it their nightly view of the world.

To other eyes, such television news would come under the category of propaganda, and probably dull propaganda at that. One British television journalist, after a visit to China, described how he could not get used to the idea of watching the main news programme on Peking television end with brief sequences or headlines of the news to be seen the *next* night.

But how much worse is that than the triviality and commercialism which

[1]Waclaw Wygledowski, head of IVN, *EBU Review* (May 1975).

surrounds news in other parts of the world? American television news people refer happily to their programmes as 'products' or 'shows', as though they were no different from other forms of entertainment, or talk about 'delivering an audience to the advertisers'.

Given that climate, it is probably unsurprising that a now-defunct American television news programme was forbidden by its cigarette company sponsors to include any shots of 'no smoking' signs and allowed only Winston Churchill to be seen smoking a cigar; or that a Caribbean newsreader regularly interrupted his own serious newscast to extol the virtue of some household product or other before resuming the catalogue of death and destruction, all without any 'ruling off' to tell the viewer where the selling began and ended.

Despite the vast improvement in communications which has made possible greater coverage of foreign stories (mostly when disaster strikes), parochialism still abounds in television news. More than ever it has become a matter of attitude, not technical limitation. As Pierre Brunel-Lantanac of the EBU once put it:

'. . . such is man's nature that a trivial incident occurring on his own doorstep sometimes involves him more deeply than an event of fundamental human significance on the other side of the globe that, without his realizing it, will affect the future of mankind.'[2]

For that reason every day, consciously or not, programme editors are applying 'McLurg's Law', named after a senior television news journalist, which says that the death of, or injury to, one person from your own country is, in terms of news value, equal to the deaths of or injuries to very much larger numbers of foreigners, depending on how far away they live; especially if there are no pictures.

On the surface, the biggest threat to the freedom of television journalists will continue to come from those who would seek to control them for their own ends. That external threat has always been present, though perhaps not so openly. No one now need have any doubt that it exists. What has not been so apparent has been the danger which comes from the journalists' own limitations.

The speed of ENG and satellite communications, for example, has at times already threatened to overwhelm the news judgements of those who have prided themselves on being editorially independent. Editors need to stand back from the fray if they are to exercise the delicate control necessary to produce programmes which are as cool, balanced, thoughtful and sensible as the constraints of daily news-gathering and presentation allow. How far 'personalized' news contributes towards that achievement will be impossible to judge until the pendulum swings back the other way.

The arguments have been raging since television news began to take its place among the great influences of society. No doubt they will continue as long as it exists in its present form. For the reporters, writers, picture editors and studio directors trapped in the middle, too wrapped up in their own work to be able to concentrate for long on such matters of great principle, there remains one crumb of comfort. Whatever developments

[2]*EBU Review* (May 1975).

may take place in television, news need have no fear of the future. One sentence from *The Task of Broadcasting News*[3], a study for the BBC General Advisory Council, says it all:

'If ever broadcasting were pared to the proverbial bone, news would have to be that bone.'

[3]BBC, May 1976.

Glossary

No editorial and production glossary can ever hope to be complete or wholly satisfy the expert, especially now that computers have begun to find their way into television newsrooms. Some terms are universally understood within television news, others mean different things to different services, still more remain unique to those who apply them. In a few areas, equipment and the process of using it is known by its trade name. The definitions listed here are those I have come across personally and are, I believe, among the most widely used and generally accepted. In deference to some of my older colleagues I have included a number which refer to the television eras nostalgically known as *BE* (Before ENG) and *BEG* (Before Electronic Graphics).

ABC (1) American Broadcasting Company; (2) Australian Broadcasting Company.
Access time Interval between the selection of a computer function and its appearance on the screen.
Actuality Real. See *Natural sound*.
Agency tape Written material received on news agency teleprinters. Also known as *wire copy*.
Ampex Pioneers of videotape recording apparatus. Still sometimes used as a generic term for all videotape equipment.
Anchorman/woman/person Main presenter of a programme. See also *Newcaster*, *Newsreader*, *Presenter*.
Animation As used in television news, usually the technique of adding or changing information on a caption. Before electronic graphics, this was done manually with flaps, tabs or panels moved at the appropriate moment during transmission.
AP Associated Press, an American news agency.
Arriflex West German film camera. 16 mm sound and silent versions were very popular for TV news work BE.
ASBU Arab States Broadcasting Union.
Assignment sheet Written instructions from assignments editor/manager or other member of news-gathering department setting out details of an event to be covered.
Aston Makers of caption generating and other electronics equipment.
Autocue Trade name. Field and studio prompting device which enables performers to read from a written or electronically generated script while looking directly to the camera. Other makes include *Portaprompt* and *Teleprompter*.
BASIC Computer language; short for Beginner's All-purpose Symbolic Instruction Code.
Basys (Broadcast Automation Systems.) Makers of *Newsfury* newsroom computer system.
B & W Black and white.
BBC British Broadcasting Corporation.
BE Before ENG.
BEG Before Electronic Graphics.
Betacam Half-inch video format system introduced by Sony.
Betacart Carousel system for the transmission of Beta video cassettes.
Bird Communications satellite. So named after *Early Bird*, the first satellite launched after

the creation of *Intelsat*, the organization set up to establish a global system; hence *birding* for the process of transmitting material by satellite.

Brightstar Dedicated satellite system linking the United States and the United Kingdom.

Cable Authority Organization responsible for awarding franchises and supervising cable programme services in Britain.

Camcorder Combined lightweight videocamera and recorder.

Cans Earphones.

Caption Generic term for television news artwork; also *graphics*.

Caption scanner (slide chain) Form of fixed electronic camera for transmitting captions; an alternative to photographing them from pin-boards or stands in a studio.

Cassette See *Videocassette*.

CATV (Community Antenna Television). System of distributing broadcast services by cable.

CBS Columbia Broadcasting System, a US network.

Ceefax (See Facts). BBC broadcast teletext system.

Cel Transparent plastic sheet by which extra information can be added to existing artwork without permanently altering the original (e.g. new locations on a stock map); now largely out-dated with the introduction of electronic graphics systems.

Character generator Electronic method of producing on-screen lettering in a variety of type sizes and faces.

Chip Integrated computer circuit.

Clarke belt Position 22 300 miles above the equator in which orbiting communications satellites appear to be stationary; after British science writer Arthur C. Clarke who first advocated the use of satellites for broadcasting.

Clean feed Actuality (natural) sound of an event free from commentary.

Closed circuit A programme distributed privately to selected points but not broadcast (e.g. an outside broadcast recorded for later transmission).

CNN Cable News Network, an all-news channel based in Atlanta, Georgia.

Commag Combined magnetic system (BE) for recording sound on to a magnetic stripe bonded to one edge of film during manufacture; also known as *single system* sound recording; now rare in television news.

Communications satellite Man-made device positioned in space as a means of 'bouncing' television or other signals from one part of the globe to another. See also *Intelsat*.

Comsat Communications Satellite Corporation (US).

Control room/gallery Room next to or above the studio, from which production and technical operations are controlled during transmission of programmes.

Copy Written material for news.

Copytaster Journalist responsible for the first assessment of all incoming copy, especially that from news agency sources.

Correspondent Journalist employed to concentrate on a specialist subject or report from a particular geographical location.

Count down Time given in reverse order, usually spoken aloud in the control room and given by hand-signal in the studio, to ensure the smooth transition from one source to the next; mostly used in sequences between ten and zero.

CPU Central Processing Unit; the computer's 'brain'.

CSO Colour Separation Overlay; also known as *Chromakey*. An electronic means of merging pictures from separate sources, giving the illusion, for example, that a performer in the studio is set against a pictorial background.

CU Close-up.

Cue Signal given to start or stop action.

Cue dot Small circular mark made on an edited film, usually in the top right-hand corner, to indicate that it is coming to an end. Electronic cue dots are usually superimposed in the top left-hand corner to indicate the approaching end of one programme and to cue in the next.

Cut (1) An edit; (2) A deletion.

Cut-away Editing term for a shot inserted as a means of telescoping the action in a picture sequence without the loss of continuity.

Cut-away/in questions Questions repeated for the camera after interview to provide a continuity bridge between edited sections.

Cut-ins Extra shots, close-ups for example, which are edited into the main action of a scene.

Cutting/clipping Item cut or copied from a newspaper or other printed source.

Cut-off Area of a television picture naturally lost from the domestic screen.

Cuts Also known as trims or out-takes; pictures excluded from the edited story.

Cut story Complete and edited news picture item.

Database File of information held by computer; usually large and comprehensive.

DBS Direct Broadcasting by Satellite. System of transmitting broadcast signals to individual households using high-powered satellites.

Deaf aid Close-fitting earpiece through which a performer in the studio or in the field can be given instructions by editorial/production staff.

Diary story News event covered by pre-arrangement.

Dish Shaped antenna for receiving satellite signals.

Disk Electronic storage system for recording computer information.

Door-stepper Informal interview obtained by waiting for the subject 'on the doorstep'.

Dope-sheet Cameraman's detailed record of tape or film shot on location.

Double system (of recording sound on film). See *Sepmag*.

Dry run Rehearsal without the camera.

Dub To add or re-record sound to edited pictures.

Duration Exact time length of a programme or item within it.

EBU European Broadcasting Union.

Editor Executive in overall charge of a single news programme. *Editor for/of the day* is operationally responsible for the output of an entire television news service on one day. See also *Producer*.

ENG Electronic News Gathering. Lightweight video camera and sound recording system which has superseded news film; also known as EJ (Electronic Journalism).

ENS Electronic Newsroom System. Method of producing television news programmes with computers.

Establishing shot Scene-setting shot of people or subject.

Eurovision European international network for the exchange of television programmes.

Eurovision News Exchange (EVN) Thrice-daily exchange of news pictures through Eurovision links.

EUTELSAT European Telecommunications Satellite Organization.

Eyeline The direction in which the subject is seen to be looking by the camera.

FCC Federal Communications Commission, the US government agency responsible for broadcasting.

Field producer Editorial supervisor of off-base assignment. See also *Fixer*.

File Send a report.

File footage Archive/library material.

Fire brigade/fireman Editorial/camera team assigned at short notice to cover news breaks, usually abroad.

Fixer Co-ordinator accompanying units in the field. Often acts as the main point of contact between home base and teams on location.

Follow-up News report based on previously broadcast or published material.

Footprint Area covered by satellite transmission.

Format (1) Overall style and 'look' of a programme; (2) Videotape size or recording pattern.

Frame A single still picture from a moving film or tape. There are 25 film frames to the second in British television, 24 in the United States.

Frame/picture store Electronic method of storing and displaying still pictures.

Free puff News item which publicizes an event or product.

Freeze frame A single frame of videotape or film held to stop the action.

Futures file Collection of information about items for possible future news coverage.

FX Sound effects.

Gallery See *Control room*.

Geostationary Orbit in which satellites appear to remain in the same place relative to the Earth. See *Clarke belt*.

Graphics General name for artwork or artwork department.

Gun mike See *Rifle mike*.

GV General View.

Handback Performer's form of words used to signal the end of his/her contribution.

Hand-carried Equipment or material transported personally rather than sent as freight. See also *Pigeon*.

Hand-held Camera or other equipment used without a tripod or similar steadying device.

Handout Free publicity material given to news organization.

Hand-over Performer's form of words used by a newsreader, presenter, etc. as a cue for another performer (e.g. 'Now, with the sports news . . .').

Hard news 'Straight' news.

Hardware Computer machinery.

HDTV High-definition television. System of 1000+ lines offering superior quality pictures and sound.

Helical scan System which scans videotape in slanting tracks.

Herogram Effusively worded message of congratulations from base to contributor.

Hot-press machine (BEG) Device for applying selected type faces to caption cards by heat process.

In-cue Opening words of a news report.

Intake/input Department responsible for news-gathering. See also *Assignments desk.*

Intelsat International Telecommunications Satellite Organization. Originators of the global system by which television pictures, telephone calls and other signals are beamed from one country to others. See *Communications satellites.*

Intervision Eastern bloc counterpart of *Eurovision.*

Inject 'Live' contribution to a news programme from a distant source.

Intro Introduction; opening sentence of a news story.

Instant lettering (BEG) The sheets of rub-on lettering used in non-electronic artwork.

In vision/on camera (story) Item or part item read by performer in studio without further illustration.

ITN Independent Television News. Company responsible for providing national news for Independent Television in Britain.

IVN Intervision News Exchange.

Jump cut An edit which destroys pictorial continuity by making a subject appear to jump from one position to another in consecutive shots.

K Kilobyte. Measurement of computer memory.

Keying colour Colour chosen to activate *CSO.*

Key light Chief source of artificial light for a camera scene.

Key shot Master shot.

Lay-on Arrange coverage.

Lead (1) Opening item of a news programme; (2) Opening sentence of a story, usually written for presenter.

Lead in See *Intro.*

Leader Portion of tape which precedes the first frame of picture; usually calibrated in seconds to aid *count down.*

Library material/tape See *File footage.*

Line Telecommunication circuit between transmitting and receiving points.

Line-up Period immediately before a recording or programme transmission during which the final technical checks are carried out.

Live As it is happening.

Location Geographical position of an event.

LS Long shot.

Magazine programme Programme which is a mix of 'hard' news and feature items.

Mic/mike Microphone.

Microcomputer 'Personal' computer system.

Minicam Mobile electronic camera unit with live capability.

Modem Modulator/demodulator which allows computer signals to be transmitted by telephone.

Monitor Screen for displaying television pictures or computer-generated data.

Monochrome Black and white.

Monopod Single extendable pole fitted to the base of a camera to keep it steady.

Multilateral Shared use by three or more broadcasting services of Eurovision, communications satellite or similar links. See also *Unilateral.*

Multiplexer Vision and sound switch that allows several videotape sources in succession to be routed at high speed on to one line for transmission.

Natural sound Sound recorded on to tape at the same time as the pictures are taken.

NBC National Broadcasting Company, a US network.

Neck/personal mike Small lightweight microphone which clips on to clothing or is hung from a cord round the neck.

Network (1) National broadcasting system; (2) Linked computer devices.

News director (US) Executive in charge of news department.

News editor Senior journalist; in television usually concerned with news-gathering. See *Assignments desk*.

Newsreader/newscaster Main presenter of a news programme. See also *Anchorman*.

Newstar Computerized newsroom system.

News-writer Newsroom-based journalist responsible for assembling and writing programme items.

Noddies Reporter's simulated reaction shots for use as interview cut-aways.

NTSC National Television Standards Commission which gave its name to the US system of colour television.

OB Outside broadcast.

OC On camera. See *In vision*.

Onion bag String bag used for carrying videotape cassettes, so called for its resemblance to the bags in which onions are sold.

OIRT International Radio and Television Organization, based in Prague.

OOV Out of vision. Commentary spoken by unseen reader in the studio during transmission, also known as *voice-over*.

ORACLE Optional Reception of Announcements by Coded Line Electronics. British Independent Television broadcast teletext.

Out cue The final words of a news report.

Output News department responsible for the selection and processing of material for transmission. Counterpart of *intake-input*.

Out-takes See *Cuts*.

Over-crank To run a camera motor at faster than normal speed. When seen the picture appears to be in slow motion. See also *Under-crank*.

Overlay Editing technique for matching a recorded sound-track with relevant pictures.

PA (1) Press Association, a British domestic news agency; (2) Production Assistant.

Package Self-contained pictorial news report usually containing a number of different elements.

Paint box Electronic system for the creation of graphics.

PAL Phase Alternation (by) Line. Colour television system.

Pan Camera movement on (1) the horizontal plane (pan left to right, pan right to left), (2) the vertical plane (pan up, pan down).

PASB Programme As Broadcast. Detailed record of a programme for file and payment purposes; includes names of contributors, interviewees, duration and type of videotape inserts, etc.

Peripheral Printer or other device linked to a computer.

Piece to camera/stand-up (per) Report spoken directly to the camera in the field.

Pigeon Traveller entrusted with passing film or tape between a camera unit and their base.

Pixel Picture element.

Producer Person responsible for (1) entire news programme or (2) item within it.

Program Set of instructions compiled to enable a computer to carry out a specific function.

Presenter See *Anchorman/newsreader/newscaster*.

Quadruplex Videotape machine with four vision heads recording across a magnetic tape two inches wide.

Quantel Makers of electronic production equipment, particularly for computer graphics.

Quarter-cam Quarter-inch format video system.

Quarter-inch tape Quarter-inch wide audio recording tape.

Radio mike Microphone used with small transmitter; needs no cable link with recording equipment.

RAM Random Access Memory. Main computer memory; anything put into it is lost when the machine is switched off.

Reuters British-based agency supplying foreign news.

Reversal film Film type which emerges as a positive after chemical processing; very popular for tv news work in colour BE.

Reverse phase Electronic means of changing (film) negative to positive for transmission purposes.

Reverse question see *Cut-away questions*.

Rifle mike Directional microphone with rifle-shaped barrel.

Roller caption (crawl) Mechanical device for displaying moving lettering vertically or horizontally across the screen.

ROM Read-Only Memory. Program permanently built in or added to computer.

Rostrum camera Camera mounted on the photographic enlarger principle to control filming/taping of static objects (maps, etc.).

Rough cut First completed assembly of tape or film edited to its approximately pre-selected order and duration.

Running order/rundown Order of transmission of items in a programme.

Run through Rehearsal.

Run up The time considered necessary for technical equipment to reach its full operating speed.

Rushes (Dailies) Exposed tape or film in its unedited form

Scanner Mobile control centre serving outside broadcast unit. See also *Caption scanner*.

SECAM Sequence Avec Memoire. Colour television system.

Sepmag Separate magnetic system of recording sound on film. The sound is recorded separately on to a tape recorder run in synchronism with the film. Also known as *sync sound*.

Shot list Detailed written description of each scene in edited tape or film, from which the commentary is made to match the pictures; usually measured in seconds; essential preliminary to quality commentary writing.

Single system (of recording sound on film) See *Commag*.

SMATV Satellite Master Antenna Television. System of sending satellite pictures to community dishes for distribution by cable.

Soft (1) A shot that is slightly out of focus; (2) A news item considered interesting rather than important.

Software Computer programs.

SOT Sound on tape.

Sound track(s) Area of tape on which sound is recorded.

Soup Processing plant for film.

Sound bite (US) Sound (usually speech) segment of tape chosen for inclusion in edited news package.

Sparks Electrician or lighting assistant working with camera crew.

Split screen A picture composed of two separate elements, each occupying half of the screen area. (A picture with more than two elements is usually known as a *multi screen*.)

Steenbeck German-made film editing machine, much in television news use BE.

Stick mike Stick-shaped microphone much favoured for news work for its speed of preparation and ease of use.

Still A single picture.

Still frame See *Freeze frame*.

Stock Raw unused tape or film.

Stringer A freelance contributor employed on a regular basis.

Stripe The narrow band of magnetic sound track used in the commag (single) system of recording sound on film.

Studio spot (Usually) a contribution made live in the studio by a performer other than the main presenter.

Superimposition Usually abbreviated to *super*. Electronic or optical combination of two or more pictures to give extra information on the screen (often the addition of a speaker's name or title).

Talk-back One-way sound link between control room and other technical area.

Talking head Any interviewee; also pejorative: to have too many talking heads in a news programme is considered unimaginative.

Telecine Projector/tv camera mechanism for transmitting film on television.

Teleprompter See *Autocue*.

Tele-recording Process of recording programmes or items by filming direct off high-quality monitors.

Teletext Broadcast *videotex*. On screen text information transmitted on unused lines within television signal.

Terminal Computer keyboard. See also *VDT, VDU*.

Tilt Vertical panning movement of the camera.

Transponder Transmitter/responder. On board satellite equipment which receives and passes on a telecommunications signal.

Tripod Adjustable three-legged stand fixed to the base of a camera to keep it steady.

TVRO Television Receive Only.

Two-shot A shot of two people.

TX Transmission.

U-matic Three-quarter inch videotape recording system first introduced by Sony.

Under crank To run a camera motor at slower speed than normal. When the picture is replayed at the correct speed the action seems faster than it should be. See also *Over crank*.

Unilateral Exclusive use by one broadcasting organization of Eurovision, communications satellite or other links.

Upcut US term for the accidental overlapping of two sound sources (e.g. live commentary running into recorded sound).

VDT/VDU Visual Display Terminal/Visual Display Unit. Display screen linked to computer.

Videotape (VT/VTR) System of recording television pictures and sound on magnetic tape for instant reproduction.

Video(tape) cassette Container which allows tape to be threaded automatically into cameras and recorders.

Videotex 'Written' information distributed to television/display screens from central computers.

Viewdata Non-broadcast videotex accessed over telephone.

Vision story See *On camera*.

Visnews International television news agency.

Voice over See *OOV*.

Vox pop Vox populi. A series of usually very short interviews on a specific topic, often with people selected at random, and edited together to give a cross-section of opinion.

Whip pan (zip pan) Very high speed panning movement of the camera.

Wild track/wild sound Recorded sound which is related to but not synchronized with the picture.

Wipe (1) A production technique often described as an 'electronic method of turning the page'; (2) to erase.

Word processing Using a computer to write and edit.

Worldwide Television News (WTN) (Formerly *UPITN*) Television news agency.

Zoom lens A lens giving a variable focal length.

Further Reading

A History of Broadcasting in the United States (3 vols.), Eric Barnouw (OUP, 1966–70).
A Survey of Television, Stuart Hood (Heinemann, 1967).
Bad News, More Bad News, Glasgow Media Group (Routledge & Kegan Paul, 1976, 1980).
BBC Broadcasting Research Findings (published annually) (BBC Data).
BBC Handbooks (published annually) (BBC Publications).
Broadcasting in Britain, 1922–72, Keith Geddes (HMSO, 1972).
Day by Day: a Dose of My Own Hemlock, Robin Day (William Kimber, 1975).
Effective TV Production, Gerald Millerson (Focal Press, 1976).
Factual Television, Norman Swallow (Focal Press, 1966).
Here is the News, Richard Baker (Leslie Frewin, 1966).
I Counted Them All Out and I Counted Them All Back, Brian Hanrahan and Robert Fox (BBC, 1982).
In and Out of the Box, Robert Dougall (Collins Harvill, 1973).
Penguin Dictionary of Telecommunications, (Penguin, 1983).
Prime Time: the Life of Edward R. Murrow, Alexander Kendrick (Dent & Sons, 1970).
Really Bad News, members of Glasgow Media Group (Writers' and Readers' Publishing Co-operative Society, 1982).
Report of the Committee on the Future of Broadcasting, Chairman Lord Annan (HMSO, 1977).
Reporting for Television, Carolyn Diana Lewis (Columbia University Press, 1984).
Reuters' Century, 1851–1951, Graham Storey (Max Parrish, 1951).
See It Happen, Geoffrey Cox (The Bodley Head, 1983).
Smile, It's Only Television, Nigel Farrell (Blandford, 1984).
Sound and Fury, Maurice Gorham (Percival Marshall, 1948).
Teletext and Viewdata, S.A. Money (Newnes Technical Books, 1981).
Television and the Riots, Howard Tumber (British Film Institute, 1982).
Television, A Personal Report, Robin Day (Hutchinson, 1961).
Television Graphics, Ron Hurrell (Thames & Hudson, 1972).
Television News, Richard Collins (British Film Institute Television Monograph, 1976).
Television News Reporting, CBS News (McGraw-Hill, 1958).
Television Newsfilm Techniques, Vernon Stone and Bruce Hinson (Hastings House, 1974).
Television and Radio Handbook (Independent Broadcasting Authority).
Television and Radio News, Bob Siller, Ted White and Hal Terkel (Macmillan, 1960).
Television/Radio News Workbook, Irving Fang (Hastings House, 1975).
Ten Seconds from Now, Godfrey Talbot (Hutchinson, 1973).
The Complete Guide to Newsroom Computers, ed. Phillip O. Keirstead (Globecom Publishing, 1984).
The Evening Stars, Barbara Matusow (Ballantine Books, 1984).
The Fog of War, Tom Hopkinson, Derrik Mercer, Geoff Mungham and Kevin Williams (Secker and Warburg, 1987).
The Handling of Press and Public Information during the Falklands Conflict, (HMSO, 1983).

The History of Broadcasting in the United Kingdom (4 vols.), Asa Briggs (OUP, 1961–69).

The Least Worst Television in the World, Milton Shulman (Barrie & Jenkins, 1973).

The Media and the Falklands Campaign, Valerie Adams (Macmillan, 1986).

The Mirror in the Corner, Peter Black (Hutchinson, 1972).

The New Priesthood, Joan Bakewell and Nicholas Garnham (Allen Lane, Penguin Press, 1973).

The Ravenous Eye, Milton Shulman (Collins, 1973).

The Shadow in the Cave, Anthony Smith (Allen & Unwin, 1973).

The Task of Broadcasting News, a study for the BBC General Advisory Council (BBC, 1976).

The Technique of Television Announcing, Bruce Lewis (Focal Press, 1966).

The Universal Eye, World Television in the Seventies, Timothy Green (The Bodley Head, 1972).

The Work of the Television Journalist, Robert Tyrrell (Focal Press, 1980).

Today and Yesterday, John Timpson (Allen & Unwin, 1976).

To Kill a Messenger, Television News and the Real World, William Small (Hastings House, 1970).

TV News – Whose Bias? Professor Martin Harrison (Policy Journals, 1985).

War and Peace News, Glasgow University Media Group (Open University Press, 1985).

Index

DATE DUE